W9-BUU-125

The Jossey-Bass Nonprofit and Public Management Series also includes

The CarverGuide Series on Effective Board Governance, *John Carver, Miriam Mayhew Carver*

Boards That Make a Difference: A New Design for Leadership in Nonprofit and Public Organizations, Second Edition, *John Carver*

The Board Member's Guide to Fundraising, *Fisher Howe*

The Board Member's Guide to Strategic Planning, *Fisher Howe*

Nonprofit Boards and Leadership, *Miriam M. Wood, Editor*

Reinventing Your Board: A Step-by-Step Guide to Implementing Policy Governance, *John Carver, Miriam Mayhew Carver*

The Fundraising Planner, *Doug and Terry Schaff*

Transforming Fundraising: A Practical Guide to Evaluating and Strengthening Fundraising to Grow with Change, *Judith Nichols*

The Budget-Building Book for Nonprofits, *Murray Dropkin, Bill La Touche*

Saving Money in Nonprofit Organizations: More Than 100 Money-Saving Ideas, Tips, and Strategies for Reducing Expenses Without Cutting the Budget, *Gregory Dabel*

Winning Grants Step by Step: Support Centers of America's Complete Workbook for Planning, Developing, and Writing Successful Proposals, *Mim Carlson*

Achieving Excellence in Fund Raising, *Henry A. Rosso and Associates*

Rosso on Fund Raising: Lessons from a Master's Lifetime Experience, *Henry A. Rosso*

Secrets of Successful Grantsmanship: A Guerrilla Guide to Raising Money, *Susan L. Golden*

Fund Raisers: Their Careers, Stories, Concerns, and Accomplishments, *Margaret A. Duronio, Eugene R. Tempel*

The Drucker Foundation Self-Assessment Tool for Nonprofit Organizations, Revised Edition, *The Peter F. Drucker Foundation for Nonprofit Management*

The Jossey-Bass Guide to Strategic Communications for Nonprofits, *Kathy Bonk, Henry Griggs, Emily Tynes*

THE POLICY GOVERNANCE FIELDBOOK

THE POLICY GOVERNANCE FIELDBOOK

Practical Lessons, Tips, and Tools from the Experience of Real-World Boards

Caroline Oliver, General Editor

Mike Conduff, Susan Edsall, Carol Gabanna, Randee Loucks, Denise Paszkiewicz, Catherine Raso, Linda Stier

Foreword by John Carver

JOSSEY-BASS
A Wiley Company
www.josseybass.com

Published by

JOSSEY-BASS
A Wiley Company
989 Market Street
San Francisco, CA 94103-1741

www.josseybass.com

Jossey-Bass books and products are available through most bookstores. To contact Jossey-Bass
directly, call (888) 378-2537, fax to (800) 605-2665, or visit our website at www.josseybass.com.

Substantial discounts on bulk quantities of Jossey-Bass books are available to corporations,
professional associations, and other organizations. For details and discount information, contact the
special sales department at Jossey-Bass.

We at Jossey-Bass strive to use the most environmentally sensitive paper stocks available to us. Our
publications are printed on acid-free recycled stock whenever possible, and our paper always meets or
exceeds minimum GPO and EPA requirements.

Policy Governance ® is a registered service mark of John Carver.

Library of Congress Cataloging-in-Publication Data

The policy governance fieldbook : practical lessons, tips, and tools from
the experience of real-world boards / Caroline Oliver, general editor ;
[contributions by] Mike Conduff . . . [et al.] ; foreword by John Carver.
        p. cm. — (The Jossey-Bass nonprofit and public management
series)
    Includes bibliographical references and index.
    ISBN 0-7879-4366-5
    1. Boards of directors.   2. Corporate governance.   I. Oliver,
Caroline, 1953–   II. Conduff, Mike, 1954–   III. Series.
    HD2745.P65   1999
    658.4'22—dc21   99-6258

FIRST EDITION
PB Printing   10 9 8 7 6 5

THE JOSSEY-BASS NONPROFIT AND
PUBLIC MANAGEMENT SERIES

To the future of boards

CONTENTS

PART ONE: HOW BOARDS GET STARTED WITH POLICY GOVERNANCE

LIST OF EXHIBITS

FOREWORD

Design of the governing board's job merits at least as much careful attention as any other element in the leadership and management of enterprise. The reason is obvious: the board has the most powerful role in any organization and the one charged with the most accountability.

Yet until recently the topic of corporate governance was relegated to a few footnotes—often not even that—in management texts. Nonprofit governance was a smattering of old ideas more blessed by tradition than by success. Governmental governance was considered merely another part of political science—with a heavier emphasis on *political* than on *science*.

Although to be sure there have been *practices* of governance, one could not speak of a *theory* of governance or even a *technology* of governance, for there was none. And if the word *model* is used to mean a conceptually coherent framework (rather than merely an "approach"), one could not even speak accurately of a *model* of governance.

Advent of the Policy Governance model in the mid-1970s changed this sad state of the art, although the model was to take more than a decade to emerge from relative obscurity. Prior to publication of *The Policy Governance Fieldbook,* there have been four books, twelve monographs, and more than 150 published articles consistent with the principles embraced by the Policy Governance model. This book is the newest—and a very welcome—addition to that growing literature.

The Policy Governance Fieldbook is a not a theoretical treatise but a practical study. Its authors are concerned with real people in real organizations with real challenges. The authors are not unconcerned with theory, however, for they know that theory may be the most powerful tool available for real issues. Along with Kurt Lewin who said it best, they know there is nothing as practical as a good theory.

In this Foreword I am happy to respond to the authors' request that I introduce their book with a few comments about the origins and philosophy of the Policy Governance model, the theory on which their study is based. I do so by focusing on how I came to produce the model, what its philosophical underpinnings are, and how I see the role of *The Policy Governance Fieldbook* as recognition of the model continues to spread worldwide.

To me, in the mid-1970s, the role of governing boards in the management context was a mystery, although I had spent years serving on boards and years working for them as a chief executive officer (CEO). The board activities I observed and those I participated in failed to have the crisp, disciplined, efficient use of human talent and time I had come to respect in good management.

Feeling confused by this situation, I tried to learn everything I could about governance from books, workshops, seminars, and journal articles. But what I found was not intellectually satisfying. Governance as presented was more a collection of specific tips and practices than a conceptually whole, rational framework of concepts.

Years of education in psychology, business, and economics gave me no help in dealing with this bewilderment. But my doctoral scientific training came to the rescue in the end, even though I was not then—and am not now—engaged in research. The scientific mind-set helped me understand the power of modeling and gave me the ability to recognize its absence. Finally I grasped the problem. In the scientific sense, *there was no model for governance;* ideas about the topic were strikingly devoid of conceptual coherence.

I must explain what I mean by *model,* for the word has several legitimate definitions that I do not intend in this context. As a child, I built model airplanes; *model* can mean a simplified representation of a particular structure. Fashion models are walking mannequins who display clothing; *model* can mean a physical frame on which various particulars can be displayed or supported. In the governance literature, *model* most often means a particular structure or arrangement of working parts. Hence, national associations will refer to various models of relating regional boards to the national entity. Community boards will consider different models of committee assignments. Corporate boards fret over the model of chair-CEO separation.

I do not mean any of these definitions. My use of the word *model*—the kind of modeling that impelled me into governance theory in the mid-1970s—is a far more demanding denotation of the word. I do not mean a structure or even an arrangement of the currently popular "best practices." I am not against those things, just not satisfied with their utility in building a solid foundation for general governance development. Of course, any useful theory has to come down to earth with concrete applications to real-life situations. But the sounder the theory, the greater its capacity is for such real-life particularization. And sound theory must run much deeper than mere structural ideas and arrangements of practices. Sound theory requires a measure of elegance in its integration of principles and concepts.

So the missing element in governance as discussed, written about, and practiced was a foundation theory or model. *A model is a collection of principles and concepts that make sense as a whole.* In fact, the phrase *principles of governance* might communicate the idea to nonscientists far more clearly than *governance model. A model is internally consistent and has external utility.* If it doesn't do any good, who cares about its pretty logic! But a model in its most elegant sense is even more than that. The best model is not just a collection of useful principles but also a logical, deductive sequence built on postulates. I have published these postulates and some of the deductive sequence elsewhere.

At any rate, it seems to me that the utility of a true model in governance would be obvious. This idea has its detractors, however. Some say there is no one model of governance—that by its very nature the art of board leadership is so peculiar to each organization's circumstances, history, and personalities that governance is immune to modeling. But that point of view is often based on using the word *model* in one of the ways I've rejected—for example, to stand for a particular structural arrangement.

In fact, I believe that those who most strongly object to a generic model would themselves agree to certain postulates about boards. For example, they would agree that any board should know its role as distinguished from other roles (such as the CEO's). They would undoubtedly agree that governing boards are accountable for the organizations they govern. They would probably agree that the clearer a board is with employees about what it wants, the more likely it is to get what it wants. They might even agree that employees function more creatively when the board gives them as much room as possible to do things their own way (short of giving away the shop, of course).

Note that these statements collectively comprise a generic snapshot of good governance. Such a list does not constitute a model, but it does presume to be true across all cases. At this very low level of what *model* might mean (a level many seem willing to accept, anyway), it is not only possible that there be a universally applicable model of governance—it is almost impossible that there not be!

But once that conclusion has been reached, one needs to develop a catalogue of universal "good governance" characteristics that is as conceptually whole as possible. To the extent that internal congruity is accomplished, one will have derived a *model* that has the high integrity to which I refer. In no way does this suggest that such a generic model is the only one possible. Governance model building is so unsophisticated at this point, however, that Policy Governance is arguably the only conceptually coherent, generic model of governance. Undoubtedly, it will later be just the earliest of a growing number of alternatives.

But the philosophical underpinnings of Policy Governance are fully as relevant to *The Policy Governance Fieldbook* as its conceptual merits. What are the beliefs on which the model is founded? What approaches to human beings and human enterprise are integral to the model? What, in fact, is the point of departure that sets Policy Governance on a different course than the conventional wisdom?

If I had to isolate one critical perspective, it would be this: *governance is a "downward" extension of ownership, not an "upward" extension of management.* The proper practice of governance, then, is more a subcategory of ownership than a subcategory of management. The concepts, conduct, and concerns of governance must then be more allied with owning an enterprise than with running it.

Because most boards do not themselves and by their own rights own the organizations they govern, they are owner-representatives rather than true owners. As owner-representatives, boards act on behalf of others' ownership rights, not their own. This introduces the economic and legal problem of agency, for board members have interests that may not always align with the interests of their principals. Although there may be procedural safeguards to minimize the problem of agency, the philosophical solution is the "servant-leadership" ideal identified by Robert K. Greenleaf.

Boards, then, have a moral obligation primarily to an "ownership" and secondarily to the broader social order. The obligation to the owners is that the owned asset produce for them what they wish. The obligation to the social order is that law, probity, and ethics be observed. Because this is a moral issue more than a strictly legal one, it matters little whether there are owners in the sense of shareholders. Indeed, the owners may be members (for an association) or the general public (for a public school system or a municipal government). The differences between equity corporations on the one hand and nonprofit or governmental bodies on the other hand are more legal than moral. The servant-leadership obligation boards have to their owners is the same no matter whether the ownership status rests on legal or on moral grounds.

Accountable for an entire organization's conduct, achievement, values, and destiny, a board has no choice but to exercise unambiguous control. To do less is to cheat the owners of their one authoritative voice in the on-site leadership of the organization. But the imposition of controls can be as destructive to owner interests as it is favorable to them. Control that stultifies creativity, for example, is myopic, for the very lifeblood of an organization is destroyed by oppressive, small-minded, or niggling control. Consequently, a board needs to exercise a type of control that safeguards owner values while optimally empowering the human beings employed in the enterprise. This balance is a challenge at which traditional governance has proven particularly inept.

So the four philosophical foundations of Policy Governance are accountability, servant-leadership, clarity of group values, and empowerment.

- *Accountability.* Given its owner-representative role, the board's obligation to the true owners is to see to it that the organization achieves what it should while avoiding unacceptable activities and situations. Governance is part of ownership, not part of management. Defaulting to staff, to vocal consumer groups, or even to individual board members is a dereliction of this stewardship. Assuring this accountability and being at arm's length from its fulfillment must coexist.
- *Servant-leadership.* As owner-representative, the board is both servant to and leader of the ownership. Failing in either part of this dual trusteeship—whether because of conflicts of interest, self-aggrandizement, or even simple passivity—is an abuse of authority. Thus the board adds value to the owners (not to the managers), in that owners not only have their wishes served but also become more enlightened, responsible owners. Providing leadership to the owners and being their servant must co-exist.
- *Clarity of group values.* The board is vested with group responsibility and group authority, whereas no single member has any. Yet the platform of authority afforded by board membership tempts members to impose individual desires on the organization. Expressing individual values is requisite to the forging of group values but is not authoritative outside the group. Group wisdom that emerges from this active interchange must be made explicit in order to be expressed with certainty. Rigorous diversity and group wholeness must coexist.
- *Empowerment.* Although staff are employed to serve the board's will, both productivity and humanity are better served if the staff's latitude to make decisions, to try new ways, and to make mistakes is maximized. The board is accountable for the organization's ethics about people and promises, just as with any other aspect of organization. Productivity and human dignity must coexist.

So what role does *The Policy Governance Fieldbook* play in boards' consideration of their weighty challenges? Simply this: the model is a rational framework, *a prescription for what governance can be rather than a description of what it is.* Ideals toward which to aim serve an important role in human affairs. Religion, political philosophies, ethical codes, and even weight-loss programs all paint a vision that we might try to realize. Their value is as much in motivating our reach as in our achieving the grasp. So it is with the Policy Governance model.

Some boards will implement the Policy Governance model with more precision than others. The model promises great gains in the integrity of accountability, servant-leadership, clarity of values, and empowerment if its tenets are strictly honored.

But what of real organizations, real boards, real people? Do they actually implement the model completely. If so, are the promised gains realized? If not, why not? Does the model simply fail to serve their needs, or does it demand more discipline than board members have? Are certain parts of the model more difficult than others? As to completeness of implementation, is it better for a board to have half of the Policy Governance loaf than to have none? Is it possible that board members chosen for the skills appropriate to conventional governance are not the right board members for the new paradigm? If so, what should give way for better governance in the long term—the people or the paradigm? Is such a transition best made swiftly with transitory pain or slowly with more gentle moves?

The Policy Governance Fieldbook does not and cannot answer all these questions. But in having authors who can expertly discern the nuances of Policy Governance and in reporting real-life situations, it is the first book to start down what is surely to be a very long road. For that boldness, I am in its authors' debt. But more important, boards everywhere and those who rely on the integrity of governance—that means all of us—are in their debt, as well.

April 1999   John Carver
Atlanta, Georgia

PREFACE

Boards are worthy of close study because they are the ultimate form of leadership in almost every sphere of human endeavor. It is therefore curious that so little material about boards is currently available. Look on any bookshelf and see how many more titles are addressed to chief executive officers (CEOs) and senior managers than to chairpersons and board members.

It is also curious that when it comes to the scant writing on boards, Policy Governance seems to represent virtually the only innovative approach. It seems to us that every other approach to governance in current circulation is basically a variation on an old tune. We, the authors of this book, do not assert that Policy Governance is the only way for boards. However, we do maintain that it is, thus far, the only coherent approach to distinguishing governance as a particular form of leadership.

Our commitment is not to Policy Governance for its own sake. Our commitment is to the possibility of boards' fulfilling the missions of their organizations. And for as long as Policy Governance remains the most powerful expression of that possibility, we are committed to assisting boards in developing it. In that spirit, the purpose of this book is twofold: (1) to assess how Policy Governance is working in practice and (2) to learn what we can from boards' experience of applying Policy Governance.

How This Book Was Written

In preparing this book, our first step was to identify organizations in which Policy Governance is being practiced. We contacted people who were active in the field and asked them for case material. From the responses, we produced a list of thirty possible organizations. Of those thirty, we selected eleven organizations. They reflected a range of organization types and various stages of progress with Policy Governance. We wanted our sample to represent the diversity of boards' implementation experiences and the reality that the path to implementation is not always smooth.

Collectively, we authors have a wide range of experience of working with organizations on Policy Governance, and this has informed our writing. However, we have attempted to listen rigorously to the organizations that contributed material and to make the book reflect what they have told us. In fact we considerably altered our original outline for the book after analyzing the organizations' experiences.

Three cornerstones for success emerged: (1) the extent to which the whole board truly saw the *possibility* of Policy Governance for its organization, (2) the extent to which the board made a real *commitment* to implementing Policy Governance, and (3) the extent to which the board instituted a clear *process* or *structure* to realize that commitment.

What surprised us was that these elements don't all have to be present at the same time and that it doesn't seem to matter which comes first. If a board is clear about the possibility, the commitment and process usually follow. If board members are committed to Policy Governance, the possibility will live on and the process will develop. If the board has a clear process, the possibility and the commitment can arise from the struggle of applying it. This is a message of hope, for boards and organizations are made up of human beings. Like perfection, Policy Governance is an ideal worth aiming for, not a permanent state.

The writing of this book has been a team project from beginning to end. As a team, we believe that we have modeled many of the very principles of Policy Governance that we espouse. We have spoken throughout with one voice, and it has been unbelievably easy. Our commitment to effective governance is so strong that, for instance, when it came to agreeing who was going to write which chapter, the whole process took two minutes! Our decisions have been primarily policy decisions. We have trusted each other to perform our roles within agreed-on parameters. We have focused on our broadest values and have thus created a powerful overall context from which the detail has naturally flowed. Incredibly, throughout the writing of the book we have had only one meeting. This book could not have been written so quickly and efficiently without e-mail, but most important it could not have been written at all without our three touchstones: possibility, commitment, and structure. We hope you enjoy our work and that something of our shared spirit will touch you and make a difference for your board.

What the Book Provides

The Policy Governance Fieldbook relates and assesses the real-life experiences of organizations in applying the theory of Policy Governance. Thus it provides field experience to inform the inquiry that naturally arises when one considers how any new theory really works. As such, we believe that this book contributes to a full body of information about Policy Governance, which includes the theory, advice on its implementation, and the experience of using it.

Each part of this body of information supports and informs every other part. Relevant field experience cannot exist without the theory. In turn, the theory—and advice on how to use it—requires well-documented and well-critiqued field experience to substantiate and inform it. This book does not pretend to be a quantitative research study. It does claim to provide a small but varied sample of organizations' real-life experiences and the lessons that can be drawn from them. It has been assembled by a group of people well acquainted with the possibility of the theory and the challenges it presents in practice.

At the end of this book Resource D, "The History of Policy Governance in Practice," makes it clear that there is much more to be done. We hope there will be many more works like this one that will seek to establish whether Policy Governance can deliver on its promises of greater role clarity, greater accountability, and greater benefits for people in real life. We have no hesitation in asserting that this book is true to life. We have not glossed over the struggles boards have faced in sustaining the model over time. And we have not underplayed the way Policy Governance has helped boards see their importance in an entirely new and positive light.

The Policy Governance Fieldbook looks at what board life is like for organizations using Policy Governance. How have they balanced all the information—the theory, the how-to advice, and the real-world uncertainties and circumstances? We often interpret theory and act on it in different ways. Even when we know what to do and how to do it, we might not do it, or we might do "our version" of a recommended action. How have organizations carried out John Carver's recommendations? How have their various interpretations worked?

Getting Started

To benefit fully from *The Policy Governance Fieldbook*, you will need a fundamental understanding of the Policy Governance model. The best way to gain such an understanding is probably to read one of John Carver's main works, *Boards That Make a Difference* or *Reinventing Your Board*, which Miriam Carver coauthored (see Resource C at the end of the book for details about these titles). Even if you have read one of these, you may wish to read "The Principles of Policy Governance Explained" at the beginning of this book.

How the Main Chapters Are Organized

The topics of the main chapters derived from the experience of the organizations that gave us source material. The chapters can be read in the order they appear (they are loosely organized into parts according to the typical stages of development of Policy Governance) or in any order you choose. You should be able to dip into any topic of interest to you and find something valuable there.

Each chapter begins with a section called "The Challenge," which introduces the importance of the topic, the questions the chapter will address, and the way its conclusions will be translated into action points for the reader. The backbone of every chapter is the section titled "The Experience," which describes the experience of the boards we have surveyed in relation to the questions asked in "The Challenge." Where relevant, we have added some material from other organizations known to us. The "Key Learnings" section that follows gathers the lessons from the experience. These lessons could help other organizations facing the same issues and challenges.

We believe an organization must follow the model's principles consistently in order to realize its promise. Yet we also believe there are many ways to put Policy Governance into action. We intend to offer pathways, not prescriptions. Organizations have to choose how they will apply the principles on the basis of their current situation. Hence the next section of each chapter, "Taking Action: Strategies for Where You Are Now," invites you to look at where your organization is starting from and leads you into the final "Practical Tips and Tools" section. In this last section you will find a host of suggestions to move your board forward from wherever you are today.

Resource Sections

As many of the tools referred to in each chapter are relevant to more than one chapter, we have indexed them in Resources A and B, the two Tool Finder charts for board development and group process. Looking at these charts, you can quickly access all the tools in the book that are relevant to your particular need. Resource C, the "Further Reading and Resources" section, cites the main works mentioned in the book and lists many other useful resources. Next we offer Resource D, "The History of Policy Governance in Practice," which gives some perspectives on how the practice of Policy Governance has developed, the extent to which it influences boards today, its place within the broader context of current thinking about governance, and the type of criticisms it has incurred. Finally in Resource E, "About the Source Organizations," we give you more information about the organizations that provided the source material for the book.

ACKNOWLEDGMENTS

The authors of this book would like to acknowledge how grateful they are to the following people:

John Carver and Miriam Carver

Clearly this book would not have been written without John Carver's work in developing and pioneering the Policy Governance model. What was not so obvious is that he would have been so open and generous in his support of our work. His only condition for contributing the Foreword was that the book not betray the integrity of the model; we are delighted to find that we have met this condition. Far from feeling that this condition inhibited us from criticizing the model, we have always treated it in the spirit it was given; John welcomes criticism based on a full understanding of the model.

Our thanks go to John for creating and pioneering Policy Governance, for introducing us to it, for encouraging our book project from the first time we mentioned it, and for responding to our numerous questions.

Similar thanks are due to Miriam Carver, who has cowritten much of the most important recent work on Policy Governance and who has also been immensely supportive of our efforts.

In addition, a special mention must go to Ivan Benson, the Carvers' most excellent assistant, who has dealt with all our requests with speed, efficiency, and a wonderful courtesy.

Contributors of Source Material

The following people have added immeasurably to our work by generously providing full descriptions of their organizations' experiences in implementing Policy Governance. Their only recompense has been the knowledge that their work will benefit you the reader and that the proceeds from this book will help promote knowledge of Policy Governance implementation. These board and staff members have shared more than just their experiences with us; they have shared their struggles, their triumphs, and their dreams. Their generosity and their commitment to making a difference are truly inspiring.

Tom Atterton, chair of the United Way of Burlington, Hamilton-Wentworth, Ontario, Canada.

Darby Bradley, president of the Vermont Land Trust.

Kendra Coates, past chair of the United Way of Burlington, Hamilton-Wentworth, Ontario, Canada.

Michael A. Conduff, city manager of Bryan, Texas, USA.

Catherine Corrick, member of the policy secretariat staff for the Law Society of Upper Canada, Toronto.

Abe Feinstein, bencher and chair of the Governance Re-structuring Implementation Committee of the Law Society of Upper Canada. He is based in Ottawa.

Joseph Fera, staff member of the San Francisco AIDS Foundation with special responsibility for board liaison for Ends policies.

Tammy McCormick Ferguson, executive director of the Early Childhood Community Development Centre of Saint Catharines, Ontario, Canada.

Dan Galvin, council member and mayor pro tem (from 1997 to 1998) of Bryan, Texas, USA.

Michael Graham, chair of the Southern Ontario Library Service, Ontario, Canada, from 1993 to 1997.

Laurey Irvine, chief executive officer of the Southern Ontario Library Service, Ontario, Canada.

Gil Livingston, vice president of operations for the Vermont Land Trust, USA.

Jannice Moore, principal of Jannice Moore & Associates, a governance consultancy based in Edmonton, Alberta, Canada. She worked closely with Parkland Health District during their implementation.

Jean Morrison, chief executive officer of Parkland Health District in Saskatchewan, Canada.

Randy Quinn, executive director of the Colorado Association of School Boards, USA.

Kandy Rose, council member at large for the City of Bryan, Texas, USA.

Robin Scheu, chair of the board of the Vermont Land Trust, USA.

Ruffin Slater, founder of Weaver Street Market, Inc., of Carrboro, North Carolina, USA. He has been the general manager and a member of the board of directors since he helped found the organization.

Lonnie Stabler, mayor of Bryan, Texas, USA.

Linda Stier, president of the board of directors of Weaver Street Market, Inc., in Carrboro, North Carolina, USA.

Fred Treischl, director of human resources development for the YMCA-YWCA of London, Ontario, Canada.

Barbara Wagner, vice president of land conservation for the Vermont Land Trust, USA.

Other Contributors

Our thanks also go to the following people, who have given us advice and information.

Jeffrey L. Brudney, Ph.D., professor of political science and director of the Doctor of Public Administration Program at the University of Georgia, USA.

Brenda Gainer, Ph.D., Royal Bank Professor of Nonprofit Management and director of the Nonprofit Management and Leadership Program at York University, Toronto, Canada.

Raymond Lemieux, a governance consultant with Raymond Lemieux Gouvernance, who works with nonprofit and public organizations in Quebec and throughout Canada.

THE AUTHORS

Mike Conduff has been city manager of Bryan, Texas, since 1992. He has also served as city manager of Manhattan, Kansas, and of Pittsburg, Kansas. He has served on dozens of boards in his career, including several to which he was gubernatorially appointed. Conduff has worked with numerous cities to help them implement Policy Governance. He is a past member of the board of directors of the Texas City Management Association, has chaired the International City County Management Association Public Policy Committee, and is the past president of the Kansas Association of City and County Managers. Conduff holds a B.S. in civil engineering from the University of New Hampshire and an M.B.A. from Pittsburg State University.

Susan Edsall is a private consultant working with not-for-profit organizations on large-scale systems change. She has worked in the not-for-profit field for more than twenty years as a governing board member, a volunteer, and a chief executive. She works with organizations on board development, strategic planning, systems and process improvement, and team learning. She has a national client base in the United States. Edsall holds a B.A. in English literature from Montana State University.

Carol Gabanna is the chief executive officer (CEO) of the Health Association of Prince Edward Island, a nonprofit organization that provides board development and support to regional health boards and CEOs. She also consults with boards of other nonprofit community and public sector organizations. Gabanna is a certified facilitator, working with groups of all kinds to ensure that their meetings generate productive results by drawing on the knowledge, ability, and creativity of individual group members. She has a B.B.A. in business administration from the University of Prince Edward Island.

Randee Loucks is manager of trustee development at Southern Ontario Library Service, an organization providing resource sharing, training, and development to 256 public library boards. She has presented the Policy Governance model to a number of these boards and has worked extensively with 7 of them to implement the model. Prior to working in Ontario, Loucks was a senior cultural consultant with Alberta Culture and Multiculturalism, where she worked with a variety of organizations in seventy-five communities surrounding Calgary. She has been involved in board development and training in Ontario and Alberta for more than a decade. Loucks holds a B.Sc(N) degree from McGill University and a B.F.A. and an M.A. from the University of Calgary.

Caroline Oliver is a founding partner of The Leadership Team, a Canadian organization that focuses on board leadership issues. She has consulted with organizations in Canada and the United States, including several of the organizations established under the Regulated Health Professions Act of Ontario. She has also held senior executive and board positions for several national organizations in the United Kingdom and has served on national and European government committees. Oliver has acted as general editor of this book and as overall coordinator of the project, which has involved eleven organizations and eight authors.

Denise Paszkiewicz is executive administrator for People Inc., a human services agency in western New York with a 1500-person staff. She works with the executive director on governance issues on a daily basis and has led the agency's senior management staff in the transition to the Policy Governance model. She has been instrumental in developing the board of directors' view of governance and has facilitated the development of the agency's current governing policies. In addition, Paszkiewicz has consulted with agencies throughout the United States. She holds a B.S. degree in organizational management from Houghton College in Buffalo, New York, and has studied nonprofit management at the State University of New York and at Niagara Community College.

Catherine Raso is principal of CMR Governance Consulting, which specializes in board development. From 1986 to 1996, she was executive director of a $3 million (in Canadian dollars) nonprofit organization. Since becoming a full-time consultant in 1997, she has helped dozens of organizations implement the Policy Governance model. She also has extensive experience as a board trainer and a workshop facilitator with the Leadership Development Services Program of the United Way. She has worked as an instructor at the Volunteer Management Program at Mohawk College in Hamilton, Ontario, and at the National Non-Profit Sector Management Certificate Program at McMaster University in Hamilton. Raso holds a B.A. in economics and an M.B.A. in health services from McMaster University.

Linda Stier is a coach, a trainer, and a consultant committed to empowering boards to lead their organizations effectively and to achieve their missions. She works with boards in the public, private, and nonprofit sectors and specializes in training people in the theory and the implementation of Policy Governance. She has served as a board member, a board officer, a volunteer, and a staff manager in a wide variety of fields, including statewide arts, professional performing arts, countywide strategic planning, women's issues, horticulture, sustainable agriculture, retail cooperatives, and leadership training. Stier holds a B.S. degree in mathematics from Hofstra University and a certificate in nonprofit management from Duke University Continuing Education.

THE POLICY GOVERNANCE FIELDBOOK

THE PRINCIPLES OF POLICY GOVERNANCE EXPLAINED

This book is intended for those who already understand the Policy Governance model. The purpose of the following explanation of Policy Governance principles is to refresh that understanding.

1. The Trust in Trusteeship

Because board members act as trustees on behalf of a larger group (which is called the "moral ownership") and because the board is a subset of that group, the board must do the following things: (1) clearly identify who that larger group is and (2) make certain that the organization achieves what that group wants it to achieve. This requires the board to communicate (or link) with its owners.

2. The Board Speaks with One Voice or Not at All

Although unanimity is not required, the board's group decision must be unambiguous, recorded in policy, and upheld by all members of the board as if it had been a decision that each made individually. No member has the authority to speak for the board unless specifically authorized to do so by the whole board. The board's policies are the board's voice.

3. Board Decisions Should Be Policy Decisions

Because the board's voice is expressed in its policies, board decision making is always an amendment of, or an addition to, existing policy.

4. Boards Should Formulate Policy by Determining the Broadest Values Before Progressing to Narrower Ones

By "nesting" policies, boards can delegate details and concentrate on why those details matter. For example, instead of deciding that staff members should receive a certain number of vacation days each year, the board could decide that fair and competitive staff treatment is a board value. Board members can then leave it to the chief executive officer (CEO) to interpret their words, or they can go to the next level of specificity.

5. A Board Should Define and Delegate Rather Than React and Ratify

If a board truly chooses to govern, then it must not be led by staff members or by its own committees. The board itself should work incessantly, continually, and obsessively to define the results the organization is to produce (Ends policies) and to define the "acceptable boundaries" (Executive Limitations policies) within which it can delegate the achievement of those results to the CEO. If truly governing, the board should not be simply reacting to and ratifying staff or committee ideas.

6. Ends Determination Is the Pivotal Duty of Governance

On behalf of the moral ownership (which cannot conveniently assemble on a regular basis), the board must paint the target toward which the staff should shoot in terms of the benefits to be produced, the people to be served, and the cost of meeting these goals. There is no greater governance job than this, and it cannot be delegated.

7. The Board Can Best Control Staff Means by Limiting, Not Prescribing

Although boards often try to develop complete "to do" lists for CEOs, for other staff members, or for committees, boards cannot oversee all the detail involved. It is easier, and in fact more complete, for a board to tell the CEO what should be achieved on behalf of the moral ownership (in Ends policies) and then to allow the CEO to use his or her expertise and experience to determine how best to get there within the limits of law, prudence, and ethics (Executive Limitations policies).

8. A Board Must Explicitly Design Its Own Products and Processes

Because the board's governance function is distinct from the staff's management function, the board must determine its own definition of governance and then decide how it will actually govern. All board members should clearly understand why the board exists; the purpose is not to oversee staff but rather to define the future on behalf of the moral ownership and to ensure that that future is achieved in a legal, ethical, and prudent manner.

9. A Board Must Form an Empowering and Safe Linkage with Management

Role clarity means that the board clearly knows its own role and the staff's role and that the staff has a similar understanding. If both understand each other's roles, if these roles do not overlap, and if both parties agree to adhere to these roles, then staff members can function freely yet be fully aware of their limitations. Board members essentially tell staff members, "We will not interfere if you can achieve the Ends without violating Executive Limitations."

10. CEO Performance Must Be Monitored Rigorously but Only Against Policy Criteria

In a fair contest, contestants are only judged if they know the rules. Similarly, in Policy Governance the board judges the staff only according to the board's own rules, and the staff will know those rules because they have been stated in policies.

These principles have been abridged from *CarverGuide 1: Basic Principles of Policy Governance*. See Resource C, "Further Reading and Resources," for details.

HOW BOARDS GET STARTED WITH POLICY GOVERNANCE

CHAPTER ONE

EXPLORING POLICY GOVERNANCE

☐ The Challenge

This chapter looks at the very initial stages of an organization's move to Policy Governance. Therefore it examines questions of particular value to organizations that have not yet considered Policy Governance or that are just beginning to think about it.

First we examine the experience of our eleven organizations in relation to the following questions:

- What attracts boards to Policy Governance?
- How do boards consider whether Policy Governance is right for them?
- What kinds of organizations consider Policy Governance?
- What variables affect whether Policy Governance will be attractive to an organization?

Next we present key learnings about what makes an exploration process successful. Finally we invite you to look at where your board is in the process, and we give some advice, tips, and tools to make it work for your board.

■ The Experience

What Attracts Boards to Policy Governance?

Boards are attracted to Policy Governance for two main reasons. First, some boards are not satisfied with the way things are. For example, they may feel that they are spending too much time approving committee reports or that they need to sort out board and staff responsibilities. Their organization's future may be threatened. They may recognize the need to be stronger leaders or simply sense that they are not really making a difference.

Second, rather than wanting to fix the way things are, boards may be attracted to Policy Governance because it offers something new and potentially valuable. Similarly, a couple might buy a new house either because their old one is falling down or because they have seen another one that captivates them.

The eleven organizations studied in this book, along with many of which we have personal knowledge, have decided to move to a new way of governing. How did they get there?

Someone Hears Something.   The very first thing that happened at the Colorado Association of School Boards was that the chief executive officer (CEO) and another staff member read *Boards That Make a Difference* by John Carver. At the San Francisco AIDS Foundation, it was the chair who first heard about the model. It really doesn't seem to matter who hears about it first.

At the City of Bryan, Texas, a council member and the city manager attended a municipal leadership conference at which Carver was the featured presenter. Several board members and two senior staff members of the Southern Ontario Library Service heard Carver speak at the Ontario Library Association Conference in 1992. Similarly, Parkland Health District's board heard about Policy Governance from several members who had attended presentations sponsored by their provincial association of health organizations.

Some organizations come across Policy Governance as part of a general exploration about how they can improve their process. The board of the United Way of Burlington, Hamilton-Wentworth, had already been gathering information about governance issues and some members had seen Carver's video when their treasurer went to a Policy Governance training session. The board members of the Vermont Land Trust had been reviewing their roles and responsibilities when a senior staff member attended a workshop that introduced some of the Policy Governance principles in a very general way. Similarly, the board members of the

Early Childhood Community Development Centre had already decided to look for a new governance model when, as part of their research, their CEO and a board member attended a two-day training program on Policy Governance.

Organizations also find out about Policy Governance through the grapevine. Weaver Street Market heard about Policy Governance through other cooperatives and through the work of a university outreach specialist who was spreading the word about the model. At the Law Society of Upper Canada there was a meeting of the minds; a board member had heard about Policy Governance through other organizations in his community, a new CEO had come from a system that was using Policy Governance, and their chair was interested in the model as well.

They Want to Find Out More. For matters to go any further after people first hear about Policy Governance, they must have heard something that motivates them to learn more. The CEO and the senior staff member at the Colorado Association of School Boards were "interested from the start" and invited Carver to speak at their statewide school board convention in 1990. The city manager and the council member from Bryan were "intrigued with Carver's message of Ends and Means" and teamed up with another council to invite Carver to speak at a follow-up presentation.

The training session attended by the two representatives of the Early Childhood Community Development Centre "appealed to both the executive director and board member, confirming that the Policy Governance model would achieve the criteria the board identified for . . . a model to govern the organization." At the next board meeting, the representatives made a presentation about the model's benefits. Similarly, when the three members of the YMCA-YWCA of London returned from their session with Carver, they were "enthusiastic about the model, feeling the board should pursue it." The board then invited Carver to provide an orientation session for the entire board and invited other local agencies to attend so as to help defray the cost.

Many organizations proceeded with finding out more in a very thorough manner. The Law Society of Upper Canada created a "governance restructuring task force to consider the model carefully." The chair and vice-chair of Parkland Health District were "very interested in the potential of the model and did further homework, speaking to users of the model and comparing the approaches of consultants." The Vermont Land Trust's board members did not get really interested until they were in the middle of their introductory workshop. At that time, their consultant took them through a discussion using first their existing process and then Policy Governance principles. At the end of this discussion, the board decided to proceed with another workshop.

The Boards See a Possibility. After a board has been introduced to Policy Governance, the future depends on the extent to which the whole group sees that the model has possibilities for their board. Obviously, all eleven boards discussed in this book did see something. But what was it?

The selected boards had all sorts of hopes for Policy Governance. One hoped it would be able to stave off or manage crises by using the model. Others saw the possibility of greater board discipline and unity. Another was keen to reduce the number of its committees, which had become more powerful than the board itself and which had "staff on a treadmill supporting them." Three overarching possibilities clearly emerge for boards that use Policy Governance: role clarity, mission accomplishment, and workload manageability.

Role Clarity. Of all the boards we examined, most thought Policy Governance could clarify roles and make their relationships with their CEOs and staff members more productive. The board of the Law Society of Upper Canada, for example, was appointing a new CEO and wanted "a real CEO to be accountable for operations, not someone who was second in command under the chair." The United Way of Burlington, Hamilton-Wentworth, had been suffering from a "mixed understanding about who did what both on the board and in the operations." The City of Bryan believed that "councils could govern more effectively. Staff could work more aggressively." For the CEO of the Colorado Association of School Boards, Policy Governance "just made sense. I've been in the business of working with school boards for twenty-nine years, and there is a constant struggle to decide who does what. All the checklists on earth have never accurately divided the line of responsibility." The Vermont Land Trust "understood that their minute evaluation of individual staff decisions did not add value." The YMCA-YWCA of London wanted a governance approach that would better "define the staff and volunteer partnership that is so much a part of the organization's philosophy."

Mission Accomplishment. Most boards also thought Policy Governance would help them focus on accomplishing their organization's mission. The Colorado Association of School Boards says, "Another attraction for using Policy Governance with school boards was that it forced them to deal with things that matter, which is the source of most of our problems regarding effectiveness." Before Policy Governance, members of the Southern Ontario Library Service board "were finding that the traditional model was requiring them to spend a lot of time on the wrong questions (such as details of vacation leave) and preventing them from making a real contribution to the organization." The Vermont Land Trust found that "people were not excited about coming to the meetings—although they were very excited about the mission. Typically three or four people would talk about the projects and everyone else [would] disengage."

Board members of the Early Childhood Community Development Centre wanted their organization "to be the best place it can be," and they clearly saw Policy Governance as offering that possibility. The City of Bryan considered a further benefit: "Citizens of Bryan could be engaged in . . . thinking about the future of the community in concert with the council. In the final analysis, it was this promise of reconnecting with the citizens and the council that proved to be the most alluring."

Workload Manageability. Some organizations believed that Policy Governance would enable them to handle the volume of work with greater ease. For the City of Bryan, "In the press of business it never seemed there was time to talk about dreams—only immediate concerns. Carver's model seemed to be a breath of fresh air!" Certainly many boards have too much for a small group of part-time people to do. One organization reports, "The board was meeting directly with groups of staff and approving all operational policies at all levels." In another organization, "All committees met the night before a board meeting and reviewed the myriad reports from staff. The committees usually accepted the staff recommendations, forwarding them to the board for approval. The next day the whole board reviewed the recommendations once again—and again approved them."

How Do Boards Consider Whether Policy Governance Is Right for Them?

Once board members have heard enough about Policy Governance to see that it has some possibility for them, they have to consider more closely whether it really is right for their organization. They must prepare to make the decision to adopt or not to adopt. In this section we will concentrate on how boards consider adopting Policy Governance. In the next chapter we will look at how they actually decide.

Examining Governance Options. Boards use a variety of methods to consider whether Policy Governance is right for their organization. Some boards, such as that of the Law Society of Upper Canada, look at all the governance options they can find. Others hire a governance consultant to identify the board's governance needs and to recommend the best way to proceed. In all these ways, boards attempt to gain a general understanding of the field of governance.

Introducing the Model to the Whole Board. Having decided to take a closer look at Policy Governance, boards usually seek someone who knows enough about it to give them a good introductory session. Unless a board or staff member has an extensive background in the model, board members look for external specialists. Some boards bring in John Carver (often sharing the cost with other boards). Others find Policy Governance consultants through their professional networks. In most cases, these people have been personally trained by John and Miriam Carver. Policy Governance introductory sessions normally last at least a full day and often involve senior staff members as well as all board members.

Seeking Other Resources. In most cases boards supplement this session with other educational resources:

- Policy Governance books (see Resource C, "Further Reading and Resources," for a list of the main titles). The book most used as a starting point is Carver's *Boards That Make a Difference.* Many boards purchase several copies of that book and distribute them among board members. One board had each member read two chapters and report back to the full board.
- Other Policy Governance reference materials, such as audiotapes, videotapes, booklets, and the bimonthly newsletter *Board Leadership* (see Resource C).
- Discussions with other boards (preferably of similar organizations) that have implemented the model.
- Conversations with anyone and everyone, internal and external, who has some knowledge of Policy Governance. Several of the boards covered in this book had board members or staff members who had worked with other Policy Governance boards.

This learning process should teach the board and especially the CEO two main things: (1) what the principles of Policy Governance are, and (2) what impact Policy Governance will have on the board's behavior and outcomes.

What Kinds of Organizations Consider Policy Governance?

All kinds of organizations consider Policy Governance. In preparing this book, we deliberately selected eleven organizations that represent a broad range of functions: health, regulatory, fundraising, association, environment, municipal, recreational, educational, child-care, cooperative, advocacy, government, and library. Our wider experience also shows that Policy Governance is taken up by organizations operating in every field.

Public and Quasi-Governmental Organizations. Structural circumstances affect the kinds of governance challenges a board faces. For instance, boards that are subject to legislation—such as professional regulatory bodies, school boards, colleges, hospitals, and municipal governments—know that they have to operate within a system that is often incompatible with Policy Governance. However, as five of the organizations in our selection are subject to considerable legislative influence, it seems that this situation does not deter boards from considering Policy Governance. Boards with publicly elected members also know that if they use the model, they will need to change their electorates' expectations. Again, this does not seem to have dissuaded the relevant organizations in our selection.

Fundraising and Advocacy Organizations. Boards such as the San Francisco AIDS Foundation and the United Way come from a tradition in which a large part of the organization's purpose, as well as the board's purpose, is to raise funds. Organizations in which the board has had a direct and major role in fundraising, advocacy, or any other nongovernance activity must consider how they will handle this role under Policy Governance. Their choices are either to delegate fundraising to the CEO or to retain it as a board responsibility, which can create additional challenges in sustaining the discipline of Policy Governance. Again, this factor did not deter the organizations in our selection from considering Policy Governance.

Small and Large Organizations. The boards we selected came from organizations of all sizes, ranging from fifteen to almost one thousand staff members. In our experience this is representative of the organizations that are attracted to Policy Governance; they can be small or large. Board size does not seem to be a factor in the consideration of Policy Governance, either. Large boards will face additional challenges in maintaining the kind of discipline required, but the ones in our sample didn't let that put them off from further exploration.

What Other Variables Affect Whether Policy Governance Will Be Attractive to an Organization?

In this section we will briefly look at whether boards turn to Policy Governance when they are old or new, doing well or facing trouble.

Age. From the eleven experiences we have studied, the age of an organization is an unlikely predictor of whether it will be attracted to Policy Governance. The Law Society of Upper Canada was, for example, founded in 1797, whereas Parkland Health District was founded in 1994. In theory at least, a brand-new organization might find the practice of Policy Governance easier, because the organization lacks the baggage of old habits and practices, but we have insufficient evidence to make that assertion definitive.

Presence or Absence of a Crisis. From the experiences in our sample, it seems that most organizations are not in a serious crisis when they begin considering Policy Governance. Apparently, the San Francisco AIDS Foundation had no need for change and no pressing governance issues. The chair says relations on the board were "harmonious" and notes that the agency was "well run." Some would say, "If it works, don't fix it." But the board felt that it needed to "find its role, its voice" and believed that Policy Governance would help it do so.

Although most boards that consider Policy Governance are not in an organizational crisis, many do have some concerns about their current governance process. These vary from minor irritations to situations in which the board is meddling in operations too much. In the latter scenario, staff members can become frustrated and alienated, or board members so overloaded that it is difficult to recruit new board members. Such difficulties are inherent in traditional governance practices. Whether Policy Governance can remedy these problems is one of the main questions this book seeks to answer.

☑ Key Learnings

As the eleven organizations told us how they came to consider Policy Governance, we drew the following conclusions.

It Doesn't Matter Who Gets the Ball Rolling

It doesn't seem to matter who first brings Policy Governance to the board's attention or how board members hear about it. The only important thing is that someone be motivated enough to discuss it with the board and persuade board members to learn more.

But the Board Must Pick Up the Ball

Although any member of the board or the staff can initiate interest in Policy Governance, successful governance change ultimately results from the board's momentum.

And the CEO Must Be at Least Willing to Run with It

It is the board's responsibility to govern well, whatever the CEO's attitude is. However, in practice, it seems to be important that both the board chair and the CEO be interested in learning more about the model. Once the board uses Policy Governance, the board chair and the CEO will each serve separate leadership functions. That is, the board chair will lead governance while the CEO will lead the management and support the governance function. Eventually, both parties must be committed to Policy Governance. Although commitment is certainly not required at this stage, strong interest in learning more about Policy Governance definitely is.

Policy Governance is easiest to consider when an organization is strong and when the board chair and CEO both understand and champion the model. Ideally, the chair will be able to provide structure and leadership in the exploration process, and the CEO will be able to provide support, information, and linkage with the staff. When the CEO takes the lead alone, as sometimes happens, the board may never pick up the ball or, more often than not, it will eventually get dropped. Ultimately, the CEO cannot do the board's job for the board members.

The Board Must Be Ready to Learn

Right from the start, well before the board even begins to examine what Policy Governance is about, board members must be interested in learning something new and willing to address what may be, as yet, unarticulated governance concerns.

Policy Governance Has Three Main Attractions for Boards

The three principal attractions of Policy Governance seem to be role clarity (between board and staff), a reorientation of the board's energy (toward mission accomplishment and away from the detail of operations), and the establishment of manageable workloads. These goals may not be well articulated when a board first considers Policy Governance. Nevertheless they exist in the minds and experiences of board members and cause the board to be open to potential change.

The Board Must See the Possibility for the Organization

Unless a board truly sees what a change to Policy Governance could mean for the organization, it will remain an interesting idea. Policy Governance is a major shift in thinking and practice—not just something extra that will happen at board meetings.

Any Board Can See the Possibilities of Policy Governance

Boards from any sector, boards of any type, size, or age, and boards in any situation except a dire crisis seem to be attracted to Policy Governance.

○ Taking Action: Strategies for Where You Are Now

At this moment, your board may not even have begun to consider changing the way it governs, or it may already be exploring a change. The next two sections give some advice and tips, whatever your board's starting position.

If Your Board Has Not Yet Been Introduced to Policy Governance

If you are thinking of introducing your board to Policy Governance, you will need to be clear about its possibilities for your board. Avoid making your introduction sound like a criticism of current practice. Unless everyone is dissatisfied with the way things are, you may get a negative reaction. It will be very helpful if you can cite other organizations in your field that have successfully implemented Policy Governance. It will also be beneficial if you can think of someone with a thorough knowledge of the model who could make a full introduction at a special board session.

If Your Board Is Currently Considering Policy Governance

Your board may already be considering Policy Governance or some form of governance change. If so, make sure that both the board chair and the CEO are heavily involved in discussions that could have a huge impact on their work. Perhaps they should have a leadership role in such conversations. Encourage everyone to read, to conduct other research, and to talk to others as much as possible. See the next section for ideas about how to make this exploration more effective.

▶ Practical Tips and Tools

Here are some tips and tools for exploring Policy Governance.

Reflect on the Purpose of a Board

Ask board members why they think boards exist. It can also be useful to ask why we have CEOs and to contrast the answers to the two questions. Finally, ask board members what boards and CEOs need in order to work together. Such an inquiry is likely to help the board start considering what Policy Governance has to offer.

Reflect on How the Board Would Like to Develop Its Governance

Ask board members what aspects of their governance they would like to develop in the future. This is a good way to articulate your board's specific governance issues. For example, is the board confused about its role in relation to the staff's role? Does the board want to reduce the number of its committees? Is board member dissatisfaction or turnover a problem? Is there a desire to do more to ensure that the organization is really improving the quality of clients' lives?

Create a List of What Any Good Governance Model Should Provide

List the criteria that any good governance model should provide. Whatever the concerns or the reasons for wanting a change in governance, they should be articulated and documented so that the board can choose a model that specifically addresses those issues.

Invest in Learning

Have the board consider how much good governance is worth to the organization. Boards often devalue their own importance, but if they have really pondered the questions mentioned earlier, they should realize that it is worthwhile to invest time and money in improving their governance. You may want the board to read books on Policy Governance and to get the video- or audiocassettes. You might want to bring in a knowledgeable person to do a full introduction. Board members might reject these expenditures as unnecessary or frivolous unless they understand them to be an investment in the board's capital.

Find Out What's Available

See Resource C to find out what's available in terms of Policy Governance. Your local college may offer training in Policy Governance. Ask other organizations who are using the model about what has been useful for them. Visit the Policy Governance web site, *www.policygovernance.com*, for information about John Carver's courses. Ask people in your professional network if they can refer you to a trained consultant in Policy Governance.

CHAPTER TWO

DECIDING IF POLICY GOVERNANCE IS RIGHT FOR YOUR ORGANIZATION

☐ The Challenge

This chapter examines how boards move from having seen the possibility of Policy Governance to deciding to adopt it. If your board is in the process of making this commitment or if it has already made the commitment but you have concerns about the strength of that commitment, you will find much of value here. As the chapter will explain, adopting Policy Governance is a crucial step toward actually being a Policy Governance board. It represents a commitment to operate under Policy Governance as soon as reasonably possible. This is a very serious commitment not only because the board will have to invest considerable time and effort in developing policy but also because, if all goes well, it will forever change the way the board operates.

The chapter begins by reviewing the experience of the organizations we have studied in relation to the following questions:

- How do boards achieve commitment?
- How do boards decide to adopt?
- What happens when there is not unanimous agreement?
- When is a board ready to implement Policy Governance?

From the answers to these questions we draw some conclusions about securing the kind of commitment needed when implementing Policy Governance. We then invite you to examine the strength of your own board's commitment and give some advice, tips, and tools on creating or re-creating that level of commitment.

■ The Experience

How Do Boards Achieve Commitment?

The main way boards achieve commitment is by clearly, fully, openly, and respectfully addressing all the concerns board members have. There can be many. A senior staff member from one organization that could not sustain the process of implementing Policy Governance claims that the board members "didn't understand what they were buying." Board members did not have a true understanding of the change, so they did not fully engage with Policy Governance.

Raising Common Concerns. Here are some of the main concerns board members raise in the course of adopting Policy Governance.

We'll Be Saying We've Been Wrong All Along. Sometimes enthusiastic board or staff members present the model in such a way that the other members only hear a repudiation of past practice. This can create a powerful resistance from board leadership, both past and present.

It's a Fad. Is Policy Governance just the latest fashion? Will it become outdated? Will we be embarrassed?

We'll Be Out on a Limb. Who has done this before? Does Policy Governance work? Is it tested? Is it tried? According to one staff member, the board chair feared that "we were going down a track that no one had been down before and we were going to regret it."

People Will Think We Are Abdicating Our Job. The board is concerned about what the people around them will think, because people have come to expect the board to address operational items at meetings. This is an especially real issue for membership association and public boards. For example, a school board that refrains from making staff hiring decisions could worry that the public will see it as not fulfilling its duties.

It's a Guru's Dream. The fact that Policy Governance is the personal creation of one man, John Carver, can make it hard for boards to adopt it as their own. There is a natural resistance to buying into someone else's model. One CEO says of a past chair, "The fact that it wasn't his idea diminished it for him."

The CEO Will Have Too Much Power. Some board members find it hard to see the adoption of Executive Limitations policies as anything other than a big giveaway of their power to the staff and feel they will become disenfranchised.

We'll Lose Touch. Board members have fears about losing touch with what is going on in the organization and not having enough information to keep them interested and in control.

This Isn't the "Real Work." For board members who have been service volunteers—people who do the hands-on work of helping staff members—the new governance model isn't what they signed up for. Boards that are currently directly engaged in fundraising, advocacy, and special committees are likely to be concerned about what will happen to their work under Policy Governance.

The Board Won't Have Anything to Do. Once board members begin to see the amount of work they can safely delegate to the CEO using Policy Governance, they sometimes worry that there will be nothing to do instead.

There's a Cultural Clash. Boards may have concerns about whether the Policy Governance model fits well with their current culture.

Something Else Has Come Up. Sometimes boards simply become overwhelmed by unexpected events and feel that they have to put their Policy Governance work on the back burner.

The Staff Members Have Concerns. Some boards meet with resistance from staff members, who have gotten used to determining the organization's direction through their own day-to-day decision making. A staff member says, "One of the ironies that came out of all this is that the board had been doing staff work and the staff had been doing board work. Staff [members get] the jitters. They think, 'Who are these people on the board? What makes them capable of making these decisions when it is *we* who devote our lives to this and know the issues?'"

Handling the Concerns. There is no way to avoid facing these issues (and there are undoubtedly more that come up). Boards simply have to tackle them head-on.

What follows are some pointers from the experience of the organizations covered in this book.

Get Satisfactory Answers. A lot of unnecessary damage can be done when a question is not fully answered. Board members are making a very big decision. Their concerns and fears are real, and they deserve good answers. It is well worth investing effort and, if necessary, money to obtain the required level of Policy Governance expertise, whether in-house or external. This is the stage when reluctant or skeptical board members need to be able to ask the hard questions that someone new to the model will probably not be equipped to answer.

Check Understanding. There is a danger that the powerful effect of an eloquent expert or consultant or the enthusiasm of a board member or the CEO can persuade board members to make a decision to which they are not really committed. The board must truly understand the issues being addressed and the implications for board operations.

Stick to the Model. It is vital to look at every issue raised in terms of the principles and practice of the model. As one CEO says of an introductory board retreat facilitated by a Policy Governance specialist, "There wasn't a question asked that the Policy Governance model couldn't answer."

Make It Specific to Your Business. Rather than taking part in an introduction for several organizations, it is a great advantage if board members can ask all their questions in a context that is specific to their own organization. Having a free exchange of concerns with someone who knows the Policy Governance model and who can relate to your kind of organization also helps bring together theory and practice.

We're in This Thing Together. There is also great benefit in simply convening the board in one place to hear the same thing at the same time. This creates consistency and helps with team building. The chair of the Southern Ontario Library Service board says its initial retreat "was key because we all had the same experience together."

It May Not Work for Everyone. Some issues are particularly difficult and may lead board members to decide that Policy Governance is not for them, which is a decision they have every right to make. For instance, if service volunteers form a large part of the board, it may not be able to implement Policy Governance successfully. The Southern Ontario Library Service chair believes that "if the board is a mix of governance and service volunteers, there may not be enough clarity of purpose to undertake the shift to this model successfully." As some boards in our study adopted Policy Governance, service volunteers left. The boards were, however, able to make this a harmonious process by ensuring an alternative way for these service volunteers to continue serving the organization.

Try It On. At the Vermont Land Trust, a consultant led the board through a discussion of a topic using the board's typical process and then led the same discussion using the principles of Policy Governance. One board member reports that "in the discussion that followed the old model, there were all kinds of helpful questions like, 'Did you consider . . . ?' (to which the staff always answered yes) and 'Tell me about . . .' (which was nice and anecdotal but not value-added). In the discussion that took place using Policy Governance principles, there was a light bulb that went on for people. This might have been the conversation that convinced people this was the way to go."

Try It Out. Another board took an organizational topic for which it might develop Executive Limitations and simply asked the members, "What are your fears?" The members were able to develop an Executive Limitations policy based on their concerns. In this way, they practiced Policy Governance without having adopted it. One board member says, "This was the first time I felt like I could really contribute to the discussion." They discovered not only that they were competent at applying the model but also that the model would enable them to govern in the truest sense, not just react to individual issues.

Try It Out Some More. Boards know their agendas will change under Policy Governance. But what will that change look like? Going through mock meetings really helps boards get the feel of Policy Governance and start reframing some of their concerns. For instance, once boards start discussing Executive Limitations, they can see that they actually have more oversight and control over the multitude of possible issues. When they start having their Ends conversations, they can see how unaccountable they were before because they were not explicitly stating the outcomes they seek.

Ignore It, and It Won't Go Away. The advice of numerous CEOs and board members is to allow plenty of time for discussion and not to ignore the resistance. The model *can* answer difficult questions that arise for board members. The Southern Ontario Library Service chair describes what made the process work for that board: "Interest came from board members themselves and was allowed to grow at its own pace. With each discussion, more questions were grappled with and answered to some degree of comfort, and more board members came on side."

Talk to Other Policy Governance Boards. Talking to other boards that are truly using Policy Governance is one of the best ways to learn what it's like to live with the model and to assuage fears and concerns. One board says the testimonials it received from similar boards were "compelling."

Keep the Benefits Clear. Keep the possibilities that the board first saw alive and well. If board members are to understand the model fully, they must discuss not only their concerns but also the benefits of the model. The city manager of Bryan, Texas, asserts that the "clear benefit needs to be articulated." He describes his council as "less than enthusiastic in the early going." Members have overcome this by constantly keeping the possibility of Policy Governance in the forefront. When the board members of the Southern Ontario Library Service met and formally voted to adopt Policy Governance, they very clearly stated its potential benefits: "The Policy Governance model would enable the . . . board to play a more significant leadership and advocacy role on behalf of its stakeholders, and board time currently spent on reviewing internal issues could be spent discussing issues of community concern."

How Do Boards Decide to Adopt?

Having examined the pros and cons of Policy Governance, boards need to take the formal step of agreeing to adopt the model. In this section we examine how boards go about taking that step.

The Adoption Process. A major word of caution: When people talk about "adopting" or "implementing" Policy Governance, they may not mean the same things. We need to define our terms.

Generally (but by no means always) the process goes like this:

1. The board agrees to *consider* Policy Governance (the subject of Chapter One).
2. The board agrees to *adopt* the model (the subject of this chapter). By *adopt* we mean making the decision to become a Policy Governance board.
3. The board agrees on all its policies (Executive Limitations, Board-Staff Relationship, Governance Process, and at least a holding statement on Ends) and is ready to *implement* Policy Governance (the subject of Chapter Three). By *implement* we mean enact and live by the policies. Only at this point is Policy Governance truly in place.

This picture of the usual process is complicated by the fact that some boards, as you will learn in the next chapter, start operating under some Policy

Governance principles before they have developed the policies and are in a position to implement the model fully. Others decide to develop the policies before formally adopting Policy Governance. For example, Bryan's city council and the Vermont Land Trust had their policies in place before they officially adopted Policy Governance. For these organizations, therefore, adoption and implementation occurred simultaneously.

Most boards covered in this book have followed the three-stage exploration-adoption-implementation process described above. The road to adoption can be a long one. For example, the Early Childhood Community Development Centre decided to adopt Policy Governance at the meeting following the board's one-day Policy Governance introduction. However, this decision was also the culmination of much prior investigation and education. Similarly, the Law Society of Upper Canada unanimously voted to adopt Policy Governance after having several meetings with John Carver, doing much research, viewing the video, and drawing on the organization's in-house expertise. The San Francisco AIDS Foundation decided to adopt Policy Governance at a board retreat with Carver one year after an introduction that it had shared with two other organizations. The board had also had two people trained at the Policy Governance Academy, reviewed books and tapes, and had several internal discussions.

The Southern Ontario Library Service took just under a year to get from the board's first exposure to Policy Governance to a daylong orientation session with Carver. An informal poll after the session was "overwhelmingly in favor" of adoption, but two members supported partial implementation. To investigate this possibility the board established a committee for which almost half of the members volunteered. Two months later the committee came back to a meeting of the board and the committee chairs with a recommendation to adopt the model in its entirety and to hold a policy development session at the next board meeting. This recommendation was tabled as a motion at the next full board meeting and approved.

Decision making about adopting Policy Governance can only be done by the whole board itself. Establishing subgroups of the board to reflect on governance issues can be dangerous, because the board loses ownership of designing its own job. In one case we studied, only the members of the subgroup were committed to Policy Governance. When all of those members retired, so did the momentum for Policy Governance.

Establishing Agreement. In order to adopt Policy Governance, a board obviously needs a majority agreement. However, of the eleven organizations covered in this book, those who successfully implemented Policy Governance did not necessarily have unanimous votes in favor of adopting the model. Generally the board chair and the CEO (who usually does not have a formal vote) are two crucial players who do need to agree with the decision to adopt Policy Governance, having understood its implications for their respective jobs. In nine of the eleven organizations, both the CEO and the board chair supported the move to Policy Governance.

Whatever the size and composition of the vote to adopt, achieving true commitment is one of the most important requirements for implementing Policy Governance successfully. The process of achieving this commitment requires a degree of discipline and rigor that boards may not anticipate. Because Policy Governance is so different from traditional governance, board members have no previous experience on which to base expectations. It would be fair to say that once the board decides to adopt Policy Governance, its real work begins. Even though, more often than not, board members have already committed a significant amount of time to learning about Policy Governance and how it will benefit their board, there is a lot more to do. Without real commitment to using the model, the board will not have enough motivation to stay on track.

Commitment does not mean going along with the rest of the board. It does not mean making the governance subgroup or the eager board chair happy. It is perfectly possible for boards to agree to adopt Policy Governance but not to have a real understanding of what that decision means. For these boards, adoption is certainly not the same as commitment, and a rocky road lies ahead as they try to develop and use their policies.

What Happens When There Is Not Unanimous Agreement?

The fact that a vote to adopt Policy Governance is not unanimous can reveal that real commitment is absent. More often, it simply means that a few people are not in favor of the move, revealing nothing about the commitment of the board as a whole. The vote at the Southern Ontario Library Service, for example, was not unanimous (although very nearly so), yet the board has tackled the challenges of Policy Governance with considerable success.

Some individual opposition will likely melt away as Policy Governance progresses. One organization reports, "The opposition wasn't really opposition to the model. Some just couldn't understand their role. Some stuck it out and, to their surprise, have found a comfortable role." In other cases, opposing members have slowed down the postadoption process and made life difficult but not brought the process to a halt.

Diversity of views is more than welcome in a Policy Governance board. Members who tend to raise objections frequently trigger more thoughtful action. As long as board members are ultimately committed to the principle of "speaking with one voice" and that voice is completely committed to Policy Governance, it will be successful.

This is particularly well illustrated by the two organizations in our sample in which the board chair voted against adoption. A member of the first organization reports that "the chair was a hard sell. He raised every issue in the book. Fortunately this only reinforced the strength and consistency of the model. Once the board voted, he accepted the vote and immersed himself in the model. He did lots of reading and interacted with other people that he met on the Internet [who were] practicing the model. He tried honestly to make it work." And it has worked. In the second organization, the chair was opposed, but the board as a whole has continued successfully with the implementation process.

In most of the cases we studied, the chair or the CEO or both could definitely be described as "champions" of the model. In only one of the eleven boards did board members leave as a result of the adoption of Policy Governance. However, we suspect other boards may have had the same experience.

When Is a Board Ready to Implement Policy Governance?

Once the board has agreed to adopt Policy Governance, it is ready to start developing its policies prior to full implementation. Or is it? Here's another way of asking this question: How do you know, even after the decision has been made to adopt Policy Governance, that your board's commitment is real enough to carry you through to implementation? The next chapter looks at preparing the board for success in implementing Policy Governance. Here we examine the factors that influence whether a board is ready to go there at all.

The Board Understands What the Model Can Contribute. It will certainly help if your board addresses concerns and benefits as described in this chapter and thereby clearly identifies the results it wants from Policy Governance. You can envision these results when the going gets rough and use them as the criteria for evaluating success once Policy Governance is being used. For instance, is the key goal clarifying roles? Improving leadership? Delegating better to staff? Being more accountable? Or just understanding the board's job and doing it well?

The Board Feels That It Owns the Model. The boards that moved forward most easily with Policy Governance had internalized this new approach to governance. They didn't just adopt the Policy Governance model or become "Carverized." Instead they truly made it their own.

The Board Has No Immediate Problems. The board is just about to take on a major chunk of work—developing its policies. Once it has gotten through this phase and actually implemented Policy Governance, life will become a lot easier. But is the board in good enough shape to make it?

The board with no immediate problems certainly has a head start. A senior staff member at the San Francisco AIDS Foundation sums it up in this way: "The agency was very well run, and that certainly was a *key* to [its] ability to be comfortable with the model. Management was stable. The CEO had the confidence of the board [and] wasn't a beginner. The agency was on a strong fiscal track. Also the board [members were] able to transition to Policy Governance because they were harmonious."

A few of the organizations covered in this book were experiencing major difficulties when they adopted Policy Governance. It is hard for board members to talk about their fears and to create a new operating structure when they feel like the house is burning down around them. They simply will not be able to devote the necessary time. A member of one organization that struggled with the policy development process says, "There were so many issues impinging on the organization that it was difficult for the board to concentrate on developing policies." Another notes that "having interim CEOs has had a negative effect on board momentum." The organization needs to be feeling reasonably strong if the transition to a new method of governing is to be feasible.

For the organization swept up in a crisis, this is a double bind. The board members can't address Policy Governance because they don't have the time to do the work to put it in place; they don't have the time because they are not using Policy Governance. This book gives several examples of organizations that met crises farther down the Policy Governance road and felt that they were able to handle them far more effectively because they were using Policy Governance.

The Board Knows How to Combine Member Turnover with Its Shift to the Model. Two of the organizations debated about the timing of implementation. That is, they wondered whether they should postpone policy development work until the new board was elected or whether they should do the work themselves and pass this legacy on to the new board. Both boards decided to develop policies immediately. That way, one of their criteria for selecting new board members could be their suitability for working with Policy Governance.

Boards need to look at the kinds of skills required to be on a Policy Governance board. These include the ability to think about the future and to deal with abstract, qualitative ideas. Traditional boards are more likely to require members with skills that mirror organizational operations, such as managing finance, fundraising, public relations, and personnel. Under Policy Governance, board members need to give up the satisfaction usually associated with making short-term concrete decisions and being involved in day-to-day operations; instead they will be linking with owners and shaping the organization's long-term future. See Chapter Eight for more on recruitment and orientation of new board members.

☑ Key Learnings

This chapter has looked at how a board moves from exploring Policy Governance to deciding to become a Policy Governance board. In the process, it commits to doing all that is necessary to develop policies and to start actually *being* a Policy Governance board. What follows is a review of what we have said about this crucial stage.

Concerns, Concerns, Concerns

Understandably, as a board moves toward making a real commitment, many concerns and fears arise. These all need to be brought into the open and addressed. Avoiding them will only hamper the Policy Governance process later. The concerns could become magnified over time. Addressing the concerns together is also a great way of increasing everyone's understanding of the model.

Get Good Answers

The board deserves good answers to questions on matters of such importance. The answers to all the questions can be found in the design of the Policy Governance model itself. Thus it is important that the board consult with an expert who has a thorough knowledge of the model. Keep checking for understanding. Don't let the board be bowled over by sheer charisma or pulling power. It will also help if the person answering the questions understands your particular kind of organization.

Try It On, Try It Out

One of the very best ways to understand Policy Governance is to try it out. Take a current issue and see how it would be treated under Policy Governance. Look at a mock agenda. Have an Ends discussion about a particular topic. Using your expert will bring out all the learning value.

Keep the Possibility Alive

Don't just talk about the concerns. Keep examining the benefits, too. The things that attracted your board to Policy Governance in the first place, and any further possibilities you see as you go through the exploration process, will ultimately carry you through—or not.

Adoption Doesn't Have to Be Unanimous

Not everyone has to agree in order for the adoption of Policy Governance to work. Inevitably some people who vote for the model (even after all the preparation and discussion) may not completely understand what they have gotten themselves into. A vote to adopt Policy Governance is not a guarantee that everyone is truly committed to it.

Some Disagreement Is Fine

If a few people on the board are uncommitted, either the commitment of the majority will pull them through to the point that they start seeing and believing in the benefits or they will leave. Either way, the board as a whole can succeed and can even welcome or at least tolerate the resistance. Some resistance is a drag, but constructive critics are needed on every board.

You Are Ready to Move Forward When Your Board Is Committed

Adoption works when it reflects true commitment. Your board can only be truly committed if you have addressed all concerns fully, openly, and honestly and if you have been clear about the possibility you are pursuing. You are ready to begin creating policies and implementing Policy Governance if the following is true: you know what you are doing and why, you see Policy Governance less as someone else's idea and more as your own, and you are reasonably confident that you can make the time and will devote the energy to pursue Policy Governance.

○ Taking Action: Strategies for Where You Are Now

At this stage, your board may have become very enthusiastic about Policy Governance, or it may be stuck in stated or unstated disagreements about whether it is the right way to go. The next two sections provide some advice and tips for wherever you are.

If Your Board Is Ready to Go

If your board members are raring to adopt Policy Governance and get on with developing their policies, it is still worthwhile to check their common and individual understanding before moving on. Are the board members truly committed to change, or are they just going along with the rest of the board? Are they clear about how it will change their work, how much time they will need to invest in developing their initial policies, and how they will operate until all the policies are in place? Do they really understand what Policy Governance is?

If Your Board Is Still Debating

If your board is currently trying to handle opposition or fears about Policy Governance, are you taking the concerns seriously and documenting them, or are you trying to gloss over them? Have you invested enough time and money in learning about Policy Governance and discovering what Policy Governance will mean to your board? Has your board clearly articulated which aspects of governance it wishes to improve? This is a critical step for both evaluating success after implementation and determining whether Policy Governance is the right governance solution for your board.

If There Are Individual Concerns. Are there board members with serious concerns about Policy Governance? Some may simply have a different vision of what governance is about. What is their vision? You may find that, as individuals, they wish to continue doing hands-on work, in which case there is nothing to prevent them from continuing to volunteer. The only difference is that under Policy Governance they would be volunteering like any other volunteer; their work would not be considered a board function. They also need to be aware that it takes discipline to wear two hats.

Other board members may be concerned about losing touch or losing control. What are their fears exactly? How could they be addressed in policy? What could happen under Policy Governance in a worst-case scenario? What could happen under the current form of governance in a worst-case scenario?

If the Whole Board Is Concerned. In addition to the above concerns, which the whole board could share, you may find that the entire board and staff want the board to continue playing a part in fundraising or in some other function. If so, do they want board members to do this as volunteers, or do they want the board to retain the function as a direct board responsibility? In the latter case, can they distinguish the board and staff roles sufficiently to keep from backsliding into a situation in which no one is truly accountable?

If Your Board Is Definitely Split

If it is clear that board members have had all the information and discussion time they need and if the board is definitely split, the members need to decide how they wish to proceed. How would the minority suggest that the board as a whole resolve the matter? Should the board decide not to move without consensus, or should it just go with the decision of a specified majority? Would the majority be willing to defer the decision until just before the next election so that current members who are unwilling to operate under Policy Governance can serve out their full terms? If the board is split 50–50, with what frequency should the issue be reviewed? Should potential new members be told of the debate? What process should be used in any future review? Are there discussion and decision-making tools that the board can use now or in the future to help the process along? What other ideas does the board have?

▶ Practical Tips and Tools

Here are some tips and tools for helping your board make its decision about Policy Governance.

Get the Concerns on the Table

Encourage and welcome skepticism so that real concerns can be addressed. See Exhibits 2.1, 2.2, and 2.3 for some techniques to ensure that you are really listening. People need to buy in at their own pace, which may be sooner for some than for others. Board members should not feel like they are being sold something; Policy Governance should be something they want. As board members learn about the model, make sure that they all have an opportunity to learn the principles of Policy Governance (individually and as a group) and that all have a chance to articulate their questions or concerns.

Create a Worry List

Document board members' concerns in a worry list so that they can be dealt with, either right then or later, when the group investigates the benefits of Policy Governance. Keep the list of concerns in front of the group, and tick them off the list when people agree that the concern has been sufficiently dealt with. Make sure all the tough questions have been addressed.

Create a Possibilities List

The board will probably have some clear ideas about why it is attracted to Policy Governance. Now that board members are ready to develop policies, it is time to revisit and refine this list. This will help the board keep the possibility alive as it moves through to implementation. As an example or a guide, Exhibit 2.4 presents the list generated by the board of the Southern Ontario Library Service.

EXHIBIT 2.1. LISTENING TO DISSENTING VOICES.

When people disagree, they often push their own ideas harder. At best, they try to persuade. At worst, they just override objections.

For good group process, start with the assumption that all group members have something important to offer in terms of perspective, expertise, or thoughtfulness. When others disagree with you, therefore, the ideal stance is to be curious about how they arrived at their point of view. If you listen to dissenting voices, you are likely to discover that

- Others are missing some important data that you have that would cause them to change their mind.
- Others have additional data that you didn't know about that would cause you to change your mind.
- Others are operating with a different set of assumptions or goals, in which case the group must resolve a bigger area of disagreement than just the specific issue.

In all cases, listening to dissenting voices can improve the group's work, because it ensures that all information is shared. This approach requires people not only to have a point of view but also to clarify how they arrived at that opinion.

EXHIBIT 2.2. BALANCING ADVOCACY WITH INQUIRY.

Balance advocacy with inquiry as the board makes its decision. Advocacy means making your thought process visible to the group. You state not only your viewpoint but also the logic with which you arrived there. Inquiry means investigating the thought process of another person, particularly one with whom you disagree. Both processes involve asking yourself or the other person, "What leads you to that view?"

Balancing advocacy and inquiry ensures that all voices are heard and that the thinking that informs each member's viewpoint is fully expressed and understood. This rule is one of five ground rules for "skilled discussion" elaborated on in *The Fifth Discipline Fieldbook*.

Source: P. Senge and others, *The Fifth Discipline Fieldbook* (New York: Doubleday, 1994).

EXHIBIT 2.3. A DIFFERENT POINT OF VIEW.

Purpose: Group members will look at an issue or problem from different points of view. This technique can be used when a group wants to broaden its thinking, explore issues from several perspectives, and ensure diversity in viewpoints.

Technique: Ask each group member to consider the issue from three points of view. For example, if your board is developing Ends (specifically considering the question "What good for which people?"), ask board members to identify people's needs from the perspectives of a senior citizen, a teenager, and a single parent.

This technique could also be used when a board is determining effective methods of linkage with the ownership. Tell board members to assume three different identities and to ask themselves, "If I were a _____, how would I want to express my thoughts to this board?"

Test Understanding

To determine the level of understanding of the ten principles of Policy Governance (see "The Principles of Policy Governance Explained" in the beginning of this book), try asking all the board members to explain, in their own words, what each principle means to them. Similarly, ask the board how they think meetings will be different. List the answers and discuss them.

Do Some Mock Work

Do some mock Policy Governance work, such as the following:

- Hold an Ends discussion in a particular arena of your current work.
- State a concern in Executive Limitations language.
- Identify the broadest board value from a very specific concern.
- See what policy category an issue might fall into.
- Use Policy Governance principles to analyze how a recent board decision would have been handled under Policy Governance. Compare that with the way it was handled under the existing model of governance.

For example, in relation to Executive Limitations policies, think of an arena where a board should show oversight. Financial condition and budgeting are two concrete examples that board members can usually relate to easily. Ask, "What,

---

EXHIBIT 2.4. REASONS WE ARE PURSUING POLICY GOVERNANCE.

- The board will no longer simply rubber-stamp staff actions.
- The board will use its time more effectively.
- There will be a clear distinction between board and CEO roles.
- The board will have the opportunity to build linkages with its ownership and with other library community stakeholders.
- The board will fill a leadership role in the public library community.
- Board concern with Ends values and Executive Limitations will facilitate measurement and evaluation.

Source: Southern Ontario Library Service.

---

as board members, should we be concerned about?" List all the concerns. Compare these concerns with the sample policies in John and Miriam Carver's book *Reinventing Your Board* (see Resource C). Develop your own policy.

Have someone really knowledgeable on hand to make sure that any mock work you do is accurate and to draw out all the learnings.

Test Commitment

Try asking yourselves these questions:

- Is there at least one board member (not a staff member) who is willing to champion the process of adopting and implementing the model and whose leadership is acceptable to the group?
- How much time do we think it will take to develop the policies, and how and when will we create this time?
- How will we operate in the meantime?
- Are we confident that we can keep the existing system running while building the new one?

Do Background Reading

Refer to John Carver's article "Nine Steps to Implementing Policy Governance" in the newsletter *Board Leadership* to help your board prepare for the next parts of the journey. See Resource C for more details about this and other titles.

CHAPTER THREE

BEGINNING TO IMPLEMENT POLICY GOVERNANCE

☐ The Challenge

As with any new endeavor, when boards choose to adopt Policy Governance, they essentially step into the unknown. They have considered the potential benefits of Policy Governance, discussed their concerns, and looked at possible risks. They may also have sought to learn from other boards' experiences before making their commitment. Yet they realize that the impact of Policy Governance on their own organization cannot truly be known until they have implemented the model for themselves. With varying degrees of trepidation and anticipation they therefore embark on a journey to find out how Policy Governance will work for them and how they can operate the model to provide vital leadership for their organizations.

Starting to implement Policy Governance can seem overwhelming. A board needs to develop Executive Limitations policies, Board-Staff Relationship policies, and Governance Process policies, and it should at least begin developing its Ends policies. In the meantime, the board still has to do its everyday work. There is so much to do, the model is new and unfamiliar, and the skills and discipline of the board members are untried.

Every board has a different set of circumstances, so there are no "recipes" to fit every organization's situation. However, organizations that have implemented Policy Governance do have common experiences, which can teach us much about the pitfalls and the success factors. Knowing what others tend to go through can help your board implement Policy Governance successfully.

In this chapter we examine boards' experiences in implementing Policy Governance. To that end, we consider the following questions:

- How can boards set themselves up for success?
- Can boards ease into Policy Governance?
- What difficulties do boards face in getting started?

We draw conclusions about successful implementation, which leads us to an inquiry about your board's current situation. Finally we offer some ideas, tips, and tools for helping your board implement the model well.

■ The Experience

How Can Boards Set Themselves Up for Success?

As with any great endeavor, preparation pays.

Confirm Members' Understanding of the Principles. As suggested in the previous chapter, a key factor in successfully implementing Policy Governance is fully understanding the principles. It is not the speed of implementation but the understanding of the model that is most important.

Of the organizations we surveyed, some took more than a year to implement the model fully, and others were able to move far more quickly. Success in all cases hinged on understanding the model. Organizations that went through various "steps" of implementation but lacked a full, conceptual understanding did not realize the full potential of Policy Governance. It must be noted, though, that even these organizations feel that their governance has improved as a result of the process, and they have not given up.

Another reason full understanding is so important is that it enables a board to design a process that suits its specific situation. Although Policy Governance works for organizations that operate in all arenas and that come in all shapes and sizes, the implementation process varies with the boards' circumstances. Are your board members operating essentially as hands-on volunteers who want to be more future oriented? Is your board overloaded and uninspired by the operational discussions that dominate board meetings? Does your board have several champions of Policy Governance who are willing to lead the board through the implementation process? Are you a public board with active constituents who expect the board to handle their individual concerns? Your board's situation will determine the course of your implementation process. Knowing the model fully will help you develop good processes that fit both your board and the model.

This emphasis on understanding the model is not just for current board members beginning to work with Policy Governance. It also applies to all new board members. Numerous organizations say they have significantly increased board discipline and focus by thoroughly orienting new board members to the model.

Have Strong Leadership. The experience of the organizations we surveyed was that strong leadership is essential for implementation, preferably but not necessarily from the board chair. One board chair was clearly a skeptic. He kept asking, "Who else is doing this?" He had no patience with developing Executive Limitations policies because, compared with talking about the program details (which the board had been doing for years), developing policy statements was dry stuff. He repeatedly wondered, "When are we going to get back to the real work?" This did not help the board understand that the policy work was the real work. In this case, other board members held their ground. One of them, the champion for Policy Governance, comments, "The board chair was a weak facilitator, and that didn't help." From another organization, a CEO reports that "since neither the outgoing nor the incoming chairs were champions of the model, it was difficult to move forward."

Another board clearly saw the importance of the chair's leadership for Policy Governance success. In this case, a very articulate board member with a lot of informal power did not trust the CEO and therefore was unwilling to let any significant decision occur without the voice of the board behind it, thus jeopardizing the board's move to Policy Governance. According to the tradition on that board, that member was next in line to be board chair. Another board member saw what would happen to Policy Governance if his colleague became chair, so he ran for the position himself. It was his positive stand on Policy Governance that caused him to be elected chair. The person who was expected to be chair has since lost his informal power, and the board's adherence to Policy Governance has been smooth. There is nothing quite as good as having the chair as the primary champion. A close second is having at least one other strong board member or the CEO as champion.

Generate CEO and Staff Support. Because staff members will ask most of the initial questions, the CEO's understanding of staff members' roles is critical. As one astute staff member puts it, "The first thing is to get the board out of the staff's work. The second thing is to get the staff out of the board's work." In organizations without Policy Governance, staff members often make policy decisions about direction while the board goes through program details with a fine-tooth comb. This staff member goes on to say, "The dirty little secret of nonprofit organizations is that the staff is constantly manipulating their own board."

In this organization, it was not the board members who felt they were losing power so much as the staff! One staff member says, "At times it feels like you are giving away a very big piece of organizational decision making. I might make different choices than the board is making." He adds, "The quality of the board's thinking has relieved me of my concern. My fear was they couldn't have a values conversation, since we'd never had one before."

The staff can play a critical role in helping the board understand the values choices to be made and the trade-offs of those choices. Without a strong CEO or at least a strong staff person in support of the board, the quality of the board's decision making might be jeopardized—or at least slowed down—early on.

It is still possible to adopt Policy Governance successfully if the staff is unsupportive of the move or if the relationship between the board and the CEO is strained. However, in these cases you absolutely must have a strong board leader, preferably the chair. For one organization, tensions between the board and the staff created such an atmosphere of distrust that some board members called for a management audit. The chair's strong leadership in the move to Policy Governance did not further strain the board but provided the answer that board members had sought. As a result of developing Policy Governance, the CEO and the board now have mutual respect and trust. According to the chair, this is a direct product of the work they did on articulating values and vision through their policy development process. The CEO is "working as a partner with the board in providing the organization with effective leadership."

Do Transition Planning. Transition planing will help board members know how they will move from the old way of doing business to the new. A board can take some concrete steps to move toward Policy Governance.

Whether they are in their exploration process or have already decided to adopt Policy Governance, boards have found a governance action plan very useful. Various organizations have called the plan by different names—a work plan, a master schedule, a transition plan—but the idea is essentially the same. It is a way for the board to see all that needs to be done, to put tasks in a sensible order, and to assign some deadlines or expectations. An advantage of a governance action plan is that it is the board's work plan for itself, not its work plan for the staff or for the CEO. Another advantage is that it helps the board maintain its overall perspective. In the middle of policy discussions, board members can easily lose track of where they are and where they plan to go. A master plan helps the board attend to the work it must do at that moment and keeps board members clear about how everything fits into the big picture.

The Weaver Street Market board took a daylong retreat to list and prioritize all of its activities. Members created a master schedule for the entire year. The schedule became a transition plan. The board made some compromises; it would continue serving the organization's business needs (for instance, setting goals for the next fiscal year) without doing the visioning and Ends work that it would ultimately like to have done. But the clear intent was that the process was provisional and that a big task of the board that year would be building the Policy Governance framework.

The board took a full year to establish all policies except Ends. Each time board members addressed an issue required by the business, they dealt with it from a Policy Governance perspective. They asked, "What is important to the board about this particular issue?" With the help of sample generic policies, the board developed one policy at a time. When board work took longer than expected or when other issues came up, the Weaver Street Market board maintained its discipline by scheduling the work into its master schedule. The board chair was unrelenting in keeping the board's actions consistent with Policy Governance principles on every item that came before it. This intense work meant that by the end of that year, board members had become very practiced in all aspects of Policy Governance.

In contrast, the council of the City of Bryan, Texas, began more quickly, opting for a "policy blitz." For two days the city council worked from a set of generic policies and developed all but their Ends policies. The council proceeded to formally adopt Policy Governance and operated with the model from then on.

Whichever route they take, organizations that have been successful in implementing Policy Governance have operated with a board work plan of some sort. It is important to restate that the work plan outlines the board's own tasks, not its goals for the organization.

Install Supportive Structures. A board can put simple structures into place to help itself become effective and proficient in the new model.

List of Reasons for Adopting the Model. As we saw in the previous chapter, one simple structure several organizations use very early in their process is a list of reasons for adopting Policy Governance. They can then revisit this list when the going gets tough or use it as an evaluation instrument to see if their expectations match their experience. Exhibit 2.4 provided an example.

Streamlined Information. In terms of the month-to-month management of the board under the new model, boards often find it helpful to determine what information they need and in what form. After doing this analysis, some boards choose to do some of the following things:

- Eliminate the standard CEO reports
- Eliminate staff reports on various programs
- Color-code material to help differentiate between the following:

  Briefing notes for policy discussions
  Information-only material in compliance with the Communication and
      Counsel to the Board policy
  Monitoring reports
  Policies in the different policy categories (Executive Limitations, Board-
      Staff Relationship, Governance Process, and Ends)

- Send out background information that illustrates various points of view on a policy topic that has been discussed in the past or that is coming up for discussion

The specific choices boards make aren't important here. What is essential is that the board decide what kind of information it needs, in what format, and with what frequency.

These choices have led most staff members to produce very different kinds of reports and to spend less time preparing reports for the board. One staff member says, "Incredible amounts of staff time were freed up from having to prepare [program] reports. The time of the staff is now deployed differently. Previously when the board met monthly . . . there was very heavy preparation, which was a terrible, awful headache. That is all gone now."

Transition Meeting Schedule. In the transition phase, almost every board in our study wanted to address the length and frequency of board meetings. Some boards created a transition schedule with more frequent and lengthier meetings so the boards could get policies and processes in place. Other boards moved to a permanent schedule that differed from the one they had been using. All boards discovered that they needed longer meetings or retreats. However, many boards also met less frequently. As the staff member responsible for board liaison at the San Francisco AIDS Foundation notes, "Three- to four-hour monthly meetings at the end of a workday didn't work anymore." After a series of monthly Saturday morning work sessions the board moved to quarterly meetings. Longer meetings not only accommodate a new kind of conversation at board meetings but also help develop the relationships needed for values-based discussions. As the chair of the Southern Ontario Library Service's board says, "A board that meets for only two hours per month may find it difficult to develop the rapport necessary for this type of work."

Policy-Oriented Agendas. The boards we studied also found the need to alter the way they put together their agendas. The agendas no longer have a long list of reports to the board. Rather, board agendas are dominated by well-framed policy discussions. For example, Parkland Health District's board moved to an agenda format that explicitly links every agenda item to a policy. Following good Policy Governance practice, that board starts every board discussion by asking, "What have we already said about this matter in existing policy?" This method ensures that the board has a discussion that adds value.

Use of a Policy Governance Consultant. Finally, every board we interviewed that successfully implemented Policy Governance worked with a consultant who either gave board members a solid introduction to the model and the processes or who worked with them more extensively. In these latter cases the consultant acted as a coach at board meetings to help the board develop good habits and processes. Two staff members at the Vermont Land Trust state, "We don't see how any board could do it without a consultant." This does not mean that boards cannot in fact implement Policy Governance without a consultant. Indeed, having a consultant is not a guarantee of success. However, having access to some form of real Policy Governance expertise is vital, and having independent facilitation can be a great help.

Develop Process Skills. Group process skills for board members are another key to success. The nature of the discussions at board meetings will obviously change under Policy Governance. Discussions will be about much larger issues with much more critical trade-offs. Whenever you ask, "What benefits, for whom, at what cost?" you are talking about not only what you will do and for whom but, perhaps more painfully, what you will not be doing and who will not be served.

This kind of discussion requires a board atmosphere of trust, respect, and rapport. This will come about more fully if it is attended to explicitly. The Southern Ontario Library Service board members used the Myers-Briggs Type Indicator as a way to help them understand one another and the strengths each member brought to the group. Their board chair says the time they spent on this was "very important to developing the trust and safety to tackle the big issues." He adds that the trust affected "the way we experimented at meetings."

Another board, which suffered from lack of trust between the board and the CEO, used the entire process of policy development and monitoring to begin building trust. One of the issues the members tackled first was what decision-making method they were going to use. Discussing and deciding this up front reduced confusion and conflict when they faced difficult values choices later on.

Members of many of the organizations we studied wish they had had training in discussion and decision making much earlier in the process. One staff member says, "The board's self-governance as a group should have been on the table earlier. They should have had training in dialogue and meeting management. Bad individual behavior is a barrier to the kinds of discussion that Policy Governance requires. Bullying happened at the board table, and that needed to be nipped in the bud." According to a CEO with similar concerns, "Boards need discussion skills that are much higher than what they come with. They need training in specific skills beyond the admonition to 'do better.'"

Basic attitudes affect group process. Noting that the model "requires discipline and rigor," one organization suggests that successful implementation is difficult for boards that dislike that kind of work. In another example, the board was not interested in having the future-oriented, conceptual discussions that the Ends questions required. Members considered such conversations "a waste of time" and made comments such as, "Navel gazing is very interesting, but let's get on with the work."

Several practitioners of Policy Governance found the descriptions of the model incomplete because they do not sufficiently describe and emphasize the extent to which the model depends on more effective group processes. A typical comment from one chair was that the model "could be enhanced by encouraging all boards to become more self-aware." The specific skills mentioned by various practitioners include the following:

- Managing meetings
- Listening
- Developing ground rules for discussion
- Setting up discussions
- Conducting skilled discussions

(Tools for helping boards develop all these skills can be found at the end of this chapter.)

Can Boards Ease into Policy Governance?

Sometimes boards believe that if they ease into Policy Governance, it will make the whole process less threatening and easier to swallow. The experience, however, does not always reflect that hope. The San Francisco AIDS Foundation reports that "living in two worlds was very tough." In *Reinventing Your Board* (see Resource C), John and Miriam Carver advise boards to keep old governance systems in place until policies have been developed in all categories except Ends. Only then should a board jump into Policy Governance. The Carvers also recommend developing the policies as quickly as possible to avoid living in two worlds for long.

The Weaver Street Market board took a unique route with its previously described transition plan. According to one member, "The plan charted a way by which the board [members] could operate within Policy Governance principles at the same time that they were building the framework of Policy Governance policies. The board could also provide what the business had normally expected the board to provide while building a bridge to the future in which board input would occur at a different level." The board had several important ingredients for making its easing-in process successful: strong leadership, a clear plan, a serious time commitment from members (agreeing to have three-hour board meetings twice a month during the first year), and a process for running its meetings in accordance with Policy Governance principles.

"Easing in" seemed to work for several organizations in relation to eliminating committees that would no be longer required under Policy Governance. One organization let go of many of its standing committees, whose main function was to help staff. But the organization held onto several committees, including the finance committee. The organization reports that the reluctance to let go of this committee was "of such magnitude that if the board had been forced to relinquish the committee, it might very well have chosen not to proceed with Policy Governance at all." The board members opted for an incremental approach. Eventually, they eliminated the finance committee, because their policies and monitoring processes became so strong that they felt comfortable enough to do without it. They say, "There are times when a board is simply not ready. . . . It took time and acquiring confidence that the model does indeed work before [we] were ready to lower the safety net [of a finance committee] gradually."

As we have seen, the City of Bryan's council did not ease in at all. It completed a policy blitz in two days, adopted the model, and was off and running. The lesson here is that you must decide how fast to go based on the needs and culture of your board. There is not one right way.

Experience indicates, however, that certain ways create problems. A board inevitably requires some period of "double duty" as it moves safely from its old form of governing to Policy Governance. If "easing in" means that the board addresses all the day-to-day matters that it has always dealt with and then tries to develop Executive Limitations or Ends policies as extra work within the time frame of normal board meetings, there is going to be a struggle. Many boards find that developing strong policies in the Policy Governance sense is so time-consuming and so out of sync with the traditional way of operating that policy development consistently gets pushed off the table. One staff member says, "At the current pace set aside for Ends policy development, Ends policies cannot be dealt with on normal agendas, so [we] would need many more board meetings each year. Ends policy development seems overwhelming when added to the day-to-day board work, because it seems like an extra effort." As we have already seen, a transition board work plan and meeting schedule can be vital tools for a board moving to Policy Governance.

What Difficulties Do Boards Face in Getting Started?

Boards face a variety of challenges as they begin developing the policies and processes that will allow them to implement Policy Governance fully.

Resistance. Even after a board has decided to adopt Policy Governance, some members of the board or staff resist the change. Instead of viewing this as a drag on the process, boards find it helpful to locate the source of the resistance and to deal with it directly. Often the resistance arises from legitimate fears that can be addressed: the fear of losing power; the fear of losing connection; the fear of adopting the latest fad; or the fear of no longer getting to do hands-on, fun activities. See the previous chapter for more on typical concerns.

In whatever form it takes, resistance can tire out the board members. One CEO says, "The biggest detractor from the board's enthusiasm was the two or three board members who were really resistant to getting their hands out of the things they had been in. By far the majority of the board wanted to move ahead to set policy and talk about bigger issues, but a few members kept bringing up concerns that were no longer board concerns, and constantly dealing with their resistance was wearing. This made life difficult for staff and board for a year."

Fortunately, the majority of boards' experience is that once the discussion of Ends and of linking with the ownership is under way, there is an increase in interest and in the sense of connection to the organization. At the Vermont Land Trust, board members believe that "the most thoughtful, compelling conversations we have had have been in the last year on the Ends. . . . Conversations are of a much higher quality and [are] more exciting. . . . The board feels it is adding value to the organization." Sometimes the board may need to be reminded of the power of its discussions and clearly shown how it is adding value and influencing the organization's future.

Loss of Momentum. Most boards hit a slump while making the transition from their old way of doing business to Policy Governance. The primary reason for the slump is usually the tedium of developing Executive Limitations policies or a desire to avoid actually putting them in place.

One board was so restless about dealing with Executive Limitations and so critical of its "lack of connection to the real work of the organization" that the CEO worried that the board would shift back to the old way. The board's response was to move to the Ends work before completing all the Executive Limitations work. The CEO notes, "It is hard to start with Executive Limitations and not lose energy." He felt "very disconnected" during the slump, particularly since he did not have a clear sense of how the board would come out of it. He was not convinced the Ends work would bring them out, but it did, and the Ends work has been the source of this board's inspiration ever since.

Other boards lose confidence in what they have created. One board completed all its policy work in a blitz session but got bogged down in what it would actually mean if the CEO made many decisions without board approval. The CEO has this advice: "Expect some rough moments when you get to the point of operationalizing [Policy Governance]."

Internal conflict can also lead to a loss of momentum. One CEO confides that during times of disagreement, some board members blamed all the board conflict on the model. He notes that "after more conversation, the board was able to say, 'The model isn't causing these problems; we've had these problems all along.'" The model made them talk about their organizational values and discover that they had very different views.

Hot Topics. Some boards have such strong policies and such clear discipline that the staff simply deals with controversial or "hot" issues within policy and keeps the board informed. But controversial, highly public, or political issues cause other boards to take a detour. They go off track by assuming that if it's controversial, it must be board work. Publicly elected boards have a special challenge in maintaining good governance in the face of controversy. (See "Special Challenges for Certain Types of Boards" later in this chapter for more on the problems confronting public boards.) Some boards get derailed only momentarily, but several go seriously off track for months or even years. One board reports that concerns about funding and relations with the City diverted it from its focus on Policy Governance for two years.

Inappropriate CEO Requests for Board Approval. Sometimes a CEO brings a difficult issue to the board for approval and wants support for a decision that is the CEO's to make. In an effort to be supportive, the board is tempted to decide on a course of action, thereby reversing its previous decision to delegate that matter. See the next section for more on this topic.

Lack of Discipline and Focus. Maintaining the discipline required to be successful in Policy Governance can be tiring. It is very easy for boards to drift and find themselves right back where they were. Sometimes they have more fun solving a problem, stating a point of view, or talking about program ideas.

One organization that was ultimately unsuccessful in fully implementing the model reports that board members had a "lack of desire to engage in abstract thinking." Fundamentally, the members wanted to "continue to be involved in operations." Similarly, another board found it "hard to maintain enthusiasm because of the disappointment of some board members who preferred to be involved in hands-on decision making." They didn't feel that they were doing their job unless they were directly involved. As a result, when the CEO brought issues to the board as "information only" (not for board decision), the members began to discuss and advise. These problems reinforce the notions that board members need to understand the model and that with many service volunteers on a board, it might be hard to implement the model successfully.

Another organization that has been very successful with the model still slips occasionally. The CEO reports that the board members "have a strong incentive to stray into the day-to-day operations. . . . Service expectations are high, and when customers complain, well-meaning [board members] want to 'solve' the perceived problem." This board's consultant concludes that in "the real world of implementation . . . there will be some falls, but over time the skill is acquired. In each case, the board has learned from its fall and become better at being true to the principles of the model."

An Excess of Cooks. If the board is large (fifteen or more people), board size is a governance issue that may need to be addressed, because the high-quality discussions involved in using Policy Governance are more suited to a smaller group of people and less effective in a large-group setting. Large boards are often created in an attempt to represent various groups (for instance, government, union, minorities, and clients) or for fundraising, political, or public purposes. However, Policy Governance reduces the relevance of oversized boards because it offers a way to hear more fully from constituents and to design more effective oversight of operational accomplishment.

Special Challenges for Certain Types of Boards. Public boards have the biggest challenge in governing and therefore the largest obstacles in adopting Policy Governance. The public has strong expectations about how the board should respond to its particular needs. A school board routinely gets input on all kinds of administrative issues from the public, which expects the board to solve its problems. Citizens complain to the board rather than to the CEO about their concerns. This is simply how the public has been trained to act.

Policy Governance alters the rules. If a public board doesn't prepare the public for this change in rules, a serious backlash can result. The CEO of the Colorado Association of School Boards tells us that public boards "have to pay particular attention to the political and public environment. . . . There are lots of people . . . who will show up at public meetings and want the board to talk about nonboard issues. And then they get on a tirade when they discover it is not board work. Educating the public is front and center for public boards." The city manager of Bryan, Texas, when asked about lessons learned in implementing Policy Governance, said "Educate, educate, educate the community about the model."

Another special consideration for public boards is that, because their members are publicly elected, they have less control over who their colleagues are. Trust, collegiality, and respectful dialogue are essential when board members address the issues at the heart of Policy Governance, so the mix of people at the board table is critical. Because Policy Governance requires a commitment to a particular kind of discipline and outlook, gaining a board member who does not accept the model can be detrimental. One CEO points out that the ability to sustain Policy Governance is "an actual measure of how deeply ingrained the governance model is in the [current] board." This argues for serious education of candidates and orientation of new members. Any board runs the risks associated with board turnover, whether or not it is using Policy Governance. But public boards using Policy Governance have far less control over the recruitment process than most other boards.

Other boards that may face special challenges in implementing Policy Governance are those that take on additional responsibilities, such as fundraising and advocacy. See "Fundraising and Advocacy Organizations" in Chapter One for more on this.

☑ Key Learnings

Three factors seem to contribute more than any others to organizations' success in the early stages of implementing Policy Governance.

- *Strong board and staff leadership.* Ideally, leadership for the implementation process comes from the chair and the CEO, but at the very least the organization needs strong, identifiable leadership in both board and staff arenas. Policy Governance cannot fix a weak organization and cannot be implemented effectively without strong leadership.
- *Thorough understanding of the principles.* All board members must fully understand the principles. Policy Governance is not just a series of principles about meeting management that a chair can impose. It is a way of thinking. If most board members do not understand the principles and philosophy, it is unlikely that they will be able to exercise the necessary discipline and rigor to make the

transition to the Policy Governance model and to sustain the thinking required. Although there are generic policies (see Chapter Four) that provide a starting point for developing Executive Limitations, Governance Process, and Board-Staff Relationship policies, the bulk of the board's work is going to be work that they design with processes that they develop. They cannot do this well without a complete understanding of both the principles and the purpose of Policy Governance.

• *A plan.* Board members need a work plan or a transition plan. The work of crafting and implementing Executive Limitations policies or devising a way to tackle the Ends questions can be daunting. The tedium or the complexity can easily cause board members to lose their bearings in the middle of the task. A clear work plan can help the board deal with the specific issues it is working on and to place itself in the big picture. This work plan can, of course, be modified as issues come up, but if the board is to remain in charge of its work, it must stick to a plan, not address whatever comes up in the moment. This is not only entirely possible but also necessary if the board is to focus on the future.

If these three basics for success are in place, the other important issues in the implementation process become much easier to handle. The experience of the organizations we have studied indicates that these include several other ingredients:

• *Board process skills.* The board needs to build its skills in dialogue, discussion, listening, and understanding underlying values. These skills are a must if boards are to engage in the kind of thinking, decision making, and communication that Policy Governance involves. Building these skills can help board members become more self-aware, develop a sense of team spirit, and welcome the diversity of views around the board table and among the ownership.

• *Well-planned sessions.* Board meetings that are thoroughly planned help the implementation process go smoothly. Board members need information in advance, and the discussions must be organized so that issues and options are clear. However, the board also needs to develop a tolerance for the complexity of some issues involved in making values choices.

• *Discipline and preparedness.* A board moving to Policy Governance may need to be willing to lose service volunteers. It can try to find a way for these volunteers to keep contributing in a manner that satisfies them and benefits the organization. Staying connected is extremely important, and every board needs to consider ways to make that possible without compromising its determination to govern. But the board shouldn't hamper the success of Policy Governance by continuing to deal with hands-on issues as a way of staying connected or pleasing service volunteers.

The board is bound to hit some snags and traps. It should avoid being seduced into the old ways of governance as a result of hot or controversial topics, being asked to give approvals to insecure CEOs, or giving in to a desire to deal with an operations issue because it is interesting. Otherwise, it will soon find itself right back where it started. A board needs to maintain the discipline of working within the Policy Governance principles even if the discipline seems contrived at times. A board should know that it is likely to hit a slump and prepare for it in advance. Sometimes just acknowledging the slump can give the board the room it needs to move through it. Other times, the board will have to take more aggressive action.

○ Taking Action: Strategies for Where You Are Now

Just because your board has decided to adopt Policy Governance doesn't mean that the going is always easy. Now the board really sees the implications of its decision. Your board may be progressing beautifully; mulling over concerns; getting bogged down in discussion; or feeling distracted, trapped, or downright lost. The next sections provide some advice for wherever you are.

If Policy Governance Is Really on Its Way

If your board is developing its policies with enthusiasm and discipline, the main issue is how to keep it that way. Keep revisiting your list of reasons for deciding to adopt Policy Governance (as in Exhibit 2.4), or generate a list if you don't have one already. Keep looking at your governance action plan to check your progress toward your goals. Celebrate the milestones.

If the Board Still Has Concerns

Previous concerns may be arising again, or people who have been swept along may be starting to speak up. If so, it's time to go back to listing your concerns. In the next "Practical Tips and Tools" section, see "Deal with Slumps," which presents a more advanced version of the worry list exercise mentioned in Chapter Two.

If the Board Is Bogged Down in Discussion

If the board is struggling to discuss issues without "making each other wrong" or "getting personal" or is simply getting lost in the kind of complex discussions required by Policy Governance, you may need to invite board members to think about the kind of skills that would enable them to have better discussions. Board members could generate a list of past experiences or training from which their communication has benefited, then develop a plan to further increase their skills. See the next "Practical Tips and Tools" section for some ideas.

If Meetings Go All over the Place

Are your agendas helping you create discipline? Analyze a past agenda. Can you create a tighter structure that relates directly to the Policy Governance model? See the next "Practical Tips and Tools" section for more guidance.

If the Board Is in Danger of Falling into Traps

If all is going well but you can see that your board could fall into common traps, you need to consider them ahead of time. Prevention is a lot better than cure. See "Avoid the Traps" in the next "Practical Tips and Tools" section to identify the potential pitfalls for your board and to discuss ways to avoid them.

If the Board Doesn't Know Where to Go from Here

If your board has become really lost in several different interpretations of the Policy Governance model and it has all become very hard work, board members could probably benefit from some outside help. Be specific about what the board needs and how those needs can be met. If you have not already done so, consider reading materials, checking out video- or audiocassettes, and subscribing to the *Board Leadership* newsletter (see Resource C for a full list of titles). You could also invite members of other Policy Governance boards to talk with you about their experiences either in person or in a conference call with the whole board. If you think you need to hire a consultant, list specifically what you want that consultant to provide and how you will know if you are getting what you need.

▶ Practical Tips and Tools

The following tips and tools should help you keep in good shape for your work in implementing Policy Governance. See the Tool Finders in Resources A and B at the back of this book for more ideas.

Improve Your Discussion Skills

For ground rules about skilled discussion and further information on increasing your group's skill in team dialogue, see *The Fifth Discipline Fieldbook* by Peter Senge and others; Resource C has details about this and other useful titles, as well as information on ordering an article called "Groundrules for Effective Groups" by Roger Schwarz. See Exhibits 3.1 and 3.2 for examples of exercises that your board

EXHIBIT 3.1. ROUND ROBIN.

This exercise ensures that all voices will be heard on a particular issue. It is a very quick way to get a "read" on the group members' viewpoints. Here are the guidelines for a round robin:

- Formulate a clearly worded question to pose to the group.
- Go around the room, asking each person to give a one-word, one-sentence, or otherwise brief answer to the question, stating his or her current viewpoint.
- Do not permit anyone to discuss another member's point of view or to interrupt or comment in any way during the round robin.

After a round robin, have the group continue to discuss the question as before.

EXHIBIT 3.2. NOMINAL GROUP TECHNIQUE.

The nominal group technique is a variation on brainstorming (see Exhibit 3.6) that allows individual members to generate ideas before reporting to the full group. Here are the guidelines for the nominal group technique:

- Make sure all members fully understand the objective of the nominal group session.
- Eliminate distractions while members individually generate a list of ideas. Give members as much time as needed to do this.
- Allow members to take turns presenting one idea from their list. Go around the room until the members have presented all the ideas on their lists.
- Do not permit members to discuss, criticize, or compliment ideas as they are presented.

After all ideas have been recorded by the group facilitator on a board or a large piece of paper, have the group clarify the list to ensure that all members have the same understanding of each idea and to eliminate duplicates. Have the group choose the best ideas from the list. The group may want to use a voting technique from Exhibit 6.3 or 6.4 to make these choices.

might want to try out. And the Tool Finder in Resource B will help you locate other useful discussion and decision-making tools contained elsewhere in this book.

Get Meetings on Track

What follows are several ideas for making sure that your meetings serve their purposes.

The Meeting Liturgy. Use a "meeting liturgy" to plan and focus your board discussions. One of the ways meetings get off track is that not everyone understands exactly what the discussion is supposed to accomplish. Everyone believes that he or she is on track but that someone else isn't. The meeting liturgy is a helpful tool for meeting management (or for discussion management if your meeting contains more than one substantive discussion). For every substantive portion of the meeting, answer the following questions:

1. What is the issue? (Put it in the form of a question.)
2. How much time do we have to talk?
3. What is needed as a result of our talking?
4. What is the decision-making method?
5. Where will this go from here?

Use this liturgy to plan the agenda. You might be surprised at how difficult it is to answer the first question. Go over the questions with the board before the discussion. If board members seem to go off track at any point in the discussion, use the meeting liturgy to redirect them. See Exhibit 3.3 for an example of how one board has used it.

Policy Governance Agendas. Create more explicit agendas consistent with Policy Governance. Exhibit 3.4 gives an example of an agenda from one Policy Governance board. At the end of each item they also show the name of the person designated to lead discussion of that item. Exhibit 8.1 shows a perpetual agenda that could act as a starting point for constructing all your agendas.

Ground Rules. The board can develop ground rules that could then become a Governance Process policy (see Exhibit 3.5 for a sample). Post the ground rules at the beginning of the meeting, and go over them with the board. Use the ground rules to point out when the board is straying from its agreements. Before developing ground rules, the board could read and discuss "Groundrules for Effective

---

EXHIBIT 3.3. SAMPLE MEETING LITURGY.

1. What is the issue?

   Do we have the right definitions for community *and* economy?

2. How much time do we have to talk?

   One hour

3. What is needed as a result of our talking?

   Direction to the work group for further Ends revisions

4. What is the decision-making method?

   Board consensus

5. Where will this go from here?

   Back to the work group as necessary; to the partners' roundtable in December

---

Groups" by Roger Schwarz, which outlines ground rules and their rationale. Ordering information is in Resource C.

Stay Connected Productively and Safely

Your board wants to feel connected to the workings of the organization without falling back into micromanaging. Have your board members think of how they can keep feeling connected in ways that support their policy work rather than detract from it. For more on this see "Deal with the Loss of Operational Involvement" in Chapter Four.

Avoid the Traps

What follows is a list of temptations or land mines that can take a board off track. Assess with your board the likelihood of its falling into the traps. Talk about how to avoid the traps and what to do if the board accidentally finds itself in one. Rate

---

EXHIBIT 3.4. A POLICY GOVERNANCE AGENDA.

5:30   Preliminaries

Focus of the meeting

Review of the agenda's purpose—Linda

5:35   Minutes of the last meeting

5:40   Automatic approval agenda

Project ratifications

5:45   Ends policy discussion

*Does the "community" Ends statement adequately cover "social-economic justice,"
or do we need to revise the policy?*

Does the proposed board work plan address our priorities?—Linda

7:45   Ends process discussion

*Presentation of the participants, format, and questions for the partners' roundtable
in September—Gary, Anne, Victor*

8:15   Executive Limitations policy

*Does our policy on Communication and Counsel to the Board reflect our concerns?
Approval of final draft needed—Bob*

8:30   Meeting evaluation

In relation to our Governance Process policies, what worked? What didn't work?

In relation to our process design, what worked? What didn't work?—Linda

---

each of the following six traps (you may come up with more) according to the like-lihood that they could take you off track. Label them "high-risk," "medium-risk," or "low-risk." For each trap, answer these questions: "What will we do to avoid it?" and "What would we do to get out of it?"

> *Trap One:* There is a hot political issue that we want to delve into.
>
> *Trap Two:* The CEO seeks our approval for something already covered in policy.
>
> *Trap Three:* We receive something from the CEO as "information only," but a board member has a point of view about it.

EXHIBIT 3.5.
SAMPLE GROUND RULES FROM A BOARD OF DIRECTORS.

- Focus on strategic, board-level issues.
- Balance advocacy with inquiry.
- Stay open to influence; be willing to move your stake.
- Agree on what important words mean.
- Test assumptions and mental models.
- Listen in order to understand; don't listen in order to debate.
- Base decisions on data.
- Have discussions or disagreements in the meeting, not outside.
- Be brief. No war stories. Don't repeat.
- Focus on interests, not positions.
- Slow down the conversation; savor important thoughts.
- Evaluate the meetings.

Trap Four: The public has a comment about something that is an administrative matter.

Trap Five: The CEO is developing a program in which several board members have expertise, but the CEO hasn't sought their input.

Trap Six: The CEO makes a decision with which several board members disagree, and they want to discuss it at the board meeting.

Deal with Slumps

If your board has hit a slump, take board members back to why they wanted to move to Policy Governance. See Exhibit 2.4 for a sample list of reasons.

If you haven't already done so, have your board create a very detailed work plan for its year. In the middle of difficult or tedious conversations, you can use the work plan to look at the bigger picture and to see how your work is moving you forward.

If the board's slump is associated with lingering concerns, try taking thirty minutes at your next board meeting and asking your board members to state all their concerns about the Policy Governance model now that they are actually working with it. Don't discuss the concerns at that point; just list them. Write each

---

EXHIBIT 3.6. BRAINSTORMING.

Brainstorming is rarely done well. People often generate a few ideas, none of which are out of the ordinary. Then people start making judgments and decisions, and ideas peter out.

Energetic brainstorming can generate a large number of creative ideas if the guidelines are clarified to the group beforehand. Here are the guidelines for brainstorming:

- All members must fully understand the objective of the brainstorming session.
- There can be no discussion of the ideas as they are presented, including criticisms and compliments.
- Creative thinking is encouraged, including ideas that are far-out and that expand on others' ideas.
- All ideas must be recorded on the flip chart exactly as presented, using two people to record if necessary.
- Do not stop when ideas slow down. The purpose is to generate as long a list as possible.
- Set a time frame within which brainstorming will occur. The group must use the entire time.

After all ideas have been presented, the team should clarify the list to ensure that all members have the same understanding of each idea and to eliminate duplicates. The team should then make decisions about list items.

---

concern with a black marker on a Post-it note, and stick it on a wall where everyone can see it. At the end of the brainstorming, group the notes into categories, and label the categories. For example, a category of concerns might be "What will we do with all the issues that currently take up all our board time?" or "How will we stay connected to the organization?" Exhibit 3.6 gives more guidance on brainstorming, which can be used for this kind of activity and for generating creative ideas on any topic.

Plan to address the concerns at a later meeting, a retreat, or a series of meetings. At these meetings, if any concern raises a new oversight issue and if you already have Executive Limitations policies in place, ask, "What should we be concerned about in terms of this new issue?" See where each concern is addressed in your current policies. If it isn't, add a line to an existing policy or create a new policy.

Give New Members Confidence

If you are orienting new board members and want them to feel confident that the model ensures proper oversight, you can ask them to develop a "worry list" of the things they ought to be concerned about as responsible trustees. Compare the list to the policies to see whether their worries are accounted for through your Executive Limitations policies. This will be a useful exercise for the whole board and may lead to new or amended policies.

Create a Transition Plan

Do you have a transition plan for Policy Governance? Take an hour out of an upcoming board meeting and develop a plan. List all the items that are now on the board's plate and all that you need to do to develop Policy Governance. Add the relevant activities to your calendar for the next few months or year.

PART TWO

HOW BOARDS PUT POLICY GOVERNANCE TO WORK

CHAPTER FOUR

DEVELOPING EXECUTIVE LIMITATIONS POLICIES

☐ The Challenge

This chapter looks at one of the most controversial aspects of Policy Governance—the board's need to ensure that the organization is sound and clarify the limits of the CEO's power and control. The mere mention of fiduciary and other due-diligence obligations puts fear in the hearts of many board members. Although board members commonly become acquainted with these obligations very early on, they also find that boards have few approaches for meeting such obligations while honoring the staff's role and while allowing for powerful and responsible delegation to the CEO.

In the Policy Governance model, boards meet fiduciary and other due diligence obligations by developing and governing with adequate policies, primarily Executive Limitations policies. This chapter looks at ways in which board and staff members address concerns about organizational behavior when using the Policy Governance model. In particular, this chapter explores the following questions:

- How do boards create Executive Limitations?
- How do boards feel about being less involved in operations?
- How do CEOs see Executive Limitations?
- How do boards manage Executive Limitations?

The answers to these questions lead us to some important conclusions about successfully creating Executive Limitations and dealing with the consequences of clearer delegation. Next we ask you to look at how confident and secure your board is feeling and how well your policies are holding up. Finally we suggest some ideas, tips, and techniques to help Executive Limitations operate powerfully for your organization.

■ The Experience

How Do Boards Create Executive Limitations?

Like any other policies, Executive Limitations policies require board considera-tion and discussion. With Policy Governance, boards need to abstract up to the highest level of policy in order to tease out commonly held values. Only then can they progress through more definitive levels of policy and finally agree that they have said all they need to say. (For more on policy design and logical containment of policies, see Chapter Three in *Boards That Make a Difference* by John Carver; de-tails are in Resource C.)

Because Executive Limitations identify behaviors, actions, and conditions that are *not* acceptable (largely because they are imprudent or unethical), board mem-bers from various types of organizations share a broad base of similar values when it comes to these policies. Certain actions are considered unethical in most situa-tions; certain conditions are considered imprudent in most settings; and there are certain areas that most governing boards want to address in order to feel in con-trol of the organization. Almost all boards see financial control as one of their most critical concerns.

Recognizing this, Carver has crafted sample Executive Limitations policies—or templates—that address these common concerns. These templates have helped many organizations implement Policy Governance. Honed through boards' ex-periences over the years, the generic policy templates make it unnecessary to start the policy development process from scratch and have become essential items in the Policy Governance consultant's toolbox. Further developed with Miriam Carver, these templates are available in *Reinventing Your Board* (see Resource C for details).

Templates typically contain drafts of the following Executive Limitations policies:

- General Executive Constraint
- (Actual) Financial Condition
- Budgeting (Financial Planning)

- Staff Treatment
- Consumer Treatment
- Asset Protection
- Communication and Counsel (or Support) to the Board
- Compensation and Benefits
- Emergency Executive Succession

Most boards that have used the templates have retained similar policy titles, but the level of detail contained in the final policies varies, and boards often create additional policies to address their unique concerns. All of the boards that contributed to this book used the templates as a foundation for their discussions. However, they did not all limit their policies to those listed here. For example, the board of the Vermont Land Trust created a Land Acquisitions policy.

Now let's look at some of the actual processes being used in the field.

The Blitz. While using templates, many organizations employ a technique called the "policy blitz" to create their Executive Limitations policies. The intent of the policy blitz is to jump-start the policymaking process, creating a skeleton of policies in the three means categories—Executive Limitations, Governance Process, and Board-Staff Relationship—in a short period, usually one session. (See John Carver's *Boards That Make a Difference,* 2nd edition, pp. 30–35, for more on policy categories; details are in Resource C.)

Ideally, the entire board is present during this important initial policymaking experience, which is why a retreat is sometimes used. Most organizations described in this book used a blitz and secured the help of a facilitator to take them through the process. A member of the Southern Ontario Library Service describes that board's policy blitz, which John Carver facilitated at the first meeting after the board formally voted to adopt the model: "During the daylong policy blitz, board members were asked to comment, paragraph by paragraph, on each sample policy provided. Informal polling was used to consider and accept or reject alternative wording. Many of the policies (except Ends) were formulated by the close of the session. Where discussion was not conclusive, items were placed in the parking lot for that policy."

The term *parking lot* refers to the practice of saving trickier or more time-consuming items for future consideration. The use of a parking lot was common among the organizations studied in this book, indicating that even with templates and a blitz process to expedite policymaking, some issues require more time for reflection. Some of these issues may be unique to the nature of the organization. Examples of frequently parked items include Conflict of Interest statements and the definition of the organization's ownership.

The Multimeeting Process. Processes other than the blitz are, at this point, less distinctly defined. The only common denominator is that they take a minimum of several months to complete. The board members of the Vermont Land Trust worked on Executive Limitations policies in small groups for four months and then discussed their drafts in a daylong board meeting before adopting Policy Governance. They report, "The biggest thing that helped here was to get people to articulate their fears. Just [answering] that question, 'What are you afraid of?' helped people. On the Lands Committee, it just came pouring out when they talked about what their concerns were. Also, they gained confidence about the process when they were able to take a specific issue and tease out . . . the values issues . . . that would apply in the future."

A Combination of the Two Approaches. The board of Weaver Street Market wasn't aware of the blitz approach, so it used the multimeeting approach. Board members adopted Policy Governance after an initial workshop conducted by a consultant. Using templates, the board "set out on the journey of creating policy over an extended period." Several months of work resulted in two policies. Renewed effort came with a new chair, who led the board in "implementing the Policy Governance model in earnest." A master schedule was created for the entire year, and within several months the basic policies were created in the three means categories. After learning of the blitz method through the chair's involvement in a Policy Governance Academy (see *www.policygovernance.com* for more information on the Policy Governance Academy), the board found that blitzes "greatly facilitated" further policy development. Henceforth, brief policy blitz sessions were included in board meetings.

The Blitz Versus the Multimeeting Approach. In hindsight, now that the Weaver Street Market board members know "the ease of doing a policy blitz," they characterize their policy development as "a long, arduous process. This was especially evident during the first six months, as several board members expressed frustration with the effort. Such an implementation process absolutely required complete discipline, which is not often easy to maintain."

Indeed the blitz technique has widespread support. The organizations surveyed see a blitz as offering speed and structure. An organization using a blitz is also more likely to draw on the Policy Governance knowledge of a trained consultant, compared with an organization that uses a multimeeting approach.

Reflecting on the blitz process at the Southern Ontario Library Service, a board member reports, "We moved quickly through large volumes of undisputed wording but were able to keep track of critical topics (large and small) that needed more in-depth discussion." The Colorado Association of School Boards also feels that the policy blitz worked. The CEO says, "I still think the only way to do it was using the blitz process. Otherwise it would have taken too long, and the energy of the board would have been sapped."

Another CEO feels that the overall benefits of the blitz carried the day but says this: "The only downside was that board members approved policies that, until they were used by me, they didn't really understand." This drawback became evident shortly after the board adopted Policy Governance.

The benefits of multimeeting approaches don't tend to be fully recognized until later in the implementation process. One chair notes a silver lining to using the more gradual process and describes its "dramatic" impact on the board:

> Board members became fully versed in working with and being consistent with Policy Governance principles. Soon [Policy Governance] became simply what the board did. This has served the board well, even as new members have come on . . . , because that discipline and depth are now a natural part of board culture. . . . [Although] the . . . policy development [process was long], it was successful in not only building the framework of Policy Governance but [also] firmly establishing a culture of rigor and discipline with the model and, per-haps most significantly, instilling true board ownership of the model and [of] the board's own work. Pioneering spirits in a new paradigm!

Whereas the blitz approach offers speed and structure, the multimeeting approach suffers from a slow pace and a structure that is vulnerable to loss of interest and loss of focus. A board member of the Vermont Land Trust explains, "The good thing about the means is they are very concrete, but they are uninspiring when you are writing them in large doses." In retrospect, some concern about "how dull putting the Executive Limitations policies together was . . . may have caused us to move too quickly to Ends before all Executive Limitations policies were finished."

How Do Boards Feel About Being Less Involved in Operations?

After the initial policy development stage, the board has put its bounded authority in place, and it no longer needs to be actively involved in organizational operations. How does this withdrawal from operational involvement affect board members?

It is safe to say that the board's withdrawal from operational involvement does not go unnoticed. Board members' reactions depend on how involved they were before and how they felt about the extent of that involvement. The shift highlights the degree to which boards were involved with, and focused on, details of the organization's operations.

Most organizations report that at least one member of their board had significant difficulty with, or resistance to, withdrawing from the involvement. Some feeling of loss appears to be a normal part of the transition and should be expected. Some of it is an inevitable consequence of using Policy Governance—a purposeful, unapologetic expectation that boards will disengage from some areas and activities. Some of it is temporary and lasts only until the board becomes accustomed to its new agenda of monitoring, evaluating, linking with owners, and developing Ends policies.

Several types of loss were noted.

Loss of a sense of connection. There was a general feeling of separation from the organization, which was sometimes further highlighted by the elimination of most committees.

An initial discomfort with the higher policy level of discussion. As one source puts it, "Sometimes [board members] just want to go off and have a nitty-gritty discussion of staff work because it's fun, it's concrete, . . . and they are good at it."

Loss of immediacy. In one organization, "Some board members experienced a loss, in that policymaking does not provide the immediate gratification that one receives when dealing with day-to-day tasks."

Less freedom to speak at will. On one board, members "were so accustomed to . . . expressing a personal opinion about everything that it really felt to them initially like a loss of power."

Loss of clarity about contribution. In another organization, "Some board members who preferred to be involved in hands-on [operational] decision making . . . didn't feel that they were making a valuable contribution unless they were hands-on."

Loss of a sense of accountability. Having, as yet, little real sense of the accountability that monitoring of Executive Limitations provides, some board members fear that they will be less accountable.

Loss of personal power over the organization. Board members who have enjoyed applying individual clout within the organization tend to have difficulty withdrawing, may drag their feet during the implementation process, and could cause disruptions.

Can the sense of loss subside? It can, and it did in most instances. For example, one board member states, "Two or three board members really liked dealing with the small stuff, and they might see this as a loss. But the board is so happy to be dealing with important issues that nobody is looking back nostalgically to the old way of doing business." Time and dedicated practice seem to pay off. A member of another board says that as board members "gain experience with the model, they can begin to appreciate that the immediate task is not always the most important thing that the board can do in terms of the organization's impact."

Sometimes individual board members who feel uncomfortable, who don't "get it," or who simply don't want to comply with the principles of the model choose to leave the board. Although one source notes that "it was painful to lose some board members who were great people" (and still supportive of the agency), most reports express more relief than remorse.

At the same time, many board members feel liberated from their involvement in operations. One notes, "I'm glad that Policy Governance has stopped the board [from] reviewing all those micromanagement reports." Similarly, the Southern Ontario Library Service chair says that the model "frees you from a lot of needless worry about things you are not responsible for. You get to worry about the things you should be worrying about!"

How Do CEOs See Executive Limitations?

Some board members may feel uncomfortable with placing restrictions on a CEO. Moreover, it certainly seems odd for a CEO to be attracted to anything referred to as an "Executive Limitation" or to embrace the policy's negatively phrased language. (See p. 79 of *Boards That Make a Difference*, 2nd edition, for more on proactive constraint; details are in Resource C.)

In fact the experience reflects a very positive response from CEOs, as reflected in these comments:

- "Clearly articulated expectations and authority delegated to the executive director empower the staff to be creative while having clear responsibility with accountability. This has proven to be the greatest benefit from the executive director's perspective."
- "Knowing the CEO role and [the] criteria . . . set by the board, [the CEO] experienced greater freedom and confidence in doing his job."
- "The CEO has been open to guidance [in the form of board policymaking], which will . . . give her what she needs to manage on the fly. Executive Limitations are very helpful, as they give a wide field to play in."

The next comment comes directly from the CEO of the Colorado Association of School Boards: "The biggest gains [in adopting Policy Governance] for me are clarity of role with the board, increased focus on expectations of the job, [and a] clear decision-making scope. Perhaps the biggest clarity is around my obligation to perform. It isn't possible any longer for me to fail to deal with things the board has said are important—and I know what the board has said. Strategic plans and goals don't hold me accountable like the policies do. This adds a dimension of accountability that wasn't there before, and I like it."

The city manager of Bryan, Texas, provides more praise for the Executive Limitations policy: "With Policy Governance the city manager is able to draw on the expertise of his executive management team to address thorny municipal issues. [City managers] are essentially free—within the confines of the Executive Limitations and [the] budget—to implement any means that brings progress toward an End. With no approval process to hide behind, we are fully responsible for these programs. Freedom and responsibility go together!"

Given their support for this method of delegation and oversight by the board, it is not surprising that CEOs should entertain the notion of using a similar management method with their staffs. A number of organizations have considered extending Executive Limitations beyond the CEO level to staff at other levels. One CEO suggests that this is not only desirable but necessary: "Mixing philosophies is not effective." To many people, extending Policy Governance principles to staff management is the next logical step.

How Do Boards Manage Executive Limitations?

A member of an organization studied in this book remarks, "One of the beauties of the model . . . is that the Executive Limitations policies are relatively stable." The word *relatively* is correct. Unlike the plans or the policies that tend to gather dust on a shelf in the boardroom, board policies under the model are meant to be constantly referred to as the source and destination points of board discussion. Boards using Policy Governance are meant to "live there," using and adapting their policies, not occasionally visiting them. Is this an unrealistic and unreasonable expectation? Or is it actually happening?

Making Policies Central to Board Work. Some organizations have reached this level of operation. The Weaver Street Market board chair reports that "ongoing policy work—identifying values, referencing existing policies for an item or report at hand, fine-tuning policy, adding policy, or completing one tagged for further work—is simply what the board does." The chair credits the "piecemeal process by which the board developed policy" with giving the board the discipline necessary to operate at this level. Having invested time up front in discussing the policies in depth, the board is very familiar and comfortable with them. Because the board views policy work as its primary job, the actual policies receive a lot of attention. They have been central to the board work since the adoption of the model, and the board's focus has not been diluted.

Struggling to Work at the Policy Level. Other experiences illustrate how easy it is to fall back into old habits. For example, during one "particularly difficult" meeting at which a consultant was present, one board found itself overly focused on a decision the CEO had made. The CEO recalls,

> The board was in a somewhat rancorous discussion about whether I had made a reasonable interpretation of policy. The consultant was pushing [board members] to keep the discussion at a policy level, not to decide as a board what they would have done in the circumstances. They finally decided that I had acted within policy and that the policy was exactly as it should be. Then at the end of this whole discussion a board member said, "But since we've been talking about this, can I give my opinion about what I think he should do?" Our consultant said an emphatic no and [added] that if the CEO needed input on this decision, the CEO could seek out the board member after the meeting. It just demonstrated how easy it is to slip back into the notion that if a board member has an opinion on something, it becomes board work.

Certainly a number of boards and CEOs do not operate their Executive Limitations policies consistently. One board reports that it had "some confusion about how the board should go about making policy, . . . specifically [about] how new policy [could] fit into the framework [that was] already developed," so it "dealt with some issues outside of the policy structure." Another organization observes that its board members seem fairly unfamiliar with their own policies, because they so infrequently make specific references to the policies.

It takes time to learn to handle issues at the policy level, but the effort does pay off. As reported by a source at the Colorado Association of School Boards, "The policy manual is now a dynamic instrument. When a decision is made, it is a policy decision. [Board members] are really getting the hang of it."

Using Automatic, Statutory, or Consent Agendas. Some boards are required by law or other ordinances to approve items that they really do not need to see. These things can clutter up the agenda and tempt the board into matters that are in the CEO's domain.

To deal with this problem, John Carver recommends creating an automatic approval agenda (see *Boards That Make a Difference,* 2nd edition, pp. 178–179; details are in Resource C). Items placed in the automatic approval agenda have already been delegated to the CEO and cannot be placed on the main board agenda unless the whole board agrees. An automatic approval agenda is similar to a statutory or a consent agenda. But with a conventional statutory or consent agenda, an item can sometimes be moved to the main board agenda if only one board member intervenes.

Parkland Health District illustrates the circumstances in which such agendas can be helpful: "Provincial regulations require that the board approve the budget, approve the health plan, and approve privileges for physicians. The health plan, for example, includes the board's Ends, which have already been approved in the board's Ends policies, as well as the CEO's operational plans for achieving the Ends. . . . The tendency is [for the board] to fall back on previous practice and spend copious amounts of time discussing the plan." However, as the board becomes better at specifying Ends statements, this tendency is decreasing. And the board is already using a consent agenda to approve physician privileges. The CEO provides a written statement certifying that the criteria according to the medical staff bylaws have been met, and the board approves the item without any discussion.

☑ Key Learnings

Several lessons can be drawn from the experiences of the boards we have studied in this chapter.

Sooner Is Better

The sooner boards can clear away the clutter of internal matters by completing Executive Limitations policies, the better. They need to create the safety net that allows them to move away from an internal operations focus and to concentrate on Ends. Only then will they begin to experience the rewards of Policy Governance—the rewards that come from being future oriented and linked to a larger community.

Even after they have developed their Executive Limitations policies, some boards feel the need to keep running parallel systems in order to build their own trust in the policies and monitoring structure. It's difficult to operate in two worlds for very long, and it wastes resources. If your board is using this transition option, clarify what rules the organization is actually running under, how long this transition period will last, and what evidence you are looking for during the transition period before you actually make the leap.

Boards Need to Test the Policies

Boards need to have confidence in the Executive Limitations policies. If a board wants to understand and own them completely, it must constantly test them as new issues arise. Boards may adopt Executive Limitations policies, but board members will not really grasp the policies until they work with them over time.

Money, Money, Money

Doing financial Executive Limitations policies first can start the process off on a positive note. Many board members need to feel comfortable with their control over the money before they can even consider other areas.

A Good Leader Is Essential

The development of Executive Limitations policies is one of the first tasks a board addresses in its move to Policy Governance. Boards need someone who knows the model well, who is willing to help focus the board at the policy level of discussion and act as a guide in unfamiliar territory. Boards come "as they are" to this process, often with only a very recent exposure to an entirely new philosophy.

The Blitz Is the Most Common Approach

A blitz is more commonly used than a multimeeting approach. The blitz can be improved on if a board recognizes the pitfalls in advance (for instance, board members' not fully understanding what they are approving) and if it takes steps to minimize them.

Extended Discussion Is a Challenge

To complete Executive Limitations successfully, board members need to tolerate, appreciate, and be skilled in extended discussion. If the board has limited patience or discipline, a facilitated blitz over one or two days is definitely the way to go with the initial policy development. (But remember that a blitz process is not suitable for Ends development.) It is the rare board that has the stamina and discipline to create Executive Limitations policies in many meetings over a long period.

Templates Make It Easy

Policy templates can serve as a helpful springboard for discussion. It seems that boards seldom tailor templates extensively; most boards share the same concerns when it comes to fiduciary responsibility and due diligence.

CEOs Really Like Executive Limitations

CEOs do like Executive Limitations policies. Many CEOS relish the freedom to operate responsibly. They want to be held accountable and are not bothered by the negative language.

Staff Members' Support Is Valuable

CEOs and staffs can jeopardize the effectiveness of Executive Limitations by luring the board back into operations. Therefore, the staff, particularly senior management, needs to be educated about the model. In addition, the board often needs the CEO and the staff to help them create the standards within Executive Limitations that will form the measures of compliance. A good deal of staff work goes into creating systems and reports, at least initially, and better understanding means better reports.

Keep the Policies at the Forefront

If Policy Governance boards do not work through operational issues in terms of their policies—that is, if they do not adhere to the model—they soon find that it is not working for them.

Boards Need to Address Uncertainties

Some boards are not sure that their Executive Limitations provide enough oversight and control, but they don't address those uncertainties. This has a negative long-term impact on commitment and confidence. All boards need to be absolutely confident that they have not abdicated their fiduciary responsibilities and that they can give that message with complete integrity to all concerned.

Addressing uncertainties often requires being prepared to stick your neck out. Board members who are comfortable with the group will find it easier to share the concerns and values that are the building blocks of policy. Discussion is better than silence. Individuals who are willing to speak up when they don't yet have the answer help the group progress.

Time Heals . . . but Not Always

Many board members feel an initial sense of loss or discomfort as they develop Executive Limitations and withdraw from operations. You can help the board feel connected again in ways consistent with Policy Governance (see the next two sections for some ideas). However, some people may never be comfortable with this form of delegation and governing. Parting company is an honorable option. Other board and staff members are usually relieved when someone who simply doesn't "get it" moves on.

Automatic Agendas Aid Discipline

Using automatic, consent, or statutory agendas can help maintain discipline in Policy Governance boards that are forced to deal with matters they have already delegated or would prefer to delegate to the CEO.

Celebrate Progress

Implementing Policy Governance, particularly developing Executive Limitations, is challenging work for boards. Remind the board of its accomplishments often, and celebrate accordingly!

○ Taking Action: Strategies for Where You Are Now

As you read about the experiences of various organizations, you may have identified with some of them. Perhaps you recognized familiar approaches taken by your board, similar difficulties surmounted, or similar challenges that still exist. You may have just begun to develop Executive Limitations policies, or they may be solidly in place. This section will help you identify where your board stands today and give you some tips and tools for moving forward.

If You Are Just Beginning to Develop Executive Limitations Policies

You may be about to decide what approach you will use in developing Executive Limitations policies (and other policies). Consider the following when making a decision.

- How familiar with Policy Governance is your board? Do members seem to understand the model's principles, the rationale of the negatively phrased Executive Limitations language, and the delegation that the Executive Limitations policies establish? If not, training board members further, giving them written materials, or having more discussions may pay big dividends later on in the process.
- What is the "temperament" of your board? Are members short on patience and group process skills? Or is it a relatively disciplined group that can maintain its focus for longer periods? How often does your board meet? Unless your board regularly demonstrates good process skills, use a policy blitz. The same applies if

your board meets less than once a month. Spreading policy development out over an extended period will increase the odds of getting off track and becoming lost in the process, especially without capable external assistance.

If Your Executive Limitations Are in Place

For those of you that have your Executive Limitations Policies in place, congratulations! You have taken a major step as a board and have made some weighty decisions about delegation to your CEO. Is there more to know? Consider the following questions to determine where you are now. If the questions reveal problem areas, see the "Practical Tips and Tools" section for possible solutions.

- Do all board members demonstrate a thorough knowledge of the content of the policies? Can members quickly identify where the line of authority in each operational area shifts from the board to the CEO? If not, this is an area for improvement.
- When was the last time you created or modified an Executive Limitations policy? Has your board ever modified one? Do you know what to do in order to modify one?
- Has the board addressed operational issues without using the Executive Limitations process—for instance, by deciding on a personnel matter at a level encompassed by your relevant policy? If so, you'll benefit from exploring this problem further. If it continues unaddressed, all that hard work in policy development could be eroded as it becomes clear that the board's policies are irrelevant—even to the board itself!
- Is there a lingering concern about the loss of operational involvement? If so, you'll need to bolster the sense of connection to the organization in ways that are still consistent with your policy and that don't violate the delegation of work to the CEO.
- Is the board reading and understanding monitoring reports? Do you know if the board is satisfied with the data provided? Monitoring is an important part of the oversight mechanism. Without real monitoring, Executive Limitations policies provide no meaningful security. See Chapter Seven for more on this topic.
- Does the CEO accept and seem comfortable with the responsibility you have delegated? Does the CEO try to get the board's blessing or involve the board in decisions that are clearly delegated to him or her?
- Is there a notable disparity in board members' participation level in discussions? Do some members seem to be carrying the load?

▶ Practical Tips and Tools

Here are some ideas for handling some of the rough spots and for fulfilling the possibilities of your board.

Increase Board Members' Knowledge of Policy Content

Board members need to be thoroughly familiar with the content of their policies. If they are not, they will tend to delve into matters that have already been delegated or handle issues in ways that contradict their own policies. Lack of familiarity with policies can also make board members feel uncomfortable about whether they have enough control or are providing enough oversight.

Keep the policies in front of the board. Each board member should have a policy manual, and additional copies should be available at every board and committee meeting. List the policies according to type for quick reference. Reference the appropriate policies with every agenda issue. Parkland Health District links every agenda item to a policy. See Exhibit 3.4 for an example from another organization.

You can also create tests so that individual board members can assess their understanding of policy content. Restate your policies with blanks in certain places. Provide multiple-choice answers, an answer sheet, and a "grading" mechanism (such as "You've got it," "Getting there," and "Back to the drawing board"). No one has to know how well anyone else did. Board members could also challenge each other to identify the policies related to a series of issues that could arise.

Enable Board Members to Take Ownership of Their Policies

Boards that have created their policies in a blitz or that have relied heavily on templates sometimes don't feel enough ownership of the results. A telltale sign that the board is not owning its policies is if it has not modified them or added new ones since it created them. To increase the sense of ownership, Weaver Street Market's board has scheduled agenda time to review and interpret Executive Limitations policies when questions arise. Parkland Health District's board reports that it is reevaluating a number of its policies a year and a half after initial adoption and is deciding to "back out of some of the inner-level policies," confining itself to broader value policies. Consider whether the board has concerns that are not addressed in the policies. Is everything in a policy needed? Can you change some wording to make the policy feel more like your own? Make sure the policy reflects your own board's values.

Ensure That Operational Issues Are Addressed Inside the Executive Limitations Framework

You've done some hard work to craft policies. Don't let it go to waste. If your board is addressing operational issues outside of the agreed-on system of Executive Limitations, it may be because the board is uncertain about how to craft policies. To remedy this, consider the following:

• You might find it helpful to isolate a discussion arena, focus on a particular issue, and then ask members, "What are you afraid of?" This question helps to tease out the board's values, which then become the basis for the policy. The task of drafting the policy can be delegated; writing policy as a group can be cumbersome. The board can then react to the draft, which could contain several options.

• Remind the board that there are no "orphan" issues. Any operational concerns can be safely delegated by way of Executive Limitations and correlated monitoring.

• Consider whether there are any "taboo" issues that the board feels uncomfortable discussing or that individual members are at least slow to mention. If this is the case, try the exercise titled "Undiscussables" on pp. 404–406 of *The Fifth Discipline Fieldbook* by Peter Senge and others (see Resource C for details).

• The board may not have mastered the discipline of viewing issues through a "policy screen." Or board members may be relying too much on one person to focus the discussions on policy instead of accepting individual responsibility. Anyone on the board can create the focus by asking questions such as the following:

Have we already addressed this issue or part of it in policy? If so, where?

What have we already said about this issue?

How have we handled similar issues?

Is this an Ends issue or a means issue? (The answer to this question will not tell you whether or not it is a board issue, but it will put the issue in a larger context and direct attention to the corresponding policies.)

• CEOs can help by reiterating policies in their monitoring reports and by providing their interpretations of policies.

• Distribute copies of *Board Leadership* no. 16, "What Do You Want from Your CEO? How to Express Board Concerns in *Unmistakable* Language," and *Board Lead-*

ership no. 4, "Free Your Board and Staff Through Executive Limitations." Discuss these articles at your next board meeting. See Resource C for more details.

Deal with the Loss of Operational Involvement

Focus on your *new* responsibilities, and let the former ones go. Boards operating under this model have opportunities to learn and experiment with exciting and challenging things. Use your creativity and energy to consider ways to link with your owners, to create the community you want, and to address weighty Ends issues. There is a lot of work to be done. Remember that discussing Ends provides a natural connection to the organization. After all, you will be speaking about creating benefits for your consumers, and that compels you to talk to everyone, including staff, owners, and consumers themselves.

Several organizations note that when the CEO provides incidental information (see Chapter Seven for more on this), it increases the board's understanding of how its policies are affecting the organization. However, boards should be aware that if they want to say anything new as a result of this information, they need to go back to their policies and express their thinking in those policies. People Inc. gives the board a monthly newsletter from the CEO that includes a regular column called "Highlight on Policy." Each edition expands on a particular policy. Exhibits 4.1 and 4.2 give examples of this column. Other staff members can be invited to provide incidental information in the form of updates on projects and other matters of common interest. Some boards will have already identified what they want to know in a Communication and Counsel to the Board policy.

Invite individual members who are having problems to do some soul-searching. Try to get at the root of why they are still experiencing a sense of loss. Is there a trust issue? Do they have concerns about an operational area that is not addressed to their satisfaction in board policy? If so, can they suggest an alternate policy wording? Would they rather be operational volunteers than board members, or can they perform both roles separately and satisfactorily? Can they work with the board's decision to use Policy Governance, or would they prefer to leave the board?

Ensure That the Board Is Reading and Understanding Monitoring Reports

To paraphrase John Carver, if a policy is worth creating, it's worth monitoring. Emphasize to the board that policymaking is a two-pronged approach that includes creating and monitoring. Chapter Seven covers this whole subject and gives ideas for keeping the board attentive to monitoring reports.

EXHIBIT 4.1. HIGHLIGHT ON POLICY: COMMUNICATION AND COUNSEL TO THE BOARD.

The Communication and Counsel to the Board policy is one of the Executive Limitations policies that the board monitors on a quarterly basis through a CEO report. The most recent report was sent out in October, and the next report will be sent out in January.

The Communication and Counsel to the Board policy plays an interesting role—it fills that space between what information must be provided to the board, due to its direct relevance to board policy, and all other information. It defines *which information,* other than that already being provided in monitoring other policies, the board wants to know about:

- Monitoring data directly addressing board policies
- Relevant trends, anticipated adverse media coverage, material external or internal changes, particularly changes in assumptions on which any board policy has previously been established
- Whether, in my opinion, the board is not in compliance with its own policies, particularly in the case of board behavior that is detrimental to our working relationship
- As many staff and external points of view, issues, and options as needed for fully informed board choices
- Any actual or anticipated noncompliance with board policy

It also defines expectations for *how* the information should be communicated:

- In a timely, accurate, and understandable fashion
- In a format that is not unnecessarily complex or long
- To the board as a whole, except when fulfilling individual requests or responding to officers or committees duly charged by the board

This policy is the place where the board defines those items it wants to know about so that it is generally well informed. So, for example, while a significant change in senior management staff would not be reported under the Staff Treatment policy, it *would* be reported under this policy, because I interpret that as a material "internal change" (which is one of the areas listed directly in the Communication and Counsel to the Board policy). I could also report other issues to the board as "incidental" information—not for monitoring or evaluative purposes, not because it is required under any board policy, but just because I think an issue might be of interest.

Source: Board Bulletin column by the CEO of People Inc., November 1997.

EXHIBIT 4.2. HIGHLIGHT ON POLICY: ASSET PROTECTION.

The board adopted a policy on Asset Protection as one of its first Executive Limitations policies on March 14, 1995. Since that time, I've provided monitoring reports on a quarterly basis, and the audit firm provides a monitoring report on the investment portion (item #8) annually. The policy was initially provided as one of the "templates," and our board adopted it with no modifications or further specifications.

There are several areas within this policy that require further interpretation, one of which is constraint #2:

"The executive director may not allow unbonded personnel access to material amounts of funds."

My quarterly response to this area has been, "There are no unbonded personnel with access to material amounts of funds." To arrive at that response, I considered two decision areas: (1) Which personnel should be bonded? and (2) What is a "material" amount of funds?

I have taken a conservative approach in addressing the first question (Which personnel should be bonded?) by having adequate insurance to cover all personnel. The coverage is applied to volunteers as well as consultants in their role as "agents" of the agency. So whether a case involves staff at a residence with access to client funds, office staff with access to petty cash, or management staff authorized to sign checks, the decision to insure (bond) broadly has made a decision on the second question (What is a "material" amount of funds?) unnecessary.

We still use common sense in determining what amount of funds is accessible in certain areas (for example, a limit of $500 on any one petty cash account, with the majority of accounts considerably less), but it has not been necessary to demonstrate this with regard to compliance to policy, since everyone with access to any amount of funds is covered under our insurance.

Two other areas of the Asset Protection policy also elicit further interpretation:

#4 "The executive director may not unnecessarily expose the organization, its board, or its staff to claims of liability."

#10 "The executive director may not endanger the organization's public image or credibility, particularly in ways that would hinder its accomplishment of mission."

I will address those two areas in future "Highlights on Policy" or through the monitoring reports. The next monitoring report on Asset Protection will be provided to the board during the month of July.

Source: Board Bulletin column by the CEO of People Inc., Summer 1997.

Take Action When the CEO Is Inappropriately Involving the Board

If the CEO continually involves the board on issues that it has delegated to the CEO, examine what is really going on.

- Is the CEO simply operating out of habit?
- Is he or she uncomfortable with the responsibility of the job? If so, you need to know why. Most CEOs enjoy the "freedom within clear limits and targets" that Policy Governance provides. Is your CEO up to the job your board requires?
- Does the CEO not understand the delegation? If not, you need to provide more education in Policy Governance. All the experiences in this book reflect that the CEO must understand the model.
- Does the CEO not fully trust that the board will actually honor the delegation? This may be an ill-founded feeling, a hangover from the previous governance system (or lack thereof), or traditional wisdom. But it may also be a reasonable fear in response to seeing the board contradict its own policies, even under Policy Governance. Because this is a sensitive area, all boards would be well advised to examine their performance periodically. Review and discuss the Board-Executive Relationship policy and see if it outlines a clear understanding between the board and the CEO. Some boards have a section under their Communication and Counsel to the Board policy that requires or allows the CEO to notify the board whenever it appears to be acting contrary to its policies.

CHAPTER FIVE

CREATING ENDS POLICIES

☐ The Challenge

Of all the chapters in this book, this is the most important. You could not have gotten to this point without all the hard work that has gone before in developing the policies (Executive Limitations, Governance Process, and Board-Staff Relationship) that enable you to turn away from day-to-day concerns and concentrate on the heart of the matter: Why does your organization exist? What difference is it going to make in the world? Why are you sitting at the board table at all?

Ends is a peculiar word invented to denote a peculiar concept. No other word in our language *(goal, result, outcome, product)* says quite enough to cover the full meaning of *Ends*. Ends policies define what results an organization holds itself accountable for producing in the world, for which people, at what cost. Ends policies thus are very distinctive statements. They are not vague generalizations about improving the quality of life. They are not about what an organization does (that is, the activities it engages in) but about the impact it intends to have. As a result, no matter how broadly stated, Ends are ultimately measurable. Thus they provide for real accountability.

This chapter starts by reviewing the experiences of organizations in developing their Ends policies. In particular, the chapter explores the following questions:

- How do boards create Ends policies?
- How are staff members involved in developing Ends policies?
- What do Ends policies look like?
- What makes good Ends policies good?
- What are the pitfalls in developing good Ends policies?
- How do boards answer the question "At what cost?"
- How does the CEO make a "reasonable interpretation" of Ends policies?
- How do Ends policies relate to traditional statements of board strategy, mission, and values?
- What do boards gain from Ends work?

The chapter then looks at the lessons drawn from these organizations' experiences. From there we invite you to look at where you are in the Ends development process and to consider the tools and techniques used by the organizations we have studied. Finally, we offer further suggestions and tips for enhancing your board's Ends work.

■ The Experience

How Do Boards Create Ends Policies?

Producing Ends challenges boards to question themselves and their owners at the deepest possible level. Boards must be able to state clearly the results or outcomes they seek, the people those results are for, and how much they feel these outcomes are worth in terms of resources. Take an extreme case—the board of a hospital specializing in cardiac care—and imagine the choices that would have to be made in answering these questions. Ultimately, the reason we, as democratic societies, have boards at all is that we do not want to leave such choices to any one individual.

Therefore, the development of Ends policies takes time. In well-crafted statements, every word counts. Every word defines the organization's future. Whether the words sound good isn't important. What matters is their meaning. Even after Ends statements have been developed, boards need to review them constantly, because the world in which they operate never stops changing.

Some of the boards that have contributed to this book seem well advanced in their Ends work. Others have made moderate progress. A few have yet to begin. However, several of the organizations are well enough into the process to draw some significant conclusions. So let's begin at the beginning of Ends.

It All Starts with Ownership. A board has the unique responsibility of creating its organization's future. But the board carries that responsibility on behalf of someone else—the ownership. Thus the concepts of ownership and Ends are very closely linked. If you are dipping in and out of this book, we encourage you to read Chapter Six in conjunction with this chapter. As you will see, all of the organizations working on their Ends policies engage their owners in the debate to a greater or lesser extent.

And Something Called a "Plug." In developing their policies, most boards start in the category in which they have the most concerns, such as Executive Limitations, and then move on to Governance Process and Board-Staff Relationship policies. At this point, they are ready to make the switch to Policy Governance; they can enact their new policies and thereby supersede all their previous statements except their constitution (or articles or letters patent) and bylaws.

The only problem is that the board still has no Ends policies, and the Board-Staff Relationship policy states that the CEO, from now on, will be accountable for the accomplishment of Ends. The board has only two ways to go. Either it can hold back on enacting its new policies until it has developed Ends policies, which could take many more months, or it can adopt a temporary "holding" Ends statement, also known as a "plug." In *Reinventing Your Board* (see Resource C for details), John and Miriam Carver use the following wording for this plug: "Whatever Ends the board has stated or implied in previous decisions or approvals will stay unchanged, pending formal adoption of Ends policies."

As an additional safeguard at this point, the board might also consider a temporary Executive Limitations policy stating that the CEO "shall not significantly alter the funding, size, or scope of current results for consumers." If board members have concerns about the CEO's using any "reasonable interpretation" of the word *significantly*, they could further define it (in terms of dollars, staffing, numbers of clients served, or other measures). Obviously as soon as the board has developed its Ends policies, this particular Executive Limitations policy should be deleted.

And Then You're Pretty Much on Your Own. The Carvers' work on Policy Governance has yielded templates for the development of Executive Limitations, Governance Process, and Board-Staff Relationship policies. These templates are relatively standard. They work for organizations of all types, whether in North America or further afield. As we have seen in Chapter Four, there has been very little modification of these policies among a wide variety of organizations.

Ends development is a different matter, and rightly so, because the purpose of each organization is unique. It seems unlikely that the cookie-cutter approach could be successful here. The Carvers' writings suggest that Ends work is more difficult. And although some excellent resources on Policy Governance (see Resource C) show what Ends policies for different types of organizations look like and how deliberation on Ends might proceed, these resources are of limited use, because the reader knows little of the organization or of the process used to develop the statements.

The preceding chapters have drawn on the experiences of all eleven boards we have studied. In this chapter we draw on the experience of the eight boards that specifically reported on their work on Ends. The experience of some of them is presented here in table format. But a word of caution: although several stages in Ends development are represented in the tables, the organizations neither went through all the same stages nor passed through them in the same order. Every board's Ends deliberation process is unique, because it depends on a variety of factors, such as the board's particular circumstances, its group dynamics, and the nature of the data it already has available. These experiences may help you greatly, but what is most important is finding your own path—the one that is right for your board. Exhibits 5.1 through 5.5 summarize several of the approaches used by boards reporting on their Ends experiences.

How Are Staff Members Involved in Developing Ends Policies?

Ends development is primarily about the link between the board and its owners, but staff members also have an enormous amount to offer. Just as a board seeks outside advice and information from experts with valuable knowledge, experience, and vision, it seeks staff input into the Ends process. In particular, staff can help the board understand the issues and illuminate the implications of different priorities. Boards rightly want to benefit from staff expertise as they deliberate the future.

In addition, although owners, not staff members, give the board the authority to make decisions about Ends, it is also the staff's task to define board Ends further and to determine the *means* to achieve the results intended by the board. Staff members need to understand the Ends process if they are to support it and translate the Ends policies into reality. When board members and staff members focus on their respective jobs, work can proceed in partnership.

The experience of our eight sample organizations shows that boards are involving staff members in their Ends work but that it can take board members time to understand the staff's role in providing input. Two examples demonstrate this. In one organization, staff members were very anxious about the board making important planning decisions and directing the future of the organization when they knew they had more direct experience and knowledge of the issues. In particular, staff members did not want the board to make a decision that would stop anything they were currently doing from being done in the future. As the discussion progressed, it became clear that, in fact, staff members had great differences about where they wanted the organization to go. It also became clear to everyone that, up until this point, the staff rather than the board had been driving the agenda.

The balance seems to have been found in this organization. A staff member reports, "Observing [the board's] commitment made me realize that I didn't have a problem. Who are we to think we are better situated than the board to make these decisions? In a very real way and in a deeper way, we have redefined the roots of the organization: community, as opposed to other tangents we got into through the strategic planning process."

A second example occurred with the Southern Ontario Library Service, bringing the board to a similar point. There was an issue over polling (an informal voting method) in terms of draft mission statements. The board very much wanted the staff involved in the discussion but found that because so many staff members were present, they had a significant effect on the vote and could alter the board's decision. Board members decided that although they would continue to value and seek staff input, final votes on Ends policies would be taken by the board alone.

For Policy Governance to work properly, there must be a strong, demonstrable partnership between board and staff. When each party understands its role, the ensuing synergy can generate outstanding results.

What Do Ends Policies Look Like?

Four sets of Ends policies appear in Exhibits 5.6 through 5.9. They are clear and largely Policy Governance–consistent examples of how boards can develop their policies through increasingly specific levels of definition.

What Makes Good Ends Policies Good?

The Ends statements in Exhibits 5.6 through 5.9 reflect the effects the organizations wish to have on their beneficiaries. The statements clearly answer "What good?" and "For whom?" Some (for example, the City of Bryan and Parkland Health District), have gotten further along the road and also answer "At what cost?" Each level of Ends policy defines the previous level of Ends policy further. Together the statements publicly proclaim the results that the board will be accountable for achieving in the community.

But aside from looking for these stated intentions, how can we tell whether Ends policies are designed to do their job effectively? The literature (such as p. 149 of *Reinventing Your Board* by John and Miriam Carver; see Resource C for details) says that Ends policies should be

- Brief, but including all three Ends components (what good, for whom, at what cost)
- Doable, not merely a wish or an unattainable goal
- Clear, but not having to bear the burden of being snappy like a slogan
- Expansive enough to embrace the fullness of your organization's intent
- Narrow enough to distinguish your organization from the larger world

EXHIBIT 5.1. ENDS DEVELOPMENT PROCESS OF WEAVER STREET MARKET.

Weaver Street Market (WSM) did not cut any corners in its move to Policy Governance. The board conducted patient and deliberate discussions and proceeded methodically and slowly. For this unique organization, the path to Ends was a dynamic, multilayered, and exciting process consisting of several steps.

Stage of Ends Development	Technique Used	Purpose	Comment
Public education	Existing newsletter	To develop ownership awareness about the Policy Governance process and about cooperatives in general	Educational articles were included in the newsletter.
Data collection	Survey	To ensure the highest-quality data from the most people in the least amount of time	The survey was distributed to owners.
Analysis		To review survey data	The survey revealed WSM's success in achieving its mission and the relative importance of various parts of the mission.
Discussion	Retreat	To debate Ends values	The board extracted values from data, sorted values by Ends and means, prioritized Ends values, and created Ends policies.
	Post-retreat meetings	To draft mega-Ends statement	
	Existing newsletter	To provide feedback to owners on draft mega-Ends statement	The feedback was sent to owners along with an article titled "Why a Renewed Mission Statement?"

EXHIBIT 5.1. ENDS DEVELOPMENT PROCESS OF WEAVER STREET MARKET (*continued*).

Discussion (*continued*)	Brainstorming	To define Ends further, to distill themes inherent in owners' feedback to the mission, and to craft further effects	The board reviewed the survey results again.
	Homework	To develop priorities among effects	Board members were asked to reflect on their personal priorities. This furthered the process and helped board members prepare for meetings. The board decided to categorize rather than prioritize its effects.
	Subcommittee	To consider values arising from the discussion and to restate them as Ends	
	Full board meeting	To consider the Ends in the context of others in the community; to reflect on progress	The board examined Ends statements of other organizations.
	Homework	To refine Ends statements further	Board members were all asked to create sample statements.
	Retreat	To develop final Ends statements; to develop "inner shell" statements	The board reexamined the draft for missing items and for items needing further development.

EXHIBIT 5.2. ENDS DEVELOPMENT PROCESS OF PARKLAND HEALTH DISTRICT.

The Ends process was challenging for Parkland Health District's board, which has undergone structural changes and massive turnover. This board proceeded through a series of distinct stages in defining its Ends policies.

Stage of Ends Development	Technique Used	Purpose	Comment
Data collection	Gathering and reviewing existing (1) needs assessment data (demographics, interviews, and community meeting reports), (2) available health status data, (3) provincial government resources information, (4) subjective needs assessment data on several health-related issues, (5) objective demographic data	To explore what areas of health might be of most concern	The new board reviewed the work of the old board, particularly ownership input.
	New needs assessments	To obtain data on target groups' health needs (youth, seniors, mental health)	Some assessments were completed, and others were planned.
Consultation	Presentations to community groups	To outline board priorities and elicit feedback	Each board member makes three presentations annually. The entire board determines the content of the meetings.
	Public meetings	To highlight past achievements; to outline planned priorities; to solicit feedback	

EXHIBIT 5.2. ENDS DEVELOPMENT PROCESS OF PARKLAND HEALTH DISTRICT (*continued*).

Consultation (*continued*)	Open board meetings	These meetings are held twice a year.
	Local newspaper and district newsletter articles and ads	To publicize changes in Ends; to request input on the relative priority of Ends.
Establishment of priorities	Framework for making decisions	To facilitate decision-making priorities	The board identified all the sources of information it would check related to each Ends issue before making a decision.
	Criteria for making priority decisions	To facilitate setting priorities	The board established a set of criteria to use as a template.

EXHIBIT 5.3. ENDS DEVELOPMENT PROCESS OF THE CITY OF BRYAN, TEXAS.

The City of Bryan, Texas, provides an important example of Ends development that has found favor with council, staff, and citizens. The council wanted to talk to citizens about Ends issues in a "nonadversarial format." The City spent considerable time and effort designing and refining an Ends development process that resulted in a multimeeting approach, which included linking with owners in a significant manner. This approach puts Ends policies before the ownership in a way that a traditional approach to governance does not. The council reports the following results: the council can articulate its vision more clearly, council meetings are spent talking about and creating this future, and this future focus has spilled over into the community, making residents feel better than they ever have about Bryan.

Stage of Ends Development	Technique Used	Purpose	Comment
Discussion	Annual retreat	To discuss values and community needs and to set priorities	The discussion provided an opportunity for newly elected council members to contribute to the Ends policy document and to help them understand their role and responsibility to the electorate. Council members are encouraged to offer suggestions that incorporate not only their individual philosophy but also that of the community.
Exploration	Multimeeting process	To discuss particular aspects of the council's Ends policies	

EXHIBIT 5.3. ENDS DEVELOPMENT PROCESS OF THE CITY OF BRYAN, TEXAS (*continued*).

Exploration (*continued*)	Experts, partners, other community groups, and members of the community at large were invited to meet with the council.	To give the council differing perspectives
	Council meetings are videotaped and broadcast several times over the local cable station.	To ensure that the public is aware of the process
Discussion	Full council meeting	To provide a forum for the council's own dialogue on "What good for which people at what cost?"
		The council discussed Ends, drafted Ends statements, and formally adopted Ends.

EXHIBIT 5.4.
ENDS DEVELOPMENT PROCESS OF THE SAN FRANCISCO AIDS FOUNDATION.

The San Francisco AIDS Foundation board has used several techniques in developing its Ends policies. The board and staff have gone to considerable lengths to integrate Ends throughout the organization. The overall Ends statement appears everywhere—in the building, in the newsletter, in speeches to the public, and in talks with staff. According to one board member, the "beauty of this model is that the board can explicitly direct the staff as it sees the changes coming. The board is very good about knowing that the Ends are a work in progress."

Stage of Ends Development	Technique Used	Purpose	Comment
Preparation for Ends meetings	Vice-chair for Ends	To facilitate and ensure that Ends development takes place	Tasks include preparing agendas and other materials in conjunction with a staff board liaison officer.
Consultation	Brown-bag lunches	To seek public input	The consultation provided an opportunity to discuss important issues.
	Open forums	To seek public comment	Forums were large community meetings focusing on a specific topic.
Exploration	One-on-one meetings	To get information from other agencies or individual owners	The meetings were attended by both a staff and a board member so that staff could answer means-related questions and board members could still elicit the information they needed.

Exploration (*continued*)	Open meetings	To hear from community members	There is concern about potential results, because community members often want to talk about means. There needs to be a way to listen to the means questions and to give satisfaction to those asking them and still to get the information the board needs.
Discussion	Mini-retreat	To provide Ends input into staff strategic planning process	The retreat is held each year.
Documentation	Binders (See Chapter Eight for more on binders.)	To create a permanent record of the process; to record a sense of the thinking that went into the deliberations; to document background information on the epidemic so that board members can look to the future	The archives contain the "developmental stages" of Ends work and insightful articles on Policy Governance and on issues related to AIDS.
Process	Meetings	To facilitate Ends discussion	Saturday mornings are the preferred format.
	Videotaped sessions	To record discussion about Ends	Videotaping allows members unable to attend to be involved in the process.
	Ends policy review	To address trends in the epidemic	Regular review of Ends is critical, because the epidemic is constantly changing. For example, when affordable housing for AIDS sufferers was identified as an emerging issue, the board was able to shift emphasis away from less-pronounced trends.

EXHIBIT 5.5. ENDS DEVELOPMENT PROCESS OF THE VERMONT LAND TRUST.

An imaginative process of Ends development led the Vermont Land Trust (VLT) board on a fascinating journey of discovery.

Stage of Ends Development	Technique Used	Purpose	Comment
Exploration	Roundtable	To elicit various points of view from experts about VLT	The roundtable took the form of a three-hour facilitated discussion with a judge, an economist, a legislator, a farmer, and a writer. The board could only watch this discussion. Many issues were uncovered about Vermont's place in the global economy and the purpose of land conservation. After the initial discussion, the board was allowed to ask questions and make comments.
	Rainbow sheets	To distill the day's conversations into a manageable format	A work group was charged with framing the board's discussion around whether the primary reason for conserving land was natural, cultural, or economic. Each rainbow sheet (paper of different colors) articulated a major focus for the organization, along with the advantages and disadvantages of that focus and ways in which the organization would have to change in order to make this a primary focus.
Discussion	Retreat	To explore the various agendas suggested by the rainbow sheets	The retreat led to a framework for the board's future discussion of Ends and to plans for meetings with partners.
Consultation	Partner meetings	To determine what other organizations were doing	The outcome-oriented discussion helped the board determine what it needed. This resulted in a work plan that outlined areas requiring exploration or consultation.

EXHIBIT 5.6. ENDS POLICY OF WEAVER STREET MARKET.

Weaver Street Market is a business cooperatively owned by its consumers and workers. Its mission is a vibrant, sustainable community defined by the following:

Flourishing, locally oriented cooperative commerce where

- Business values reflect community values
- Business and community invest in one another
- Resources remain within the community
- Trade is mutually beneficial and nonexploitative

A heightened sense of community, including

- A forum for expressing shared values
- Increased opportunity for community interaction
- A greater sense of community potential

Community members with a strong sense of individual well-being, including

- Equal treatment and respect among all community members
- Empowering and fulfilling work experiences
- Access to healthful and affordable sustenance
- Community members who have the knowledge to achieve their own well-being

The board is considering defining further levels of specificity under each sub-End.

CarverGuide 6: Creating a Mission That Makes a Difference (see Resource C for details) cautions boards to avoid verbs such as *enhance, advocate, encourage,* and *support* and nouns that signify activities. There is always the need to check whether the statements reflect actual end results or simply describe activities that may or may not achieve the results.

The wording of the mega-End, or mission, must be absolutely impeccable. From it will flow all the other statements that will eventually lead the organization to achieve results. Finding such flawless terminology is often difficult, but it is essential that boards persevere until their words have the maximum clarity and power.

The Colorado Association of School Boards helps its member school boards jump-start their own Ends process (ten of the organization's member school boards are using Policy Governance) by suggesting sample wording: "As a result of our efforts students will. . . ." Individual boards can then brainstorm the benefits sparked by the question "What good?" This discussion helps the board determine which statements reflect the needs of its unique school district. Themes emerge

EXHIBIT 5.7.
ENDS POLICY OF PARKLAND HEALTH DISTRICT.

Vision: Healthy Living in Rural Saskatchewan

The mission of Parkland Health District is to achieve results in the areas of:

I. Healthy Environment

   1. Healthy Physical Environment

      1.1   Clean air   *priority 1*

          1.1.1 Reduction of smoking in public places
          1.1.2 Public awareness of air contaminants

      1.2   Public has access to information re: environmental contaminants *priority 2*
      1.3   Safe Water

          1.3.1 Host district notified of problems with safety of drinking water

   2. Nurturing Environment

      2.1   Safe living conditions in locations where care is delivered   *priority 1*
      2.2   Social support to maintain wellness is available   *priority 2*

          2.2.1 Early recognition of symptoms of lack of social support
          2.2.2 Sense of security that support is available

II. Healthy Lifestyles

   1. Mental Health

      1.1   Increased social interaction for high risk groups   *priority 1*
      1.2   Public access to information re: the importance of the spiritual and cultural component of wellness
      1.3   Positive self-esteem for at-risk groups   *priority 1*

          1.3.1 Youth a priority area

      1.4   Skills to cope with stress

          1.4.1 Adequate school access to mental health professionals
          1.4.2 Adequate public access to mental health professionals

      1.5   Decrease in suicide attempts

   2. Physical Health

      2.1   Decreased accidents, e.g. farm accidents, ATV's [all terrain vehicles], snowmobiles, automobiles, especially [for] teens   *priority 1*
      2.2   Decrease in preventable communicable diseases
      2.3   Access to aids to independent living

EXHIBIT 5.7.
ENDS POLICY OF PARKLAND HEALTH DISTRICT (*continued*).

II. Healthy Lifestyles (*continued*)

2. Physical Health (*continued*)

2.4 Increased recreation and exercise

2.5 Proper diet

2.6 Participation in early detection and screening opportunities

3. Social Health

3.1 Decrease in substance abuse (smoking, alcohol, street drugs, smoke free tobacco) target teens; over-the-counter drugs *priority 1*

3.2 Less sexually active youth

3.3 Better parenting skills

3.3.1 Awareness of the need for adequate supervision of children

3.4 Decrease in gambling addictions

III. Healing

1. There will be adequate in-district physician coverage.

2. Physical Healing

2.1 Residents receive timely care in emergency situations *priority 1*

2.2 Timely access to diagnosis *priority 1*

2.3 Healthy delivery for mothers and babies *priority 1*

2.3.1 Delivery of low risk pregnancies in district

2.3.2 Increased number of deliveries in district

2.4 Restoration to optimum health from illness or injury *priority 2*

2.5 Maintain independent living for as long as possible with support that meets assessed and documented need *priority 2*

2.6 Dying with dignity *priority 2*

3. Mental Healing

3.1 Restoration to optimum mental well-being *priority 2*

3.1.1 Care-givers

3.1.2 Those in mental health crisis

3.1.3 Those with addictions and their families

3.1.4 Those in situational crisis

3.1.5 Those in abusive relationships

4. Spiritual Healing

4.1 Clients can access the spiritual support they feel they need

---

EXHIBIT 5.8.
ENDS POLICY OF THE SAN FRANCISCO AIDS FOUNDATION.

End the pandemic and human suffering caused by HIV.

I. End the pandemic

   A. HIV exists at the lowest possible rates

      1. New HIV infections exist at a continually diminishing rate in San Francisco

      2. Individuals most at risk have the self-knowledge, objective knowledge, skills and tools to practice safe behaviors in San Francisco

         a) People know their HIV status as early as possible after exposure to HIV

         b) People know their treatment options as soon as possible following exposure to HIV

   B. Public policies reflect an informed community, a supportive social structure and necessary funding

      1. Elected officials and other policy/decision makers create and enact legislation/decisions that promote the Ends of the San Francisco AIDS Foundation

II. End the human suffering caused by HIV

   A. People with HIV have their basic human needs met

      1. People with HIV in San Francisco have adequate housing

         a) Homelessness for people with HIV in San Francisco exists at a continually diminishing rate

   B. People affected by HIV have hope, dignity, quality of life and choice

      1. People with HIV will live for the longest possible period

      2. The human rights of people with HIV are honored and protected

      3. People have the self-knowledge, objective knowledge, skills and tools to make informed choices about HIV treatment

         a) People choosing treatment have the support they need to obtain maximum benefit from HIV treatment

      4. People with HIV have access to the best available treatment options for themselves

   C. A wide range of treatment options exist, and barriers to treatments are removed for people with HIV

      1. People know their HIV status as soon as possible after infection

EXHIBIT 5.9.
ENDS POLICY OF THE CITY OF BRYAN, TEXAS.

The City of Bryan exists so that Bryan will be a healthy, safe, attractive, and successful community for a reasonable financial burden.

1. There is a safe environment for residents and visitors

  1.1 People can move in, out and within Bryan safely, quickly and efficiently

    1.1.1 Pedestrians can move in, out and within Bryan safely, quickly and efficiently
    1.1.2 Vehicles can move in, out and within Bryan safely, quickly, and efficiently
    1.1.3 Air traffic can move in and out of Bryan safely and efficiently

  1.2 There is an adequate supply of high-quality drinking water

    1.2.1 The current supply of drinking water meets current demand
    1.2.2 The drinking water is wholesome
    1.2.3 The drinking water tastes good
    1.2.4 There is an adequate reserve of high-quality drinking water for the future

  1.3 There is efficient and effective disposal of waste

    1.3.1 Waste is collected and appropriately disposed of in a timely and cost-effective manner
    1.3.2 Recycling is appropriately utilized

  1.4 There is clean air

    1.4.1 Air is of high quality
    1.4.2 Air quality is ensured into the future

  1.5 Animals are appropriately controlled and cared for

    1.5.1 Dangerous animals are restricted
    1.5.2 Human injury from animals is infrequent and insubstantial
    1.5.3 Animal populations are appropriately controlled

  1.6 Residents and visitors are reasonably protected from emergencies and natural disasters

    1.6.1 There is a low crime rate
    1.6.2 There is low loss due to fire
    1.6.3 There is a readiness for emergencies and natural disasters
    1.6.4 Citizens have protection from flooding

**EXHIBIT 5.9.
ENDS POLICY OF THE CITY OF BRYAN, TEXAS (*continued*).**

2. The economic life of the community is stable and growing appropriately

  2.1 There is an adequate employment base

    2.1.1 Citizens are employable

    2.1.2 Workforce is employed

    2.1.3 There are adequate business opportunities to meet the employment needs

  2.2 There is a diverse recession proof economy

    2.2.1 There is an appropriate mix of small, medium and large businesses

    2.2.2 There is diversity in the types of businesses/industries

    2.2.3 Products are high quality and innovative

    2.2.4 Businesses can compete globally

  2.3 There is a dynamic, positive business climate

    2.3.1 The economic climate is favorable to businesses

    2.3.2 Businesses flourish

    2.3.3 The economic climate is responsive to the changing needs of businesses

    2.3.4 The economic climate is responsive to the changing needs of citizens

    2.3.5 There is growth in the economy

    2.3.6 Businesses contribute to the community

    2.3.7 Businesses collaborate

    2.3.8 Businesses are innovative, knowledge-based and idea-based

3. The community is attractive, clean, and aesthetically pleasing

  3.1 Neighborhoods are aesthetically pleasing

    3.1.1 Citizens participate in planning and decision-making

    3.1.2 Neighborhoods are neat, orderly, and clean

  3.2 City entrances are attractive

    3.2.1 Other organizations and industries understand the importance of first impressions

    3.2.2 Entrances are symbolic of the character of the City or neighborhood

    3.2.3 Entrances have a pleasant appearance

    3.2.4 Entrances are easily accessible and identifiable

    3.2.5 Major entrances are orderly and neat

    3.2.6 Transportation corridors are attractive

**EXHIBIT 5.9.
ENDS POLICY OF THE CITY OF BRYAN, TEXAS (*continued*).**

3.3 The city is well-maintained

    3.3.1 There is controlled vegetation

    3.3.2 There is a lack of visible junked vehicles

    3.3.3 There is a lack of abandoned buildings

3.4 There is a balance of green and developed space

    3.4.1 There is green space for both recreation and relaxation

4. Residents have a good quality of life

    4.1 People have physical, mental, and social well-being

        4.1.1 People have the information and knowledge they need to pursue a high quality of life

        4.1.2 There is a vibrant cultural life

        4.1.3 There is adequate housing

        4.1.4 People can recreate

    4.2 There is civic pride

        4.2.1 The community shares the vision of a healthy city

        4.2.2 Bryan has a distinct identity

        4.2.3 Residents are active in their community

        4.2.4 People value diversity

        4.2.5 Residents take responsibility for the appearance of the city

---

from the ideas collected in the brainstorming session, which eventually lead to subsidiary, or lower-level, benefits. Statements that are actually means or that are beyond the board's control can be dropped.

What Are the Pitfalls in Developing Good Ends Policies?

Even with the good advice provided in the literature, the road to Ends can have a number of pitfalls. Undoubtedly, Ends work demands considerable time and energy from the trustees who venture into it. Sometimes the work leads the board down unproductive paths.

Consider, for example, the experience of the Southern Ontario Library Service. In an early Ends session, the board divided into small groups, each with the task of developing a mission statement. This was done to encourage quieter members to participate. However, when the groups reconvened, they proposed six different missions, which each group proceeded to defend. It took further discussion to uncover common threads. The board then directed its informal executive committee to build on the input and to provide some options for the next meeting. In the process, the committee identified a seventh mission, which the board found "unclear and confusing." The board points out that it made several errors in the process, constantly arriving at solutions that satisfied only a small group. The board had to reopen opinions several times and ended up repeating discussions.

Another point to consider carefully is the accurate definition of ownership. The organization must be sure that it defines its own particular Ends and not those of another organization. This would seem self-evident, but boards of associations or of federations may mistakenly see the Ends of their member organizations as their own. The Colorado Association of School Boards, for example, needed to be clear that its ownership consisted of its member school boards, not the students whom those boards serve. Similarly, it was critical for the Southern Ontario Library Service to identify the library boards of southern Ontario as its ownership, rather than identifying the communities that own those boards. Defining the ownership incorrectly can lead the board astray.

Another trap is to neglect the successive definition of Ends policies. When and if the board wishes to go to another level of detail (thereby limiting the CEO's room for reasonable interpretation), each of the more detailed Ends statements should flow directly from the one before, thereby increasingly narrowing the focus. Without this discipline, Ends policies can deteriorate into just another "to do" list.

How Do Boards Answer the Question "At What Cost?"

The Ends question "At what cost?" perplexes many boards. The San Francisco AIDS Foundation reports that "the hardest questions are around 'For whom?' and 'What cost?' 'What cost?' is the most difficult to answer. It is still on the table. It is the one issue that keeps coming back." Of course, the very act of agreeing on Ends clarifies the organization's priorities; some things are in, and some things are out. However, if the board wants to dictate the overall value of the Ends (in terms of money or by some other resource measure), it needs to do more work. Indeed, the board may wish to state the relative value of individual outcomes for specific beneficiaries.

Some boards may be satisfied with a very basic pronouncement of the cost. Following are examples of some of the most obvious parameters for achieving Ends:

- A dollar figure. For example, the City of Bryan, a $140 million municipal corporation, simply states that the overall End of "a healthy, safe, attractive, and successful community" will be fulfilled for "a reasonable financial [tax] burden."
- The relative priority (such as high, medium, or low) of second-level Ends, or sub-Ends.
- A time frame.
- A percentage of resources to be used.
- A comparison between the organization and another organization.
- Competitive rates in a particular sphere.
- State-of-the-art efficiency.
- A specific level of customer satisfaction.
- Minimal cost.

Organizations might consider a "What if . . . ?" discussion to help them define the cost issue. For example, the Colorado Association of School Boards asked what would arise if one Ends priority were to be pursued over another. What happens if . . . ? What are the implications of . . . ? Who will and who will not receive benefits if the organization's funding is jeopardized? Which Ends should go, and which Ends should stay? These are difficult questions—but ones that the board must address. As yet, the board has not specified the cost in terms of either the relative priority or the estimated price tag for each End. However, the board is well aware of the nature of the issue. The CEO gives an example of the kind of question the organization faces in its Ends work: "If we agree to focus on improving public support for schools, this implies high expenditures; can we afford that choice? Is it worth it?"

Parkland Health District's board uses both a framework for decision making and criteria for decision making in its approach to setting priorities. Both these policies are included in its Governance Process policies and enshrine the principles on which the board will base its decisions. Such a discussion helps to prepare the board for the difficult and sensitive choices associated with setting priorities. See Exhibit 6.1 for more details of the framework on which the Parkland policies are based.

The "At what cost?" discussions are often complicated by a threat of serious or drastic consequences. In the Parkland Health District example, the CEO and board consultant report, "The value choices [the board] faced were significant, in some cases resulting in the closure or major change in function of a health care facility." Several of Parkland's Ends statements are designated "Priority 1" or "Priority 2," as can be seen in Exhibit 5.7.

Early in its process, Parkland Health District volunteered to be one of several Saskatchewan health districts to be audited by the provincial auditor regarding its "resource allocation process." While recognizing that the process was "evolving," the auditor nevertheless suggested several improvements:

- Consistently comparing community opinion findings [input from the ownership] with information from the province or the nation
- Improving their process of ranking priority health needs by using real health status information
- Validating their prioritization of Ends through community consultation
- Setting measurable targets for priority health needs [which in Policy Governance language would mean being more specific in defining and prioritizing Ends]
- Developing some consistent core decision principles to guide the board's decisions when prioritizing Ends
- Obtaining measurement of actual performance in achievement of Ends

Significantly, the auditor suggested actions that are clearly consistent with Policy Governance principles. For boards with nagging concerns about the model's ability to ensure compliance with fiduciary duty, this may provide substantial comfort.

How Does the CEO Make a "Reasonable Interpretation" of Ends Policies?

Ends discussion helps the board focus its attention on future outcomes. When specific outcomes are defined, it is the CEO's job to interpret those outcomes in a "reasonable" manner in any level of detail needed to contrive the means to achieve them. The more definitive the Ends policies are, the less the CEO and subsequently the staff will need to define them further.

As with all policies in the Policy Governance model, the board "stops speaking" (formulating more detailed levels of policy) when it is willing to accept any "reasonable interpretation" of its policy statements. This issue is dealt with extensively in Chapter Seven. However, it is worth discussing here in relation to the design of Ends statements.

As an example, the Ends policies of the City of Bryan are really striking in their depth and breadth. The process has allowed the council to progress further than most organizations implementing Policy Governance. The consecutive definition of Ends policies leads the way for the CEO and staff to explore what safe neighborhoods look like and what indicators can be used to prove that they have been created. However, there needs to be a balance between specificity and flexibility. The more the board defines the Ends policies, the narrower the range of options the CEO has for interpreting the definitions of success that the board might accept. The broader the range of options available for the CEO and subsequently for staff members working under the Policy Governance model, the more their own creativity and ingenuity can emerge.

When a board prioritizes its Ends policies, these priorities are also open to the CEO's "reasonable interpretation." Thus a board that stops speaking after indicating "Priority 1" and "Priority 2" could be asked to accept an interpretation that gives a little more weight to Priority 1 than to Priority 2 or an interpretation saying that Priority 1 must be fulfilled before moving to accomplish anything in Priority 2.

The board must be clear that it really is willing to accept any reasonable interpretation of what it has said. If it knows that it is not willing to accept certain interpretations of its current policy, it must proceed to a further level of detail.

How Do Ends Policies Relate to Traditional Statements of Board Strategy, Mission, and Values?

Strategic planning is a traditional process in which the organization—usually the board and the staff—maps out how it will achieve particular goals necessary for implementing the organization's purpose over a specified period. These goals are broken down into manageable components or objectives that specify how much of a particular goal is to be met by when. The strategic plan focuses on the strategies and tactics to be used to achieve these goals and objectives. It is consequently a *means* document. Doing strategic planning is often the activity that engages traditional boards most and makes board members feel that they are really accomplishing something.

The Policy Governance approach encourages the board to spend the majority of its time doing continuous, future-oriented thinking; exploring options; developing Ends; and consulting with owners. When the board has completed its work on Ends, the staff will carry on and define Ends even more specifically and eventually choose the programs and services that will achieve the Ends.

Thus there are similarities between the Ends process and strategic planning. Under Policy Governance, however, the board tells staff members what they should be planning *for*, and the staff members actually do the planning. In its ongoing Ends development process, the San Francisco AIDS Foundation goes on an annual retreat that provides input into the *staff's* strategic planning and budgeting exercises.

The distinction between Ends work and strategic planning relates to the nature of the Ends themselves. Ends could be called "goals" or "objectives" or even "strategic outcomes," but they are not Ends statements unless they clearly answer the questions "What benefit, for which people, at what cost?" And if they are not Ends statements, the chances that the board can clearly and consistently monitor progress toward them are slim.

How do the terms *vision* and *mission* fit within the context of Ends? Parkland Health District refers to its long-range Ends statement as its "vision." Many organizations adopting Policy Governance refer to their overall or "mega-Ends" statement as their "mission." Whatever a board calls the statement, the key requirement is to make sure that it answers the questions "What benefit, for whom, at what cost?"

Many boards have also worked long and hard on overarching statements, such as Guiding Principles or Values, and it is natural that they would want to hold on to them when they adopt Policy Governance. The content of these statements can usually be incorporated in Policy Governance policies, but they may need some analysis first. If these documents relate to how the board intends to do its job, they can go in Governance Process. If they basically tell the staff not to behave in certain ways, they can be put into suitable language and incorporated in Executive Limitations. If they are related to Ends, then they simply become part of the thinking that produces the Ends policy. If they fall into two or three policy categories, the board will have to pick through them extremely carefully when doing the translating. In most cases, boards find that in developing their Policy Governance policies they have actually said everything that they included in previous documents—and said it a lot more clearly.

What Do Boards Gain from Ends Work?

When Policy Governance is only partly in place and Ends work has not begun, boards can feel disconnected from their organizations. Reviewing Executive Limitations monitoring reports to check compliance with board policy is critical but hardly exciting. Board members can feel lost and unsure of their role.

The boards who have contributed to this book are at varying stages on the path of developing Ends, but they have all expressed their satisfaction with Ends work. The process has been immensely satisfying to Weaver Street Market's board and staff. They report that it has provided understanding and clarity for the board. It has also created a multifaceted approach to communicating with owners. "It is truly freeing to move beyond the details of what is happening inside the organization to see that it can indeed define, strive for, and achieve something bigger in the world." Although the Ends process is never complete, the chair reports that the Ends policies "paint a possible future that necessarily provides some direction."

For the Colorado Association of School Boards, the overall experience of Policy Governance seems to have been successful. "The board really likes this serious Ends discussion. There is overwhelming support on the board to spend our time here. No one on the board wants to go back to approving what kind of tables we buy for the conference room. . . . Our staff is able to focus so much better. We know what is expected of us. We know better now what to say yes to and what to say no to. Everything is much clearer."

Echoing that sentiment, the Southern Ontario Library Service board chair recounts that Policy Governance "was a real asset in dealing with [government officials]. I always felt quite secure that I spoke for the board and the organization.

The roles were clear. . . . I knew who I represented and what my goals were." It is also clear to the Vermont Land Trust board members that although they have a three-part agenda, which could be confusing, they understand it more clearly because of the Ends work. "We now understand that our agenda is in the interest of developing the community and the economy. In tandem if possible. And if not, then with no harm to either."

These boards have found meaning, purpose, and relevance in the discussions and retreats they have attended. They have built a sense of team. When Ends work is progressing well, boards start getting excited about *their* work. As a result, boards are less likely to be drawn into staff activities. When not actively involved in Ends determination, boards seem uncertain about what they should do. For a number of the organizations profiled here, Ends work seems to be the activity that integrates Policy Governance into the board's way of life.

John Carver challenges us with Policy Governance and especially so with Ends. These policies need to be lofty enough to motivate staff and board, practical enough to make sense to owners and consumers, and achievable enough to satisfy board and CEO performance expectations. What if the organizations we have worked so hard to create for the important purposes we have struggled to achieve (eradication of disease; creation of healthy, sustainable environments; promotion of literacy; and so on) could actually accomplish what they set out to do? Perhaps our organizations would exist on a different level. Maybe we would no longer need them. Whichever the case, our world would indeed be a better place. Policy Governance makes it just a little more possible.

☑ Key Learnings

This section summarizes what can be learned from boards' experiences in developing their Ends policies.

There Is No Template for Ends, but There Are Common Stages

Each of the boards profiled in this chapter developed its own approach to drafting Ends policies, yet a number of common stages and activities emerged:

- Collection of information
- Board exploration and education
- Preparation for Ends meetings
- Promotion of ownership awareness and education
- Consultation
- In-depth discussions

- Decision-making process
- Priority setting
- Documentation of meetings
- Dissemination of information
- Archiving of information

There is not a template for Ends policies or for the Ends process. Although other boards can undoubtedly draw on the common stages and techniques listed here, it appears that the Ends development process is not necessarily linear. Every board will not start with the first stage and progress to the last one in order. There may be points when the board has to return to a previous stage or jump ahead to another stage simply because that's what the board's process demands at the time. Put another way, the board must find its own path.

The common stages and techniques suggest areas that require serious consideration. What is most important is that boards develop Ends processes that work *for them*.

Patience Is Essential

The Ends process has many challenges. Peeling off the layers of meaning, getting to the fundamental choices, and expressing them clearly require a lot of patient work. The Ends development process can be long and involved. The process must be planned to keep momentum and to ensure that people are productively involved. Boards also need to develop their discussion skills for internal use and for use with others (owners, other boards, and staff members). Policy Governance consultant Jan Moore compares the Ends development process to eating an elephant. It must proceed "one bite at a time."

Ends Start and Finish with Owners

Involving owners in the Ends process is instrumental in helping boards create Ends policies that accurately reflect the reasons for the organization's existence. Owners' input is critical to the very special future-oriented policy work required for Ends. Once Ends policies have been drafted and approved, it is also important to elicit feedback to ensure that owners' input has been correctly interpreted. Several suggestions and tools for assisting with the information gathering and consultation phases of Ends development have emerged from this chapter and are summarized in Exhibit 5.11 at the end of the chapter. Further suggestions for consulting owners can be found in Exhibit 6.2.

Widen Your Horizons

Exploring new ideas and educational opportunities sparks the development of Ends policies. Be creative in finding and creating new activities and information to get the ideas flowing. Recognize that the issues are apt to change over time. Demographic shifts, economic fluctuations, and changes in government can all have significant effects on needs and hence on organizational Ends. The quest for the most relevant and current information is perpetual.

Staff Members Count

Staff members and other experts in the organization's field have much to contribute to the Ends discussion. Staff members in particular need to understand Ends and the board's process in delineating them because they will be both defining the Ends at more specific levels and choosing activities to achieve the desired results. The staff may be anxious that the board is making the overall decisions, but that *is* the board's domain. Once staff members see the depth and breadth of the board's Ends discussion, they will likely realize that their fears are groundless.

Watch Out for the Pitfalls

It is wise to avoid rather than stumble into the potential pitfalls and traps in Ends work. Step back frequently to reflect on where deliberations have brought you. Carefully work through each stage of your board's process, and maintain a balance between process and content.

There Are Several Ways to Determine the Costs

Boards have tackled the cost issue in many different ways. There is no one-size-fits-all solution. Each board has to find its own expression of the cost, but it should discuss the implications of all the possible alternatives. In answering the question "At what cost?" the board is dictating the relative priorities for each End—what will get dropped when resources are short and what will get expanded as new resources become available.

Prepare Carefully for a "Reasonable Interpretation" of the Ends

The more specific the Ends are and the more precisely they are stated, the clearer the CEO and the staff will be about what a "reasonable interpretation" is. The board must determine which results would be acceptable and must give staff members sufficient room to use their own expertise to make good decisions about the Ends.

Carefully Translate Traditional Board Statements into Policy Governance Statements

Most of the valuable work that has gone into a board's previous governance statements about goals, values, and principles can be incorporated into Policy Governance policies. But a board must decide which statements correspond to which category of policy. In the end, the original statements may undergo quite a change. It is generally more effective to start from scratch, looking back to check that you haven't missed something important, than to start from where you were. When translating older documents into Ends policies, make sure they really are Ends.

Results for People—What It's All About

Once a board gets to its Ends work, it has found its role and has determined what Policy Governance is all about. Boards enjoy working on Ends and reconnecting with the organization at a whole new and more powerful level. This is what most board members really wanted when they joined—to make the world a better place.

○ Taking Action: Strategies for Where You Are Now

When considering your board's approach to Ends, it is important to choose a path that reflects your board's needs. The evidence presented by the boards highlighted in this chapter indicates that Ends development really never stops, so don't be afraid of making a mistake. To some extent, when it comes to Ends development, being at the beginning is a long-term state. Some techniques will work for your board and some will not. What is important is to persevere in the work of Ends development.

Exhibit 5.10 is meant to help the board review the steps it has taken so far and determine how these steps might be modified or augmented. It asks a few questions that may help your board in its Ends work.

▶ Practical Tips and Tools

Once you have determined the areas in which you require support, refer to Exhibit 5.11. This chart lists the techniques and tools that organizations have used in their Ends development activities. You may wish to try them.

In addition, you should refer to the Tool Finders in Resources A and B. These charts provide a further range of techniques to help you keep moving.

Several articles, book extracts, and creative-thinking tools are particularly useful resources for basic Ends development. See Resource C for more details about all the titles listed here.

- *CarverGuide 6: Creating a Mission That Makes a Difference* provides a checklist for reviewing the mission or mega-Ends statement.
- *Board Leadership* newsletter has published four articles by John Carver on Ends development in different settings: a board of a trade association, a hospital board, a public school board, and a city council.

EXHIBIT 5.10. WHERE ARE YOU NOW? CHECKLIST.

Stage of Ends Development	Questions
Exploration	What perspectives might help you further your board's Ends process?
	What skills does your board require to facilitate the Ends process?
Consultation	With whom will you consult?
	What techniques will you use?
	Who will lead and be involved in the consultation process?
Discussion	What is the purpose of the discussion?
	Will you have an outside facilitator?
	If not, how will you facilitate the discussion?
	What techniques will you use?
Collection of information	What information do you already have?
	What information do you need?
	How will you get it?
Decision-making process	How has your board made decisions in the past?
	What will help your decision-making process in the future?
Preparation for Ends meetings	How would you characterize your meetings at the present time?
	What preparation do you currently do for meetings?
	What other activities might help you prepare?
Dissemination of information and education of others	With whom do you want to share information?
	What techniques have you used in the past to share information with owners? With clients? With partners? With funders?
	What techniques will serve you in the future?
Establishment of priorities	What techniques have you used in the past to determine priorities?
	What techniques and criteria will you use to set priorities in the future?

EXHIBIT 5.11. TECHNIQUES FOR ENDS DEVELOPMENT.

Stage of Ends Development	Technique Used	Description
Exploration	Roundtable	A discussion among invited informants or experts is facilitated. The board might only observe the initial discussion, asking questions and making comments later.
	Joint meetings with other organizations	Organizations with common interests are invited to discuss Ends issues.
	Challenging speakers	A speaker is invited to stimulate board discussion and deliberations.
	Expert informants	Input is sought from experts in the field.
	Open forums or meetings	At large-group meetings, owners and customers may provide information to the board. Staff members may be needed to handle means questions.
Data collection	Needs assessment	A survey is conducted to determine customers' most pressing needs.
	Impact study	A statistical study is conducted to determine the effects of the service or the program on consumers.
Consultation	Focus groups	Meetings are held with selected informants to ask specific questions.
	Brown-bag lunches	Informal lunchtime meetings are held with the public to discuss important issues.
Discussion	Brainstorming	The board uses this creative-thinking technique to generate ideas.
	Retreat	The board usually meets off-site for one or two days to have a focused, intensive discussion.
	Rainbow sheets	Major issues or concerns are summarized on notepaper of different colors and presented for consideration.
Decision-making process	Polling	Boards often use this informal voting technique in a policy blitz to help define policy statements.

EXHIBIT 5.11. TECHNIQUES FOR ENDS DEVELOPMENT (*continued*).

Stage of Ends Development	Technique Used	Description
Public education	Newsletter	This owner-member communication tool is distributed on a regular basis.
	Media releases and press conferences	Boards formally announce news items and policy changes via mail, e-mail, radio, television, or speeches at a specialized meeting.
Preparation for Ends meetings	Informal executive committee	This board committee is headed by the chair, whose purpose it is to prepare for board meetings.
	Designated board member	This board member is designated to prepare for meetings and to develop information required for board Ends deliberations.
	Homework assignments	Specific tasks are delegated to board members between scheduled meetings.
Documentation of meetings	Videotaped meetings	Ends meetings are videotaped.
Establishment of priorities	Policy on decision-making framework	A policy is outlined for the board's decision-making process in terms of Ends.
	Policy on criteria for setting priorities	A policy identifies the criteria the board will use in choosing priorities for Ends.

- The City of Bryan's six-meeting process for Ends development is described in *Board Leadership* no. 24, in an article titled "Guest Presentation."

- The process of "nesting" Ends policies and examples from a variety of organizations is described in Chapter Seven of *Reinventing Your Board* by John and Miriam Carver.

- For information on monitoring and measuring Ends, see Chapter Seven of this book.

EXHIBIT 5.12. MIND MAPPING.

Mind mapping helps you break through barriers to creativity. This method is intended to tap into your creative capacity by paralleling the way your mind organizes information through associations, rather than in perfect orderly categories like information in a library. Mind mapping is appropriate at any step of problem solving when new ideas are required. It can be used as an individual or group tool.

Here are the guidelines for mind mapping:

1. Write an issue, problem, or situation in a box in the center of a page. Think of the big categories related to this item. Draw branches out from the center, and label them with the major category headings. As ideas related to this category occur to you, draw limbs onto the branch and write the idea. As new associations continue to occur, add new limbs or draw other branches.

2. Save any evaluation or sorting until you have exhausted your thoughts. As you scan the page and see relationships between the ideas on different limbs, use markers of different colors to draw connecting lines between these ideas. This method is one of the least structured ways of stimulating nonlinear thinking and creativity. The form is of no importance.

3. In a team meeting, have each individual take ten minutes and draw a mind map of a problem facing the team. After team members work alone, have them put their ideas together on a master mind map taped to the wall. Anytime people have an idea or discover a problem, they can add an idea to an existing branch or draw in a new branch to accommodate their idea.

• Two other useful works for general background are *Collaborative Leadership* by D. Chrislip and C. Larson and *Benefits Indicators* from the RE-THINK Group.

• Exhibit 6.1 also provides a very helpful tool for decision making in Ends development.

Several group process techniques can help generate ideas. For example, see brainstorming in Exhibit 3.6, mind mapping in Exhibit 5.12, and the affinity diagram in Exhibit 5.13. (For more on mind mapping, see *The Mind Map Book* by T. Buzan and B. Buzan. For complete instructions on using the affinity diagram process and other decision-making tools, see *The Memory Jogger™ II*. Details are in Resource C.) Exhibit 5.14 explains the force field analysis technique, which can help you analyze the challenges you face in developing Ends.

EXHIBIT 5.13. AFFINITY DIAGRAM.

Using the affinity diagram helps when you need to find the major themes in a large number of ideas, opinions, or issues. In this method, you group naturally related items and then identify the one concept that ties each group together. It is a creative rather than logical process that produces consensus by sorting cards (or post-it notes) rather than by discussing the topics.

Use this method when

- Chaos exists.
- The team is drowning in ideas.
- Breakthrough thinking is required.
- Broad issues or themes must be identified.

To construct the affinity diagram, follow these steps:

1. Assemble a team of at least four people.

   They should have varied perspectives.
   They should be creative and open-minded.

2. Phrase the question that will help the team consider the issue.

   It should be broad and neutral (for example, "What are the issues connected with . . . ?" Or "What are all the barriers to . . . ?").
   It should be clearly stated and easily understood.
   Make it a complete sentence.

3. Generate and record ideas.

   Follow guidelines for brainstorming.
   Record each idea on a card.
   Don't write one-word ideas. Use complete sentences of five to eight words.
   Write complete, concise thoughts.

4. Randomly display all completed cards.

   Put them on a wall, table, or flip chart.
   Do not sort the cards while laying them out or transferring them to the wall or other surface.

5. Sort the cards into related groupings.

   Have everyone move around the display together, sorting the cards as individuals.
   Work in silence.
   Go with your gut reaction.
   Sort quickly.

EXHIBIT 5.13. AFFINITY DIAGRAM (*continued*).

If there is disagreement over a card's placement, simply move the card, rather than discussing it.

If a persistent disagreement over placement continues, create duplicate cards and place one in each grouping.

Make at least six groups.

6. Create the header cards.

Make the header concise.

Don't use one-word headers. Use a full sentence to create a complete thought that reflects the header's essence and substance.

Use fresh words, not ordinary jargon.

The header should make sense by itself. It shouldn't be necessary to read the cards beneath it to understand.

The header should capture the essential link in all the ideas beneath it and should indicate how the cards are expanding on that linking idea or theme.

Place the header at the top of each grouping.

Turn subthemes into subheaders where needed. Avoid disproportionately large groupings.

Don't stop here. This is knowledge. Push the process to find wisdom.

Find insight through the categories.

7. Draw the finished affinity diagram.

Draw lines connecting headers and subheaders with all the cards beneath them.

Bring together related groupings.

Have the team review the diagram.

Have important non–team members review the diagram and revise it as needed.

EXHIBIT 5.14. FORCE FIELD ANALYSIS.

A force field analysis is a visual listing of possible forces that drive or prevent change.

Use this method when

- You must identify what is driving, slowing, or preventing change.
- Team members want to learn to think together.
- Creative solutions need to be developed.
- Starting points for action need to be identified.

To construct a force field analysis, follow these steps:

1. Assemble a team.

   Create a group of any size.
   Choose a variety of people who collectively see both strengths and weaknesses in the current situation.

2. Agree on a question that will help the team consider the issue.

3. Draw the force field.

   On a flip chart, draw a line down the center.
   Label one column "Driving Forces" and one column "Preventing Forces."
   Brainstorm various forces without worrying about validity.
   Here's an example:

How can we educate customers about Policy Governance?

Driving Forces	Preventing Forces
We have board and staff support.	Customers want to talk about immediate issues.
Customers want to talk to board members.	We believe we have done enough.
Board members and the CEO are fully trained in Policy Governance.	We don't know how to go about educating customers.
We have some interesting topics to discuss.	We have no budget.

4. Decide which of the preventing forces to eliminate and agree on strategies for doing so.

CHAPTER SIX

IDENTIFYING AND LINKING WITH OWNERS

☐ The Challenge

Ownership is the source of boards' authority to govern. Knowing who the owners are and what they want is thus a fundamental prerequisite of good governance. This chapter examines how Policy Governance boards make the relationship with their owners a reality, becoming more open and accountable to those on whose behalf they exercise their trusteeship.

The chapter begins by reviewing the experience of our eleven organizations in relation to these questions:

- What does *moral ownership* mean?
- How do boards distinguish their ownership?
- Why do boards link with their owners?
- How do boards link with their owners?

Next the chapter looks at what we can all learn from the answers to these questions. From there we look at where your organization might be situated in terms of its linkage with owners. We make some suggestions based on what other organizations have done, and we give tips, tools, and techniques for furthering your board's linkage.

■ The Experience

What Does *Moral Ownership* Mean?

Board members have long known that they represent someone else as they sit at the boardroom table. They are trustees, which means that they hold something of value in trust for someone else. But who is that "someone else"? Board members know they are legally accountable to the people who vote at the annual general meeting. The Policy Governance literature acknowledges this obligation, but it also refers to "moral ownership," pointing board members to a broader responsibility to the various stakeholders to whom the board owes its primary allegiance.

Several of the boards we have studied have risen to the challenge of embracing moral accountability rather than purely legal accountability. The board of Parkland Health District fully recognizes its legal accountability to the government; the minister of health is the funding body and has appointed four of the board's twelve members. However, the board has defined its moral owners as "the people who live in the district, which is a circumscribed geographical area." Similarly, although the board of the Southern Ontario Library Service is an arm's-length government agency legally accountable to the government, it considers its moral ownership to be the "people of southern Ontario."

The moral ownership is not always the same as the legal ownership, but the boards of some organizations can reasonably decide that it is. Membership organizations like the Colorado Association of School Boards are a case in point. In organizations like the Weaver Street Market, the legal owners (that is the shareholders or stockholders) can also be considered the moral owners. However, even in these cases the boards recognize that they have additional responsibilities to the wider communities that they serve, and they have forged links beyond their immediate ownership.

Linking with owners is one of the main jobs a board takes on under Policy Governance. Indeed for many boards this emphasis is one of the most powerful attractions of the model. For the United Way of Burlington, Hamilton-Wentworth, an important factor in the decision to adopt Policy Governance was the promise of furthering the United Way's relationship with the community. For the City of Bryan, Texas, "The council-ownership linkage may well be the single most exciting component of the Policy Governance model."

Speaking with One Voice. One central principle of Policy Governance is that the board speak with one voice on behalf of the whole ownership. This principle can conflict with the traditional practices of representational governance. According to traditional practices, individual owners hold "their" board member directly accountable for everything. They say, "You sit on the board to represent me and my interests, and you will support my interests at all costs." Speaking with one voice can be a particular challenge for members who are elected or appointed by subsets of an organization's ownership. These members can easily feel torn between the interests of the owners as a whole and the interests of their constituents.

This problem also applies to publicly elected boards (like city councils, school boards, health boards) and many boards of membership organizations. It can also apply to organizations whose constitutions require that individuals of specific backgrounds be on the board. For instance, Weaver Street Market's board is required to have two "consumer-owners" and two "worker-owners." For health or hospital boards, legislation or bylaws may dictate that the chief of staff be a member. It is not uncommon for other boards to be required to have a staff member on the board.

With Policy Governance, the fact that members are appointed or elected to the board from different constituencies is seen as helping the board reflect the diversity of the organization's ownership. However, once appointed or elected, the board member's job is not to represent particular sections of the ownership but to ensure that the whole board is accountable to, and representative of, the entire ownership. Everyone is seen as potentially bringing valuable experience and knowledge to the boardroom table, and no individual or subgroup is seen as having more of a "right" to command the board than any other.

The board of Parkland Health District, in its Linkage with the Community policy, makes its position clear: "The board shall be accountable for the district to its owners as a whole (not as individual wards). The board shall act on behalf of the district as a whole, rather than being advocates for specific wards or interest groups." Even with such a policy, the board must remain vigilant to ensure that new members truly get the message. Jan Moore, a Policy Governance consultant who has worked with the Parkland Health District board and who is a contributor to this book, says, "New board members who are elected because they have a particular ax to grind or who believe that their job is to manage must be oriented very quickly to the model that the board has chosen to use and must be convinced that it is an effective way to carry out their responsibilities." (See Chapter Eight for more on orienting new members.)

Putting Owners Ahead of Staff and Consumers. Having staff members on a board can interfere with the board's link with the owners. When staff members are on a board, they represent the entire ownership, and the fact that they also happen to be employed by the organization becomes secondary. The challenge for these board members is to consider the interests of the owners ahead of the interests of staff members or even customers (who are not always owners).

On the Weaver Street Market board, the CEO is a full voting member. This was in place before the board adopted Policy Governance and has remained that way. The board and the CEO are aware of the potential pitfalls and have made a conscious decision to continue, at least for now. The board is satisfied that the board and the CEO can handle this "wearing of two hats." The chair says, "The general manager [CEO] has done an extraordinary job of playing dual roles and clearly exhibits complete discipline in the handling of both roles."

A recent trend in board membership is to have consumers on the board. This is usually done to ensure consumer input into decisions about issues such as access, program design, and other aspects of service delivery. Such consumer input is important, but having one or two consumers at the boardroom table is not the best way to get this input, as will be seen later in this chapter. The concept of moral ownership causes a board not only to define the ownership but also to look for the optimum ways that all the voices it needs to listen to can be heard.

How Do Boards Distinguish Their Ownership?

Some organizations can clearly identify the "who" of ownership from the start. For the board of Parkland Health District, it is the people of the district. For the council of the City of Bryan, it is the citizens. For the Colorado Association of School Boards, it is the member school boards.

For other organizations, determining ownership can be much more difficult. A particular example is provided by professional regulatory organizations. Through legislation, certain professions are granted the right to be self-regulating but must act "in the public interest." The confusion is about who the ownership is. The professionals who are usually called "members" and who are certainly "customers" of the organization's services and who are heavily represented at the board table can be forgiven for believing that they are the owners. However, as the organization's mandate comes from the government (as an agent of the public) and as the organization is obliged to act "in the public interest," the ultimate ownership undoubtedly has to be the public. This is not a popular conclusion among professionals who naturally perceive the organization as their own and who want it to act and advocate for them.

At least three of the organizations we have studied have struggled to pinpoint that "someone else" on whose behalf they are governing. The United Way of Burlington, Hamilton-Wentworth, reports that ownership is "still an unresolved issue." The organization has relations with (1) donor organizations from whom it raises funds and for whom it administers the funds, (2) member agencies to whom it allocates funds, and (3) the community, which is the ultimate beneficiary of the funds. For the moment it has defined its ownership "as the diverse communities of the region." The Vermont Land Trust has had similar difficulty with the ownership concept and says, "Often there is confusion between beneficiaries, owners, members, and funders." The board now considers its ownership to be "everyone who lives in Vermont and comes to Vermont." Taking the broad community option can be the most appropriate solution, but it can also be an avoidance of making difficult choices that could greatly enhance the organization's focus.

In defining ownership, boards sometimes ask, "Who would care if the organization closed tomorrow?" In using this question, boards need to be wary. The answer often points to the organization's customers. Although owners can also be customers of an organization, a board should delve a little deeper before finalizing its thinking.

For the following two organizations, such an inquiry produced definitions that are not immediately obvious. After "a real struggle for the board," the Early Childhood Community Development Centre now defines its ownership as "organizations/individuals involved with the care and education of children." The board of the San Francisco AIDS Foundation now governs on behalf of "those who demonstrate an active determination and commitment to hasten the end of the pandemic and promote the basic human rights and well-being of people affected by the HIV disease." These conclusions will produce very different organizations than those that might have emerged if the organizations had concluded that their owners were their current customers or their communities as a whole.

At times, the search for the answer to the question "Who is the ownership?" may seem akin to searching for the meaning of life. However, the search is worthwhile. From the answer to this question will flow the answers to many of the other difficult questions the board needs to address.

Why Do Boards Link with Their Owners?

By adopting the principles of Policy Governance, a board becomes the link with the ownership. This is one of the board's main job products, as well as one of its main activities. When asked why it would want to link with the community, the West Prince Health board identified the following reasons: fulfilling moral accountability, identifying the community's needs, educating the community about health and about the board's work, building relationships, articulating values, and receiving feedback on Ends.

The board of the Vermont Land Trust wants to have this linkage to create the future and to hear about needs, trends, and possibilities. The board worked with a small group of citizens in the first phase in its Ends work. Composed of people with a wide range of backgrounds and outlooks, this group helped broaden the board's thinking. The San Francisco AIDS Foundation has relied on small groups to inform the board's thinking about specific issues—for example, the housing needs of people with HIV.

Weaver Street Market linked with its ownership to get feedback on values, to fulfill accountability, to build relationships, to educate owners about board member recruitment and the board's approach to governing, to secure input on Ends, and to share information about Ends. Almost four years after its decision to adopt Policy Governance, the Weaver Street Market board now focuses much of its attention, and consequently its time, on ownership. "What is very evident is that, for Weaver Street Market, ownership is not simply a defined group to whom the board is accountable, but it is a fundamental aspect of what Weaver Street Market is. Ownership itself provides something to individual community members who are owners, as well as to the community as a whole."

Linking with the ownership is a major challenge for a health board like the Parkland Health District. According to the CEO, "The nature of public involvement related to health tends to be one in which people say little unless they are directly concerned. In other words, 'I won't take the time to tell you what I think until my family or I become ill. Then I want all possible health services to be available.' Thus the board must find ways to hear from the owners in a more regular way. It also needs to hear from those segments of the ownership that are traditionally the unheard voices."

If Parkland Health District's board needed any further reason to link with the community, it got that in the annual report of the Saskatchewan provincial auditor, who recommended that board members

- Validate their prioritization of Ends through community consultation
- Improve their process of ranking priority health needs by using real health status information

See "How Do Boards Answer the Question 'At What Cost?'" in Chapter Five for the full set of recommendations.

The Parkland Health District board is using policies based on the framework for ethical decision making developed by the Queen's Region Health board in Prince Edward Island. The framework is intended to help the Parkland board members make "At what cost?" decisions as part of Ends development or, in the words of the auditor, to "validate their prioritization of Ends." The framework is a variation on common ethical decision-making models. Although any type of board could use this decision-making process, the part that is unique to each organization is the inclusion of ownership values as articulated by the board. To determine these values, the board can use several methods, such as focus groups and case studies. The framework is described in Exhibit 6.1.

EXHIBIT 6.1.
FRAMEWORK FOR ETHICAL DECISION MAKING.

1. Describe the need to make the decision or to solve the problem.

   What problem are we trying to address? Why do we need to make a choice?

2. Gather data as necessary to understand the problem.

   What general information do we need to understand the problem? What are the main issues to consider in making the decision? Describe the values to be considered, and outline any potential conflicts between values.

3. Identify relevant stakeholders, say how they may be affected, and consult with them.

4. Develop alternatives, and consider their impacts.

   What are the alternatives to be considered? Project the consequences and the opportunity costs of each alternative, both short term and long term. Identify the values conflicts inherent in the various alternatives.

5. Apply criteria for decision making, and evaluate alternatives or options.

   a. Apply the value of achieving as much benefit as possible for the community with the resources available. The benefit could be measured objectively in (1) years of life gained and (2) quality of life years maintained or improved. Information about these indicators may fall under one of three categories:

      • There is clear and definitive information about the benefits or harm.
      • There is unclear or conflicting information.
      • There is no evidence.

   b. Review the alternatives in light of existing policies, laws, and principles of primary health care and in terms of increased community involvement.

   c. Evaluate and compare the relative costs. Include the opportunity cost—that is, what is the cost of not doing this as well as the cost of doing it?

   d. Evaluate the options in light of relevant values, projecting how each alternative will impinge on values.

   e. Choose the option that on balance provides the most benefit to the most people for the best cost unless it impinges inappropriately on

      i. The autonomy of individuals or groups of individuals within the community

---

EXHIBIT 6.1.
FRAMEWORK FOR ETHICAL DECISION MAKING (*continued*).

---

    ii. The access to service or the support of individuals or groups of individuals in need within the community

    iii. Emergency service or support, creating a financial, physical, or psychological threat to life

    iv. The self-reliance of individuals or communities

6. Make the decision.

Based on the information and decisions from your "most benefit" and health reform analysis and considering that on balance key values as defined have not been violated, the best decision is. . . .

7. Educate, inform, and evaluate the decision.

Source: Adapted from J. R. Williams, M. Yeo, and W. Hooper, "Ethics for Regional Boards," *Leadership in Health Services*, 1996, *5*(4), 22–26. Reprinted by permission of the publisher, MCB University Press.

Exhibit 6.2 summarizes the reasons that the boards of some organizations choose to link with their owners, as well as the techniques and tools that the boards used. Although these organizations differ greatly in nature (there is one municipal government, two quasi-public sector organizations, a for-profit cooperative, two community organizations, and a membership organization), their reasons for linking with owners are remarkably similar:

- *Accountability:* Reporting back to the ownership about the organization's performance, both in achieving results or Ends and in complying with Executive Limitations.
- *Creation of the future:* Getting input and feedback for the development of Ends and perhaps Executive Limitations.
- *Values articulation:* Hearing about priorities and about the values that should be part of the decision-making process and addressing the question "At what cost?"
- *Education:* Explaining the governing role and the model of governance, educating the owners about the concept of ownership, and expanding their knowledge and understanding of owner issues.

You will find more about these techniques and tools in Exhibit 5.11 and in Resources A and B at the end of this book.

EXHIBIT 6.2. OWNERSHIP LINKAGE TOOL FINDER.

When You Want to Link with the Ownership in Order to . . .	Try This
Be accountable	Annual general meeting Open board meeting Presentations by the board Newsletters Newspaper advertisements Annual report Information on web site
Create the future (considering owners' needs, concerns, and demands—Ends work)	Search conference Board-to-board meeting Breakfast meeting Needs assessment Various small-group processes: fishbowl, roundtables, brainstorming, affinity diagram process Expert informants Focus groups Statistics, demographic data Community profile Presentations to and by the board Board recruitment Brown-bag lunch Open forum Town hall meeting Topical community/membership meeting Focused questions Board committee
Clarify values (Ends and Executive Limitations)	Surveys Case studies, scenarios Ethical decision-making framework
Educate the owners	Presentations to and by the board Board-to-board meeting Annual general meeting Expo, poster session Newspaper articles Sponsoring speaker Newsletter
Build a relationship	Board-to-board meeting Community or membership meeting Presentations to and by board

The CEO of the Early Childhood Community Development Centre sums up the benefits of linking with the ownership in this way: "The board has created an organization that works on behalf of the ownership by talking with the ownership and creating what they want their organization to be and [determining] at what cost." Most boards intuitively believe in the wisdom of community. They would not think their governing job to be complete without connecting with those for whom they hold the work of the organization in trust. For these boards, the reasons for linkage are compelling. Linkage helps them realize a major part of the promise of Policy Governance.

How Do Boards Link with Their Owners?

John Carver identifies three types of board linkage with their owners: attitudinal, statistical, and personal. Boards might begin to forge a link by examining their own process and ensuring that it accounts for owners' needs and by seeking more information about the owners. Boards may also engage owners in a dialogue in various ways.

Examining Their Attitudes Toward Owners. Board members don't always see the importance of linking with owners to their role as trustees. They sometimes ask the following questions:

- Why would we want to meet with the community when they put us here to do a job on their behalf?
- Why do we need to meet with the community when we already know what they think?
- Why meet with the community when they don't understand all this stuff?

Such attitudes need to be challenged if linkage with ownership is to be successful. Boards that rely only on the diversity of the board member mix for linkage with ownership are missing out on the much wider and deeper pool of wisdom available outside the boardroom. Nevertheless, one very important and straightforward way for a board to link with owners is to ensure that the diversity of the ownership is represented at the board table. Boards with control over their member recruitment process can begin to link with owners by adjusting the recruitment process and by establishing qualifications for board members. If board members are to be elected, a board can publicize the criteria required of candidates for election, along with information about the governing model. If board members are to be appointed, a board can recommend criteria for candidates to the appointing body. For example, the Early Childhood Community Development Centre outlines a thorough process of recruitment and selection. The board "felt strongly that the board complement needed to be broad and reflect community ownership."

All the boards in our sample that are engaged in Ends development recognize that reviewing recruitment processes is just a start. For example, the board members of the Vermont Land Trust believe that they "are at the very beginning of [linking with the ownership] now." Yet they are conducting an impressive Ends process with all kinds of rich owner-focused questions and dialogue. In order to grapple with the "what good for which people at what cost" questions, the board invited a group of key informants for a roundtable (see Exhibit 5.5 for a full description).

This process is also known as "the fishbowl" and can be used by any board for their Ends work or in determining ownership values. (This tool is described in detail on pages 396–398 of *The Fifth Discipline Fieldbook* by Peter Senge and others; see Resource C for details.) Using such techniques, boards, like the board of the Vermont Land Trust, can reach out well beyond themselves to involve their owners in creating their organization's future.

Seeking Information About Owners. A board can learn much about its owners. Needs, demands, use patterns, fears, values, and trends can be gathered from surveys and data. West Prince Health and East Prince Health both carried out community needs assessments. The process had four parts: a survey, a community profile, an analysis of community demographics, and community meetings. Parkland Health District conducted a targeted needs assessment directed at youth. From the surveys and demographics, these boards began to get an understanding of the health needs in their communities and some notion of priorities.

In *Owners' News,* Weaver Street Market's ownership newsletter, the organization reported that it had done a survey: "The survey used the mission statement the owners were familiar with as a source to get feedback on possible effects for Weaver Street Market and Weaver Street Market values, while also causing respondents to make some choices [to prioritize] among different items. Owners were asked to check off various degrees of agreement or disagreement to selected value-based statements from the mission statement. . . . By seeking feedback on something owners were familiar with [the mission statement] and in a language they understood, the board felt it could then extrapolate possible basic values inherent in the responses."

In its four-step Ends development process, the City of Bryan included a staff-generated background paper that includes an environmental scan (a review of data and information on issues affecting an organization now and likely to affect it in the future). The board of the Early Childhood Community Development Centre conducted an impact study, which included these questions:

- What is the current impact of the Early Childhood Community Development Centre on child care in the Niagara Region?
- If we are to be successful as an organization, what should the community impact be in the future?
- How will we know if we are successful?

Members of the ownership were randomly selected for this survey. The board used the data collected from the survey to develop its Ends.

In addition to carrying out its own survey, a board could use data collected and made available by other organizations—those with similar owners or customers as well as the more obvious sources of census and other relevant data.

Getting to Know Owners. To deepen its knowledge of who the owners are and identify opportunities for interacting with them, a board may want to ask itself some or all of the following questions:

- Who are the formal and informal community leaders?
- Who are the influencers in the ownership group?
- Who else is interested in our mission?
- What else is going on (in the community) that we can be part of?
- Which are the influential and successful community organizations?
- Where and how do people gather in our community?

The payoffs from getting to know owners in person can be great, but there are several obstacles to this endeavor. On their first attempts to interact with the ownership, several boards discovered that the discussions were dominated by immediate and often individual concerns about programs and services. When owners are also customers, which is true for the majority of the organizations that have contributed to this book, the challenge is to separate owner concerns from customer concerns. A member of the East Prince Health board takes the following approach: "If a citizen calls me about a particular concern, I use the opportunity to listen and turn the conversation around, to get input on larger issues."

At each council meeting of the City of Bryan, citizens have three minutes to make a personal presentation to the council. The mayor thanks all presenters, informing them when appropriate that their issues are means issues and as such have been given to the city manager to handle. Presenters are asked to leave their names and telephone numbers with the city secretary and are informed that a staff member will contact them the next day to discuss the issue further.

Customer input can have an important impact on the development of board policies. Customers may not only have valid input on Ends but also valid concerns and worries about how they are achieved. The board explicitly addresses these worries in its Executive Limitations policies. Customers and owners can, for example, comment on board policies for the treatment of customers, which may cover issues such as access, customer involvement in program design, risk, safety, confidentiality, and competence of staff. As another example, customers may have something useful to say about how staff members are treated, which could be reflected in the board's Executive Limitations policy on the Treatment of Staff.

The important thing in personally linking with the ownership is to demonstrate to people that their concerns are taken seriously, whether by the board or by the staff. An appropriate response will help build good relationships. Board members often observe that when people have the ear of the board, they use that opportunity to vent a little. Once the venting is done, people can move more easily to "owner" issues. Owners need to be educated about the difference between owner and customer concerns. Because this is not always possible or easy, the board and the staff must be absolutely clear about the difference themselves and ensure that there are opportunities and mechanisms to hear both types of concerns.

Setting Up Opportunities for Dialogue with Owners. Connecting with a large ownership like an entire city or the people in a health district is onerous unless the task is broken into manageable pieces. Here are some ways that various boards have approached the task:

Board Organization. The board can set about its linkage work as one group or by delegation to a committee, to subgroups, or to individuals.

• *Whole-board meetings.* Many boards choose to meet their owners as an entire board so that all board members are exposed to the same information.

• *Delegation to a board committee.* Some boards delegate some of the ownership work to a board committee, making the work more manageable. The board gives tasks to the committee according to its Governance Process policies on committees. For example, Weaver Street Market established an ownership committee. Its product and authority are outlined in this board policy on Committee Structure:

Product: Options and implications for board consideration and/or, as appropriate, follow-through on board tasks with respect to the board's relations with its owners—schedule as set forth in the board's annual planning calendar or as determined by the board. This includes, but is not limited to: owners' communications, board election, and owners' meetings.

Authority: To incur resources not to exceed relevant amounts defined in the board's annual budget or as defined by the board.

• *Delegation to subgroups.* Similarly, the board of the Colorado Association of School Boards (CASB) began its linkage work by grouping the membership (or ownership) geographically, then delegating each geographic region to a subgroup of the board. All subgroups are to design "their ownership interface strategies based on the particular needs and idiosyncrasies of their region. The job of the subgroups is to go out and talk with the membership and create a live link. Some groups are putting together focus groups. Some subgroups have divided up their work so that they are able to make personal visits to [CASB member] boards [the CASB's owners] in every region over the course of a year."

• *Appointment of liaisons.* Another option is to have individual board members take on responsibility for linking with specific bodies. Parkland Health District's Governance Process policy on Linkage with the Community explains their approach: "The board members from local communities, with the CEO and/or the board chair or vice-chair, if possible, will liaise with local bodies when required, [either] to report to government on board activities or [to] respond to local issues. Such local issues shall be brought to the board for districtwide decisions."

Methods. The boards in our sample had experience developing and using a wide variety of methods to link with their owners. Here are a few:

• *Links with other boards.* Connecting with the boards of other organizations that represent the same ownership can be a productive way to form a link with owners. For a board with a very large ownership or one that is geographically dispersed, this may also be the most efficient method. Boards talk to other boards about mission and common community or ownership issues. Sometimes there is an opportunity to educate another board about Policy Governance.

The San Francisco AIDS Foundation had a series of one-on-one meetings with boards of other agencies but found that it needed to have a staff member as well as a board member at each meeting "because when you link with organizations that are not Carver, those other boards want to talk about *means.*" Now the staff can address the means questions at the meetings, and the board members can engage in the conversations they need to have. An unintended benefit of this type of linkage can be a new relationship between the staffs of organizations. The result can be joint programming or shared services.

• *Presentations by the board.* Some boards link with ownership through presentations about their work; these can take place in a variety of settings, as described in this chapter.

> The council of the City of Bryan makes presentations on Bryan Policy Governance to civic clubs and nonprofits, which represent citizens in a different way.

At a joint meeting with a board of a large provider of child care, the board of the Early Childhood Community Development Centre made presentations on ownership and Policy Governance.

Every year each Parkland Health District board member makes up to three presentations to community groups, which are selected to ensure a cross-section of the population. The entire board determines the content of these presentations, which outline the board's priorities for one to three years and state the rationale. They also include two specific questions on which the board wants feedback.

• *Presentations to the board.* Boards can also have owners make presentations to them. The City of Bryan's council has a four-stage Ends process. The partnership discussion stage involves presentations from other agencies and entities and allows individual citizens to comment on a particular Ends topic. (See Exhibit 5.3 for more on that board's whole process.)

• *Brown-bag lunches.* The San Francisco AIDS Foundation board holds lunchtime sessions to which it invites individuals to bring their lunches. Community members participate in discussion with the board on a specific issue. (See Exhibit 5.4 for the board's whole process.)

• *Focus groups.* As part of its Ends development process, the board of the Colorado Association of School Boards held focus groups with members and allied groups. At these focus groups, the board posed a series of questions, including, "What is it that the Colorado Association of School Boards should be providing in the way of member benefits that it isn't now?" The board took the ideas generated in the focus groups and began to define which member concerns were reasonable, unreasonable, or top priority. They narrowed the list to five broad statements.

• *Letters.* Periodically, the East Prince Health board writes a one-page letter on a particular topic. A database of four hundred community leaders has been compiled. The board sorts the letters according to the leaders' postal codes. Each letter is personally signed by a board member living in that postal code area. Leaders are invited to give feedback or comment by calling the board chair or the board members who signed the letter.

• *Newsletters.* Some Policy Governance boards educate owners about the ownership concept by publishing a newsletter. As mentioned, Weaver Street Market developed the *Owners' Newsletter,* "a publication of the board that is solely intended to foster a dialogue between Weaver Street Market and the owners on topics . . . related to ownership." The first issue in October 1995 explained the board's shift in its approach to governing.

- *Discovery meetings.* To further its work on Ends, the East Prince Health board developed three questions to ask about families at a series of discovery meetings:

What is your vision of the future with regard to healthy families?

How does your organization contribute to and enhance family life in this community?

What are the barriers to your vision?

The board compiled a list of organizations in the community with an interest in healthy families, and the board chair sent a letter inviting representatives from two community organizations to each meeting. The letter outlined the context for the discussions and the board's work and asked each organization to bring a one-page sheet with information about itself.

At the meeting, each organization was asked to focus on the discussion questions. The result was a three-way conversation at each meeting between three very different organizations, all with a common mission. East Prince Health then used the information from that conversation in its Ends development process.

- *Open community meetings.* Some boards take advantage of existing open community meetings to get in touch with their owners. Others set about creating open community meetings for their own specific purposes. The West Prince Health board did some preliminary Ends work using brainstorming, mind mapping, and presentations by staff on statistics and demographics. After sketching out four categories of Ends, the board set up four community meetings, one to focus on each Ends statement. Letters of invitation went to individuals and organizations. Advertisements were also placed in local newspapers. At each community meeting, the board chair did a brief presentation to set the context for the evening. The audience was broken up into smaller groups, which were each assigned three questions. The board had several purposes for the meetings: to validate what it already knew, to gain more information about and interpretations of the four Ends, and to further its relationship with the ownership in a positive way.

Two times per year the Parkland Health District board holds public meetings in which the program and the financial achievements of the prior year are reviewed and the public is informed of the board's plans. Feedback about the board's strategic direction is solicited through specific and open-ended questions. (See Exhibit 5.2 for more on that board's Ends process.)

- *Telephone polling.* The Colorado Association of School Boards put their questions on a free phone line. Owners were invited to call in and complete the survey. You will find more methods for linking with owners in the "Practical Tips and Tools" section of this chapter.

☑ Key Learnings

Other boards may benefit from some of the main points that emerge from the experiences of the boards we have studied.

Boards Want to Represent Owners

The potential to form stronger links with owners is one of the things that draws boards to the Policy Governance model. Even though boards have always considered that they represent the community, the model has encouraged them to do so in more real and powerful ways.

Identifying Owners Isn't Always Straightforward

Identifying the ownership is much more difficult for some organizations than for others. Those who have difficulties require a particularly deep understanding and commitment to the principles of the "trust" in trusteeship and the board speaking with "one voice." The challenge is often knowing who the ownership is not. Confusion between owners and customers is very common.

Boards Need to Take Owner Input Seriously

Some boards see linkage with ownership as a good thing to do, and others see it as a fundamental obligation. Boards should consider carefully what they intend to do with what they hear from the ownership. In a newsletter to clients, Jan Moore counsels boards to ask themselves, "Is the intent of connecting with owners merely to 'be seen' to be allowing ownership input, when in reality the desire is to limit the ability of the owners to effectively influence a desired decision, or is the intent to give due consideration to owners' views when making a decision?" Boards that fundamentally believe they are governing on behalf of someone else will struggle less with linkage. And boards that believe in the community's wisdom will find a greater richness in ownership linkage.

There Is More Than One Way to Link with Owners

There are various ways of linking with the ownership. All of the contributing organizations have done some linkage. Forming links through personal dialogue with owners seems to be the most common route, but the boards we have studied also provide good examples of linking through research about owners' needs. Ends work often makes this focus on owners a natural part of the process.

It Helps to Understand Why You Are Linking

Clarity of purpose helps boards construct useful methods of linking and choose workable techniques. Boards commonly link to be accountable, to create the future, to clarify values, to educate the owners, and to build a relationship with the owners.

Get to Know What Works for Your Ownership

Boards that become familiar with their ownership (whether it consists of members, citizens, or subgroups of the community) will be more successful in discovering what tools and techniques work with which group. Linking with a large ownership is tougher and will require more innovative tools and techniques. Building on existing opportunities can save time and effort.

○ Taking Action: Strategies for Where You Are Now

Linking with the ownership can be one of the trickiest pieces of the board's job for a variety of reasons:

- The ownership is hard to identify.
- The ownership doesn't know it is the ownership.
- Some people who think they are the owners are not the owners—or at least not all of the owners.
- A board is not aware of the tools and techniques available.
- A board is unclear about why it should link and what to talk about.
- People are busy.

On the other hand, linkage with the ownership can be one of the most rewarding pieces of the board's work. This chapter is meant to help your board break up the job into manageable chunks, aid you in preparing for this work, and suggest tools and techniques that are easy to use. If your board feels it still lacks the group process skills to do this work, there are several other avenues. You can hire a consultant, seek in-kind services in the community, use staff expertise to design the process, or train yourselves in group process techniques.

Allocate one hour on your next board agenda to assess where you are in regard to linking. Pick one of the suggestions from this chapter and make a plan.

If Your Board Doesn't Know Who Its Owners Are

Some boards cannot identify their owners. Until they do, the Ends conversation has nowhere to start, and ultimately there can be no real accountability. The next "Practical Tips and Tools" section gives a variety of suggestions to break through this barrier.

If Your Board Is Unclear About What to Do Next

Your board may be unclear about how to proceed with ownership linkage. If so, refer to the next "Practical Tips and Tools" section for a host of ideas.

If Your Board Is Unclear as to Why It Should Bother

When a board sees itself as already being representative of the ownership, it can seem unnecessary to make extra efforts. See the next "Practical Tips and Tools" section for ideas to provoke a more in-depth analysis.

If Your Owners (and Staff) Want to Talk About Operational Complaints

Owners are often customers too. Naturally they want to talk about the immediate, tangible issues affecting them today. No one is more aware of customer issues than frontline staff members, so how can they be expected to refrain from raising customer issues at the boardroom table? See the following "Practical Tips and Tools" section for some ideas on handling these issues.

If Your Ownership Links Are Under Way

If your board has had some successful linkages with the ownership, celebrate! Then at your next meeting take some time to assess what worked well, why it worked, and what you can do differently next time. Maybe it would be beneficial to share your success with other relevant organizations by meeting with the members of their boards.

▶ Practical Tips and Tools

Identify Your Owners

If you're struggling with the question "What does *ownership* mean?" try some of the following ideas at your next board meeting.

- Imagine that you are the board of an organization and that you are representing the stockholders. You decide to call a meeting of the stockholders in your company. Look out at the meeting room. Who would be there?
- Pretend that the stockholders have sent letters to the chair asking for a meeting with the board so the board can account for the past year's results. Who would have sent the letters?
- Imagine that your organization (and your board) doesn't exist. People are gathering around a kitchen table and saying, "There is a big need in our community, and we really need to do something about it." Who would those people be?
- If you think your ownership is quite small and focused, rethink that. Ask yourself, "Are these customers?" If the answer is yes, now look more broadly. Is it possible that your ownership is the citizens of your community? Customers can also be owners, but don't stop there. Be rigorous in your search for the moral ownership.

Work Out What to Do Next

A board may be discouraged because the ownership seems too large for any linkages to be made. If this is what your board is thinking, just do it! Take a deep breath, bite off a small chunk, pick a small group to link with, and enjoy it! Look at Exhibit 6.2, pick a tool, and give it a try.

You may need to create a context for the discussion with the ownership by doing a brief presentation at a meeting, submitting articles to the local newspaper, or perhaps sponsoring a series of shows on your local cable television or radio station. Before your discussion, consider these questions:

- What specific questions about Ends do you want to focus on?
- Which populations do you want to target, if any?
- Which owners have the information you need?
- Who can provide diverse opinions?

EXHIBIT 6.3. MULTIPLE VOTING.

Purpose

Multiple voting is a group decision-making technique designed to reduce a long list to a manageable number of ideas.

Guidelines

- Review the list of brainstormed ideas and combine redundant entries. (Be sure to combine only redundant ideas, as opposed to similar ones.)
- Have members decide on the criteria for selecting ideas.
- Have each member vote for an agreed-on number of ideas. The team decides how many votes each person can have. This usually equals approximately 20 percent of the total entries on the page. Each group member has the same number of votes.
- Members can give only one vote to an individual idea and should use all of the votes agreed on by the team.
- Members make tally marks next to the items on the flip chart they are voting for.
- Ideas with the most votes receive further consideration.
- Remove those items that receive one or zero votes.
- Repeat the process. Two rounds should be sufficient to reduce a long list to a few workable ideas.
- Allow members to make a case for an idea that is being discarded. Don't hesitate to repeat the process if new information comes to light in a discussion.

If you want to focus the discussion on a particular need, group of needs, or target population, you will most likely want to develop questions that will ensure this focus. But also make them open-ended, to elicit informative responses.

Techniques such as multiple voting and weighted voting (see Exhibits 6.3 and 6.4) can help you sort through all the ideas you will be bringing back to the boardroom.

Become Clear About the Purpose

If your board is unclear about why it should link with its owners, you may want to review Policy Governance principles that underlie linkage with the ownership. Your board members could consider these discussion questions:

EXHIBIT 6.4. WEIGHTED VOTING.

Purpose

Weighted voting is similar to rank ordering, but it reflects people's strength of feeling about various ideas rather than just their order of importance. This group decision-making technique provides a visual display of the individual and team priorities among ideas on a relatively short list. The purpose is to prioritize a list of ideas and to recognize their relative merit in the eyes of the group.

Guidelines

- Ideas are listed on a flip chart.
- Members decide on the criteria for ranking ideas.
- Each member is given a number of votes that represents 125 to 150 percent of the number of items. (If there are five items, each team member gets eight votes.)
- Members reflect the relative strength of their preference for an idea by distributing their votes accordingly. The purpose is for each team member to reflect his or her true preference, not to be strategic about "tipping the balance" of the voting.
- The individual preferences can be indicated with sticky dots or with felt-tip marks on the flip chart paper.

The flip chart clearly shows the relative weight of team members' preferences.

- What does *trusteeship* mean to us?
- Do we know everything we need to know in order to govern?
- What more do we need to know?
- Where can we find out more?

Looking at the common purposes of linkage in Exhibit 6.2 and identifying the benefits of broadening that linkage beyond the boardroom may convince your board to plan some linkage activity at its next meeting.

Ask yourselves the following questions:

- What can we learn from owners to create the future?
- Do we need to be more accountable?
- Do we need to educate our owners about what we are up to?
- Do the owners know the issues?

- Do the owners understand the needs we are trying to meet?
- Do the owners understand the root causes of the issue we are dealing with?
- Do the owners know the barriers to our making a difference?
- How can the owners be part of the solution, both through us and directly?

Deal with the Immediate Concerns of Owners, Customers, and Staff

If your board has members who have been appointed because they represent staff or consumers, try setting up a solid complaints process that outlines the roles of the board and the staff. Board members will then have comfort in knowing there is a process for dealing with customer issues. Furthermore, if an Executive Limitations policy says that the board will track customer concerns through regular monitoring reports, the board can feel more at ease. Parkland Health District's board has established this policy: "The CEO shall not fail to consult with appropriate community advisory groups when determining appropriateness of *means* for achieving the board's specified Ends." Thus the board explicitly states its value of consumer involvement. In a similar way, the board can have an Executive Limitations policy dealing with staff issues to ensure that staff issues are truly dealt with, just not mentioned at the boardroom table.

Expand the Board's Thinking

If you want to expand your board's and your ownership's thinking, try some creative-thinking processes for large groups like a search conference or some techniques for smaller groups like brainstorming and mind mapping. For more on search conferences see "Future Searches" by M. Weisbord, which appears in *Community Building*, edited by K. Gozdz. For more on brainstorming and mind mapping see Exhibits 3.6 and 5.12, as well as *The Mind Map Book* by T. Buzan and B. Buzan. Details about both works are in Resource C. Processes like these are inclusive and unthreatening to all participants. They can help any group focus on the future, and everyone usually leaves with some new learning.

CHAPTER SEVEN

MONITORING POLICIES TO ENSURE ACCOUNTABILITY

☐ The Challenge

A major part of the promise of Policy Governance is that boards will be more accountable to their owners. How boards connect with their owners to provide this accountability is discussed in detail in Chapter Six. This chapter concentrates on how Policy Governance boards gain the knowledge they need in order to be accountable. In other words, it addresses how boards monitor whether the organization is doing what the owners have a right to expect. Good monitoring is also necessary for a board to be able to focus on the future, knowing that the present isn't running out of control.

The chapter begins by looking at questions about monitoring and accountability that have been encountered by the organizations we have studied:

- What does monitoring involve?
- How do boards monitor Executive Limitations?
- How do boards monitor Governance Process?
- How do boards monitor Ends?
- What types of information do boards receive?
- How do boards evaluate CEOs?
- Does "reasonable interpretation" cause problems?

Later in the chapter you will find the key learnings from our review of these questions and some suggestions for improving your board's performance on monitoring.

■ The Experience

What Does Monitoring Involve?

Monitoring brings comfort to boards using Policy Governance. A board cannot be accountable if it does not have the information with which to provide that accountability. The Early Childhood Community Development Centre makes that link in this way: "The development of the monthly monitoring reports on scheduled policies has reinforced the power of Policy Governance in assuring accountability for the organization."

Experience has shown that it can take a fair amount of time to set up all the monitoring components. Once established, though, monitoring becomes a key determinant of the long-term success of Policy Governance. Board members often ask, "What should our board monitor?" and "When should our board start monitoring?" Essentially there are three categories of policy to be monitored: Governance Process, Executive Limitations, and Ends. In most organizations the board monitors itself on its Governance Process policies and works with the CEO to monitor Executive Limitations and Ends policies. Most boards seem to recognize that, in each instance, monitoring should start as soon as possible. All but one of the boards we have studied are monitoring at least their Executive Limitations policies to some degree.

How Do Boards Monitor Executive Limitations?

By articulating what it will not tolerate, the board essentially frees itself to focus on the future and allows the CEO and staff to use their education and experience in whatever way they believe best. For most boards, empowering the CEO through the use of Executive Limitations (see Chapter Four) involves a bit of letting go. Board members who are new to Policy Governance often think they are being asked just to trust the CEO. Understandably, many of the organizations we studied found that board members needed considerable reassurance that they were still in control. Putting their monitoring policies in place was what made the difference.

Determining Monitoring Methods and Frequency. To begin the Executive Limitations monitoring, the board discusses each policy and, as a group, decides on the method and the frequency of the monitoring. Preliminary discussion of the decision-making process can yield dividends. Most of the organizations in this book believe that a majority vote is sufficient. Even though monitoring decisions require boards to weigh the relative costs of using staff time, board time, and external services against their desire for the most thorough and objective reporting possible, the decision making seems to be a straightforward process that can be accomplished in one or two sessions.

The Policy Governance model (see *Boards That Make a Difference* by John Carver, 2nd edition, pp. 112–113) suggests three methods of monitoring: executive report, external audit, and direct inspection (that is, inspection by the board). Most of the organizations we studied use all three methods for Executive Limitations. Some have more than one method for a single limitation, especially for financial policies. For example, the Financial Condition policies of the Early Childhood Community Development Centre and of Weaver Street Market require that actual financial conditions be monitored (1) quarterly through an internal report generated by the CEO or designee and (2) annually by using an external auditing firm hired by the board.

Determining the frequency requires board members to decide how often they need to be reassured that Executive Limitations are being followed. The board members' decisions generally relate to how critical they perceive a particular limitation to be. Not surprisingly, financial policies are the ones most frequently monitored, generally on a monthly basis. In other policy areas semiannual or annual monitoring is most common. Typical board Executive Limitations monitoring schedules (see Exhibit 7.1) contain the name of the Executive Limitations policy, the monitoring method, and the monitoring frequency.

Under Policy Governance, in the board's Communication and Counsel to the Board policy, the CEO is also given the responsibility to report any anticipated or actual policy violations. Consequently the board has both the assurance of regular monitoring and the comfort of knowing that it should hear rapidly about any deviations from the agreed-on standards. Having these two assurances allows board members to say with confidence—both to themselves and to their owners—that they are not just trusting their CEOs to follow the rules. Rather they require CEOs to prove that they are adhering to preestablished criteria.

Reporting from the CEO. With the method and frequency of Executive Limitations monitoring in place, the CEO collects pertinent information and presents it in a form that helps the board readily judge adherence to the preestablished standard. The CEO's goal is to be as brief as possible while providing the data

EXHIBIT 7.1.
MONITORING REPORT: FREQUENCY AND METHODOLOGY.

Item in Executive Limitations Policy	Frequency	Methodology
1. Dealings with staff, volunteers, and citizens	Semiannually	Internal report
2. Budgeting	Annually	Direct inspection of budget
3. Actual financial conditions	Monthly and annually	Internal report and external audit
4. Information to council	Bimonthly	Direct inspection at council meetings
5. Assets	Semiannually	Internal report
6. Compensation and benefits	Annually (in October)	Internal report
7. Executive succession	As needed based on turnover	Internal report
8. Conflict of interest	Semiannually	Internal report
9. Action regarding operations of city attorney and city secretary	Annually	Internal report
10. Sharing information and being cooperative with city attorney, city secretary, and municipal court judge	Annually	Internal report

Source: City of Bryan, Texas.

and degree of specificity required to satisfy the board. These executive reports typically contain an overall conclusion and summary data that support the conclusion. In fact, having just the conclusion or just the data is not of much value to either the board or the CEO.

Having the CEO submit executive reports in this format generally ensures that boards receive far more targeted (and therefore less) information than they are used to getting. Some boards we studied therefore worried that they were becoming more distant from the organization. However, they also found that they were receiving a higher quality of information about the areas that most concerned them.

These boards learned to use their policies to solicit information about particular sources of potential problems. As areas of concern arose, the board members amended policies to reflect those concerns and subsequently required the CEO to report to them regularly on those policies. At the Colorado Association of School Boards, for example, a board member saw a particular flaw in the executive recruitment process. The board then decided to amend its Executive Recruitment policy to prohibit the filling of such positions without advertising. Correctly, the board did not chastise the CEO for any action or inaction that occurred before the limitation had been put in place.

The CEO is usually a full participant in Executive Limitations policy development discussions and is encouraged to voice any concerns. This makes sense, given that the CEO must ensure that the organization does not violate Executive Limitations. The CEO therefore has a responsibility to advise the board if a particular Executive Limitation is unrealistic.

In one example, the city council of Bryan, Texas, was considering an Executive Limitation that required that the CEO (the city manager) not allow any "unsafe" working conditions. Because some staff positions, such as police officer and electric line crew member, made potential danger an inevitable part of the workday, the city manager said he was unable to conform to this wording. After discussion, the council agreed to say that worker conditions could not be "unduly unsafe." This language allowed the CEO to account for appropriate training and accident prevention techniques when analyzing the safety of the positions.

As mentioned, most boards are justifiably concerned about the finances of the organization and often create Executive Limitations policies in this area first. During monitoring, the board should expect data from the CEO to demonstrate compliance and to demonstrate it clearly. Let us presume that in one of its financial policies the board has said that "cash balances should not fall below two months' operating expenses" and has requested monthly CEO reports. On a monthly basis the CEO will report the actual cash balance and the minimum balance allowed and will say whether or not the actual balance complies with the policy. With just two numbers and a statement, the CEO can fulfill the obligation, unless of course there is noncompliance. In a case of noncompliance the CEO should have a lot more to say!

How Do Boards Monitor Governance Process?

With the reassurance that the CEO is not going to run amok within the organization (given that the Executive Limitations corral is appropriately in place), boards usually turn to monitoring their own behavior and methods. When boards agree

EXHIBIT 7.2. BOARD SELF-EVALUATION POLICY.

Policy Name: Board Self-Evaluation   Date Approved: July 12, 1995
Policy Type: Governance Process   Review Date: Annually in March

In cooperation with the CEO, the board will establish a set of measurable standards in which the function and process of the board and individual board member performance can be evaluated.

Under the leadership of the chairperson, on an annual basis, the board will conduct a self-evaluation in conjunction with the appraisal of the CEO.

The board may request senior management or an external party or both to assist it in making this self-evaluation.

The board will evaluate itself in the areas outlined in the Board Job Description policy.

The chairperson will distribute a report to the board outlining the results of the self-evaluation.

The board will discuss and interpret the outcome of the self-evaluation.

The board will formulate a work plan that will highlight specific goals and objectives for improvement of identified areas.

The board will monitor its adherence to its own Governance Process policies on a regular basis. Upon the choice of the board, any policy can be monitored at any time. However, at minimum, the board will both review the policies and monitor its own adherence to them, according to the following schedule:

Policy Number and Name	Frequency of Reviewing and Monitoring
GP–1: Governing Style	Annually in December
GP–2: Board Job Description	Annually in December
GP–3: Chairperson's Role	Annually in December
GP–4: Board Committee Principles	Annually in January
GP–5: Board Committee Structure	Annually in January
GP–6: Reimbursement of Expenses	Annually in May
GP–7: Code of Conduct	Annually in January
GP–8: Charge to the Chief of Medical Staff	Quarterly and annually in March
GP–9: Board Self-Evaluation	Annually in March
GP–10: Board Education	Annually in March
GP–11: Board Linkage with Community	Annually in February

EXHIBIT 7.2. BOARD SELF-EVALUATION POLICY (*continued*).

Policy Number and Name	Frequency of Reviewing and Monitoring
GP–12: Board Linkage with Other Organizations	Annually in February
GP–13: Board Planning Cycle and Agenda	Annually in February
GP–14: Allocation of Capital Reserves	Annually in August
GP–15: Client and Personnel Appeals	Annually in August
GP–16: Framework for Decision Making	Biannually in June and December
GP–16.1: Criteria for Decision Making	Biannually in June and December

Source: Parkland Health District.

about what they will work on, decide how they will carry out their work, and check adherence to their own standards, they can move quickly and surely toward their predetermined goal. Exhibit 7.2 shows the Board Self-Evaluation policy from Parkland Health District.

Self-Evaluation. Monitoring Governance Process policies need not be elaborate or onerous. Several boards simply conclude each meeting by having a board member give a short monitoring report on the use of Governance Process policies. By answering a series of questions aloud, the board member charged with monitoring helps the group focus on what went right and see what could be improved in the next meeting. For this purpose the City of Bryan uses a form (see Exhibit 7.3) and records it as part of each meeting's official minutes. Members of the council are free to disagree with the monitor's viewpoint, but reportedly they rarely do so, because each strives to achieve the high standard associated with the report.

As with Executive Limitations monitoring, it is essential that a Governance Process monitoring use the policies themselves as the only criteria for judging success. In our study, the boards with the strongest sense of being a team (a sense gained from thoroughly discussing their governance approach and arriving at common values) found it easiest to agree on their own behavior and to recognize when the whole board or any board member was getting off track.

EXHIBIT 7.3. COUNCIL MEETING MONITORING FORM.

In a continual effort to improve its Policy Governance process, the Bryan city council developed this form to evaluate its progress. The scheduled council member evaluator completes this form at the conclusion of each council meeting. The evaluator evaluates the council as a whole and not individual members.

Today's date: ____/____/____

Instructions: In questions 1–5, **S** indicates Satisfactory, **NI** indicates Needs Improvement, and **UNS** indicates Unsatisfactory.

1. The council was prepared for the meeting.   S   NI   UNS

2. The council's time was appropriately spent
   on Ends as opposed to means.   S   NI   UNS

3. Each council member was given an adequate
   opportunity to participate in discussion and
   decision making.   S   NI   UNS

4. The council's treatment of all persons was
   courteous, dignified, and fair.   S   NI   UNS

5. The council adhered to Robert's Rules of Order.   S   NI   UNS

6. The council adhered to its adopted governance style:
   a. It emphasized outward vision: ____Yes   ____No
   b. It encouraged diversity in viewpoints: ____Yes   ____No
   c. It exercised strategic leadership more than
      overseeing administrative detail: ____Yes   ____No
   d. It maintained a clear distinction between
      council and staff roles: ____Yes   ____No
   e. It used collective decision making: ____Yes   ____No
   f. It looked to the future: ____Yes   ____No

7. Evaluator's comments: _____
   _____
   _____

Evaluator: _____   Signed: _____

Amended: January 24, 1998

Source: City of Bryan, Texas.

Evaluation by an Outsider. In all the cases we studied, the board itself does Governance Process monitoring. However, some members worry that the board could become complacent and that collegiality could prevent hard questions from being asked and answered. In a few cases, therefore, boards occasionally ask an outsider to observe and comment on their behavior. The problem is finding someone sufficiently well versed in Policy Governance to ensure that the reviews are consistent with the model. It is also possible that the board will be on its best behavior when the observer is present. Just going through the exercise is undoubtedly helpful, though. For information on boards' use of outsiders as coaches, see Chapter Eight.

Policy Reviews. As with any area of board policy, in addition to regular monitoring, Governance Process policies need occasional review. Especially, with board member turnover, values may change. Ideally policy reviews are done as part of a regular process, but they should be timed so that new members have some knowledge and experience of doing business under Policy Governance before the review takes place. For more on Governance Process monitoring, see Chapter Eight.

How Do Boards Monitor Ends?

Once Executive Limitations monitoring and Governance Process monitoring have been firmly established, boards can turn their attention to their most important tasks—developing and monitoring Ends. As we have seen, this is the most challenging and rewarding area for the board.

Of the eleven organizations studied in this book, only two have Ends monitoring fully in place. Two others have made a start, four are just beginning, and the remaining three have not fully developed their Ends policies and thus have nothing to monitor.

Having invested the time and energy it takes to envision the future, boards most certainly want to know that the CEO, staff, and organization are moving toward that future. For most organizations this means that once an End is adopted and some baseline information is established, periodic checking needs to be done to see what progress is being made. This information need not be elaborate. It certainly should not be monetarily or personally burdensome to collect or report. John Carver has said that "an imprecise measure of the right thing is much better than the most precise measure of the wrong thing." The board has set the targets by establishing the Ends; the CEO demonstrates progress by measuring critical components of the achievement of the Ends.

Monitoring Methods and Frequency. Just as with Executive Limitations, the board is not required to "approve" the details of Ends monitoring methodologies beyond specifying the type and frequency. In fact, the board should expect the

CEO to develop these reports. The board need only ask itself, "With what frequency do we want to monitor this End? What method should we use? An executive report, an external audit, or a direct inspection?" If an executive report is chosen, as in the vast majority of cases, then when each report arrives, the board will ask the next question: "Does this monitoring report give us the information that we need to be certain that the CEO has achieved a reasonable interpretation of our Ends?" If the answer is again yes, the board will want to ask the final question: "Given the resources that the board allocated, is appropriate progress being made toward achieving the Ends? If the answer is yes to all questions, then the CEO and the organization are on the right track.

If the board wants to talk about more detailed monitoring methodologies or Ends, the CEO should be asked to propose possible types of reports, because he or she is best acquainted with the details of operations. The board can then consider whether, if it received that type of information in the future, it could discern whether the CEO had made a "reasonable interpretation" of the Ends and progress was being made. No motion to approve the more detailed methodology is necessary. It is the CEO's methodology, and as such it needs no endorsement from the board, as long as the board later agrees that a "reasonable interpretation" has been made.

Ensuring That the CEO Submits Adequate Reports. Suppose the board concluded that the information it had received was not substantive enough to draw a conclusion about the CEO's interpretation. In this case the board would straightforwardly ask the CEO to develop alternative or improved methodologies. The board could repeatedly ask for this to occur until it got what it wanted. Because the CEO and the staff sit through the discussions and should therefore understand where the board is going, it should not take more than one or two iterations to reach the "reasonable interpretation" stage.

"Reasonable Interpretation" of Ends. In its Ends development, "reasonable interpretation," and monitoring process, the city council of Bryan begins with the mega-End (which is at the level of most mission statements) and then develops a related sub-End and a sub-sub-End in successively deeper amounts of detail. Thus the board members work until they feel they have said all that is necessary to allow the CEO to interpret their wishes further. With their need to work on a macro scale, most boards require only three or four levels of Ends.

Wherever the board stops speaking (that is, at whatever level of detail the board ceases its work), the CEO and staff will likely need to define the Ends further. Several additional levels may be required in order for the CEO to design and implement *means* in order to achieve the sub-Ends and ultimately the Ends themselves. While refining the Ends, staff members ask themselves, "As we speak to the next level and the next, what would a reasonable interpretation of the board's words be?"

Most staffs that have progressed to this point have found such questions enlightening. In this in-depth analysis staff members find themselves confronting the organization's programs, services, and systems virtually at the level of "reengineering" or of starting with a "blank page." While engaged in this process, the staff is working on Ends that are so specific and narrowly focused as to be outside the board's arena. These are not adopted Ends of the board, because the board quit speaking several levels ago, but they are Ends nonetheless.

The CEO and staff can then begin to articulate activities needed to accomplish the Ends. At this juncture virtually every activity (that is every *means*) should be able to be tied directly to one or more Ends. By using their expertise, staff members should be able to look at these activities and make good predictions about the progress the organization will make toward the broader Ends that the board has articulated.

In evaluating the accomplishment of Ends, board members sometimes talk about the CEO's or the organization's actions rather than about the outcomes. They may also insert comments about their own interpretations of Ends. They ask, "Is this what I would have done?" or "Is that the interpretation I would have made?" and they use their answers as the standards. Such a line of questioning is dangerous, for it will quickly lead the board away from a results or outcomes focus. The crucial question is, "Was the outcome a reasonable interpretation of what we previously said?" The board may not like the outcome, but if it was a "reasonable interpretation," there should be no ramifications for the CEO or the staff. Instead the board should reexamine the policy at hand and decide whether different language needs to be included or whether an Executive Limitation needs to be added or revised. Because CEOs are a critical part of this questioning about "reasonable interpretation," the CEO should certainly be allowed to explain how he or she sees the outcome as a "reasonable interpretation" of the board's Ends policy.

Developing Monitoring Indicators. Having refined the Ends as much as necessary to design and implement *means*, the CEO can now provide the board with Ends monitoring indicators (specific measures selected or devised to report progress toward the Ends). Two of the organizations we have studied, Parkland Health District and the City of Bryan, have reached this level of sophistication. These indicators do not have to be entirely precise, but they must be adequate for demonstrating to the board that the CEO understands the board's Ends and that progress commensurate with the priority and funding provided by the board is being made.

For each sub-End the CEO should articulate at least one monitoring indicator. Taken cumulatively, these monitoring indicators should give the board the information it needs to ensure acceptable progress. In most organizations some program information is already being collected. The CEO will certainly want to analyze this data to see if any of it truly addresses Ends or if it simply shows effort. Policy Governance gives no points for effort; it only rewards appropriate accomplishments. If the information meets the criteria, it is a good place to start, because it takes no additional effort to gather and report.

For example, the Bryan police department, like most such departments, is obliged to report various crime statistics to the state annually. By reconfiguring these numbers, the City staff members could supply monitoring information on the Ends related to community safety. They spent almost no new funds or effort. Information previously viewed as "bureaucratic" suddenly seemed quite relevant to the City's mission.

What Types of Information Do Boards Receive?

John Carver (*Boards That Make a Difference*, 2nd edition, p. 109) names three types of information that Policy Governance boards receive: decision information, incidental information, and monitoring information. Because information is so key to the issue of monitoring, it is worthwhile to discuss each briefly and to look closely at the roles of Ends monitoring information and Executive Limitations monitoring information in the total mix of board information.

Decision Information. Decision information is what the board needs in order to make choices. This is the arena that the board enters as it makes policy. Decision information includes environmental information and typically asserts what others are doing or perhaps what the state of the art is in a particular segment of the board's business. However, decision information may also be internal, such as information about the organization's ability to produce a certain result or information about an adverse staff reaction to a certain Executive Limitation. Because Policy Governance boards are primarily focused on the long term, decision information almost always has implications for the future.

Incidental Information. Incidental information is the information that a CEO gives the board principally to sustain the board's sense of connection with the organization. Because individual board members want different types of incidental information, a CEO generally packages it in a "take-it-or-leave-it" format. Some members read every word and wish for more, and others never open the packet. As long as the board recognizes this information for what it is, no harm is done at either extreme. It is perfectly acceptable for the board to want to know what is going on. In fact, through this incidental information the board will often find something that triggers thinking for a new policy or for a revision. It is when this incidental information is misused to judge performance that the board has wandered off course.

Monitoring Information. For true judging of the fulfillment of its policies, the board must look to monitoring information. As discussed earlier in this chapter, monitoring information from outside the board comes in two forms: Ends monitoring information and Executive Limitations monitoring information.

Ends Monitoring Information. Ends monitoring information is different from other information sent to the board in that it is highly specific to the Ends being monitored. It is also easy to read and understand, making it straightforward for board members to answer the question "Did the CEO accomplish what we said we wanted?"

The City of Bryan lists each council End, then supplies the information pertinent to that End. For example, one of the City of Bryan's sub-Ends is, "Residents and visitors are reasonably protected from emergencies and natural disasters." At the next level of specificity, one of the council's sub-sub-Ends is, "There is low loss due to fire." The CEO has interpreted this statement in two further sub-sub-sub-Ends, one of which is, "Property damage is minimized." He has then developed two monitoring indicators for this sub-sub-sub-End: (1) the number of structure fires per annum and (2) the percentage of fire calls responded to within five minutes.

In some cases, monitoring information can apply to more than one End. The City of Bryan has found it helpful simply to repeat the information. In this way council members who want to examine progress on a particular End can go to the End itself, rather than trying to deduce which monitoring information applies to which End.

Jan Moore, a consultant who works with the Policy Governance model and who has advised Parkland Health District extensively, correctly points out that "the nature of Ends related to health care frequently takes a long-term perspective," so it is difficult to find solid short-term evidence that will point to the achievement of Ends. When facing this dilemma, CEOs may tend to revert to reporting activities rather than giving the *results* of the activities. Moore also acknowledges that the art of accurately measuring health status is still relatively undeveloped. This further tempts CEOs in health care to provide measurements of *means.* She urges, "The board must insist on Ends monitoring indicators, even if they are gross indicators."

Executive Limitations Monitoring Information. Executive Limitations monitoring information is also used to judge performance. The CEO or other board-designated board member, committee, or external auditor reports on the CEO's compliance with the preestablished criteria provided by each policy. This information is also succinct and easily understood. Such compliance information is generally available in most organizations and must simply be customized to the specific Executive Limitation.

Information About Noncompliance. Most Executive Limitations policies include a policy that requires the CEO to notify the board whenever the organization is in danger of not being, or actually is not, in compliance with board policy. In addition to informing the board, the CEO is expected to provide information as to how the noncompliance occurred or is occurring, what steps are being taken to regain compliance, and the anticipated time line for regaining compliance. Depending on the nature and the severity of the noncompliance, the board may well ask for frequent updates on the organization's progress in regaining compliance.

As we have already seen, most boards monitor Executive Limitations on a biannual or quarterly basis. Parkland Health District monitors some policies at each meeting by formally placing an item on the agenda to do so. The board reads the monitoring information in advance and comes prepared with any questions about the adequacy of the information or about areas of noncompliance. When there is noncompliance, the board determines whether it wishes to receive a supplementary report before the next regularly scheduled monitoring date. But the board does not try to help the CEO "fix" the area of noncompliance. It is the CEO's responsibility to regain compliance.

The boards covered in this book seem to find that with clearly articulated Executive Limitations, the CEO stays well within policy. Knowing the criteria in advance allows the CEO to structure organizational behavior in such a manner as to achieve compliance most of the time.

How Do Boards Evaluate CEOs?

A crucial Policy Governance discipline is regular evaluation of the CEO's total performance against all the board's Executive Limitations and Ends policies. The boards we have studied provide several examples of how this can be achieved. The Southern Ontario Library Service board conducts an annual performance review of the CEO against all its Executive Limitations and Ends policies. The London YMCA-YWCA has an extensive annual process that includes assessment against Executive Limitations. Weaver Street Market uses "all the monitoring reports submitted during the year" and seeks the CEO's input when agreeing on its process.

For Parkland Health District, "The annual evaluation of the CEO has been completed as a cumulative review of previous monitoring data."

The fact that the board has made clear what it expects of the CEO and that monitoring data is routinely being collected makes CEO evaluation relatively simple under Policy Governance. But the tools are powerful; CEOs report feeling more accountable and liking it.

Does "Reasonable Interpretation" Cause Problems?

From the evidence provided by the eleven organizations examined in this book, the matter of the CEO's "reasonable interpretation" certainly does not cause problems. Only two boards cited any potential disagreements with their CEO about interpretation of their policies. In each instance the issue was quickly resolved to the board's and the CEO's satisfaction.

The design of Policy Governance leaves little room for a CEO to misinterpret a board's wishes, because (1) the board is required to say all it has to say to the CEO clearly and concisely, and (2) regular monitoring swiftly reveals any misinterpretations, which the board resolves either by further refining its policy language or by correcting the CEO. In our sample of organizations, the latter course of action had never been necessary.

☑ Key Learnings

We have learned several things about the way boards monitor and evaluate the whole range of their responsibilities.

Monitoring Is Essential for Accountability

Monitoring is the key tool for giving the board and the CEO the information they need to hold themselves accountable under the Policy Governance model. Ultimately, monitoring proves to the ownership (and to any oversight agencies) that the board is fulfilling its role responsibly.

Accountability Creates Trust and Improves Performance

In the organizations we have studied, Policy Governance seems to have produced better and more trusting relationships between the board and the CEO. There are no instances in which "reasonable interpretation" seems to have been abused, and there is some evidence that the CEO's empowerment under Policy Governance is trickling down to other staff levels.

Monitoring of Executive Limitations Is Well Advanced

Almost all the organizations covered in this book regularly monitor Executive Limitations. The financial policies seem to require the most frequent reporting and external verification. Monitoring gives boards confidence. One organization relates, "When the staff presented the budget, not for approval but to show that it met all the criteria of the Executive Limitations policy, the chair turned to the staff member and said, 'I'm so glad I don't have to turn to you and ask a pithy question about the miscellaneous line item.'"

Monitoring of Governance Process Creates a Team

Boards that are monitoring their own performance report an increase in their sense of being a team and ability to remain true to their commitment to govern rather than manage.

Monitoring of Ends Is Coming Slowly

Although boards recognize that they need to monitor Ends to measure organizational progress, this process is very much "under development" for most boards. In fact, only two of the eleven organizations have created detailed monitoring indicators for Ends. This reflects the fact that it takes considerable time and effort to develop Ends policies.

○ Taking Action: Strategies for Where You Are Now

When it comes to monitoring policies, your board may be a bit green, somewhat experienced and somewhat frustrated, or quite proficient. Wherever your organization is currently positioned in relation to monitoring, plenty of tools and tips can help you move along with greater efficiency and speed.

If Your Board Is New to Monitoring

If your board is relatively new to the model and is avoiding the monitoring component because it seems daunting, take heart. By creating the policies to be monitored, you have already done the most important piece; you have created the monitoring criteria. None of the boards we have studied found it difficult to make decisions about the monitoring method or frequency. It was simply a question of setting aside the time to put the structure in place. Look at the "Practical Tips and Tools" section that follows and the similar sections at the end of Chapters Four and Eight, which also contain relevant ideas for making your work run smoothly.

If Your Board Has Begun Monitoring but Has Become Stuck

If your board has started monitoring Executive Limitations and Governance Process policies but has become stuck on Ends monitoring, it may need to remind itself that the CEO is responsible for developing and providing the Ends monitoring indicators. Ends are the heart of the Policy Governance model, and work in this area offers the greatest rewards to the board and to the ownership. Don't fall at this last hurdle.

If the board has simply become tired or distracted, see the ideas in the "Practical Tips and Tools" sections of Chapters Three, Four, and Six for remotivating your members.

If You Are Monitoring Governance Process, Executive Limitations, and Ends

If your board is monitoring all three types of policies but is still not sure that it is getting the right kind of information, see the ideas in the "Practical Tips and Tools" section for increasing the board's confidence.

If your board is monitoring all three components well, it is among the growing numbers of boards that are truly reaping the benefits of good governance. Now all you need to do is ensure that your board is taking the monitoring reports seriously and always seeking to improve the process.

► Practical Tips and Tools

Practicing Policy Governance is not unlike learning to ride a bike. Your board will fall occasionally, but over time it will learn the skills and become quite accomplished without significant conscious thought.

Introduce Your Board to Monitoring Reports

Use the first monitoring cycle as a learning process. Observe how comfortable the board is with the content, level of detail, and format of the report. Consider the following questions when reading monitoring reports for the first time.

- Does the information presented relate directly to the policy criteria? If so, how?
- Does the information reasonably assure us that there is compliance with the policy?

Encourage discussion of monitoring reports and process by including monitoring as a specific agenda item at each meeting. Invite board members to bring up any item that concerns them. Remind board members of their obligation to review monitoring reports as their primary way of getting the information they need to be accountable.

Assuage the Board's Fears

If one of your board's continuing concerns in implementing Policy Governance is that something "bad" may happen while the board isn't looking, board members may want to create a worry list (see Chapter Two). This is a brainstormed list that puts everyone's fears on the table for discussion. Once the list is developed, the board and the CEO can discuss each fear. They can determine whether an existing Executive Limitation addresses the fear and whether a corresponding and adequate monitoring report is being provided. If so, that fear can be crossed off the worry list. If not, a new or revised Executive Limitation or monitoring report can be adopted. Using this process should reassure every member that they are behaving responsibly and that if something unpredictable and undesirable does occur, the board will be made aware of it very quickly.

Reassurance can also come from learning about the experience of other organizations. Ask other Policy Governance boards if they have had any trouble ensuring a "reasonable interpretation" or monitoring policies in general. Read relevant materials, such as John Carver's article in *Board Leadership* no. 24 called "Board Approvals and Monitoring Are Very Different Actions" or "Guest Presentation" in *Board Leadership* no. 34, which is about the City of Bryan. (See Resource C for details.)

PART THREE

HOW BOARDS KEEP POLICY GOVERNANCE GOING

CHAPTER EIGHT

STAYING ON TRACK

☐ The Challenge

Policy Governance causes boards to assume a way of life very different from the one they have traditionally known. Inspired by the possibility of having their organizations powerfully fulfill their missions, boards transform their own leadership. They create a new relationship with their own jobs and with their CEO, their staff, their customers, and their owners. Boards distinguish and articulate core values that define their organizations. They reinvent outcomes to be achieved and create structures to ensure that all people and all systems are on track.

Like any change in lifestyle, this involves discipline, perseverance, and sustained motivation. Given the inevitable distractions of a crisis-driven world and our imperfections as human beings, there can be bumps in the road. Chapter Three looked at how boards can set themselves up for success. This chapter looks at how boards can keep the initial inspiration alive as the Policy Governance implementation journey continues. We will see how boards maintain discipline and enthusiasm over time and how they get over the bumps.

In particular, this chapter reviews the experience of the eleven organizations to answer these questions:

- How do boards maintain discipline and enthusiasm?
- What jeopardizes boards' discipline and enthusiasm?
- How do boards recruit, orient, and train new members?
- What roles do the CEO and staff play in keeping boards on track?

Some very clear learnings emerge; these are summarized in the next section of the chapter. We then ask you to examine the extent to which your board is on track and give many tips, tools, and suggestions for renewing your board's commitment and sustaining your efforts over time.

■ The Experience

How Do Boards Maintain Discipline and Enthusiasm?

From the experience of the boards we have looked at, it is clear that the two main factors that contribute to maintaining board discipline are self-evaluation and self-discipline.

Self-Evaluation. Most of the eleven boards we have studied evaluate the extent to which they are being consistent with Policy Governance principles. This evaluation includes regularly monitoring the board's performance at each board meeting and conducting occasional longer assessments during the year.

The Parkland Health District board reviews its compliance with Governance Process policies at least annually. The reviews are staggered so that no more than one or two occur at any one meeting. During the policy reviews, the board examines each policy criterion and records evidence of its own compliance or noncompliance. See Exhibit 7.2 for details.

In addition to reviewing policies at each meeting, the Parkland Health District board's secretary periodically tracks the amount of meeting time spent on each category of policy. This ensures that the board "is not spending disproportionate amounts of time on monitoring or on making decisions about operational details that it [has chosen to] . . . prohibit the CEO from making by way of Executive Limitations." Parkland's board also evaluates itself by appointing a board monitor. That person uses a special note-taking form to track how well the board complies with its governing style, as defined by policy.

The Colorado Association of School Boards assesses its adherence to Governance Process policies at least annually. The board originally scheduled the yearly review to occur during a January retreat following the December election of new directors and officers. The intent was to immerse new board members in the policies and processes that guide the board. However, the new board members were at a disadvantage because of their lack of experience and found the process "awkward and uninteresting." The assessment has been rescheduled to occur before new members and officers are elected.

The Southern Ontario Library Service board reviews each type of policy over a three-year cycle to assess all of its work and to keep policies current. Governance Process is done in one fiscal year, Ends in the next, and Board-Staff Relationship and Executive Limitations in the third year of the cycle.

At the end of each meeting, Weaver Street Market's board measures its own consistency with Policy Governance principles, assesses board dynamics, and determines whether meeting outcomes were achieved. Through periodic checks during the year, it further assesses where the board is in its plan for the year (that is, which goals have or have not been achieved). The yearly plan and goals are based on the board's "job products." Thus, by following the plan and achieving the goals, the board will also be aligned with the job it set out for itself under Policy Governance.

The Southern Ontario Library Service board has incorporated an additional level of monitoring at the board level—chair monitoring reports. Given the length of time between quarterly board meetings, the chair provides "reports on the activities undertaken on behalf of the board to give members an opportunity to ask questions and react to anything done in their name by the chair." This is the chair's equivalent to CEO monitoring reports.

All of the boards that evaluated themselves feel that they have stayed focused. Although it is difficult to isolate the impact on boards when they do not self-evaluate, it is noteworthy that in our study, the boards that feel off track did not consistently monitor their adherence to Policy Governance principles or to their own Governance Process policies. One board occasionally looks at attendance or meeting times but does not consider issues of governance. Another board describes itself as not placing a high priority on adhering to Policy Governance principles, even though the policy structure is in place. It characterizes its current condition as "far from ideal." For a third board, no formal evaluating is done, and any spontaneous self-discipline by board members or by the chair is scarce. The lack of self-governance has hindered this board's focus on issues. To facilitate the board's work, the current chair is supporting board self-evaluation on an annual basis and individual evaluation of board members at reelection time. Certainly, some self-evaluation is better than no self-evaluation. But as John Carver said in *CarverGuide 8: Board Self-Assessment* (see Resource C for details), "If you want to improve performance, evaluation must be continual."

Although self-evaluation is a very tangible measure of a board's compliance with its stated policies, it does not absolutely ensure that the board is on track.

As the Bryan city council points out, "Even with the monitoring, it is hard to know in every case whether or not Policy Governance was truly followed [because] sometimes the council member on the losing side of a vote may let feelings influence perception in this arena. Even in times of calm, it is hard to measure adherence to the model from the inside." Some boards have addressed this issue by involving an external coach to help them evaluate their performance. The subject of coaches is covered later in this chapter.

Self-Discipline. Most of the boards we have studied informally use self-discipline to stay focused and on track. By self-discipline we mean board members keeping each other on the subject and in the board's domain during every board meeting. The board of the Colorado Association of School Boards finds peer pressure invaluable in sustaining board discipline. Board members catch themselves straying off subject, or they are alerted to it by the chair or another member. Usually, this is all that is required to return to the subject at hand.

For boards in which this kind of self-discipline is effective, the board is fully assuming responsibility for being consistent with Policy Governance principles. As expressed by the Bryan city council, "Board discipline rests with the council itself. . . . Each member is very proactive in pointing out whenever a perceived lapse in adherence to the model occurs. Members are reinforced in this activity by the . . . council monitoring that occurs at each meeting" (see Exhibit 7.3).

The Southern Ontario Library Service board uses individual and group self-discipline, which are "supported by a thorough recruitment and orientation of new trustees." What adds to this discipline is that board members make a "considerable effort" to screen the questions they pose during meetings. "It is not uncommon at a meeting for a board member to preface a question with, 'I don't know if I should ask this. . . .' If the chair or other members think not, they do not hesitate to say so." Such rigor was also reported in the board's early use of the model. During the self-evaluation at the end of each meeting, "the board regularly revisited a discussion to assess . . . if it stayed at the appropriate level." With this precedent established early, the board continues to use this opportunity for feedback to improve its own process.

The Weaver Street Market board also established a precedent of discipline during its early work with the model. It decided to operate according to Policy Governance principles even before the policy structure was fully in place. Thus whenever an item came before the board, it was examined with respect to where it would appropriately be considered under Policy Governance. Over the course of a lengthy implementation process, such rigor meant that board members became fully versed in applying Policy Governance principles. Discipline "is now a natural part of board culture," even with the turnover of board members.

EXHIBIT 8.1. SAMPLE PERPETUAL AGENDA.

Board of Directors
Notice of Meeting

Agenda

1. Call to order
2. Minutes approval
3. Board policies
4. Monitoring confirmation
5. Ownership linkage
6. Ends
7. Incidental information
8. Board evaluation
9. Adjournment

Structures and Other Tools. Most boards surveyed support their own discipline with structures and tools, such as policy-linked agendas, a board annual calendar, a perpetual agenda, and a governance action plan. These aids help to ensure that the work the board does is indeed board work. On the Early Childhood Community Development Centre board, the board chair uses a perpetual agenda to restrict the issues discussed at board meetings to a policy level. A sample perpetual agenda is shown in Exhibit 8.1.

For the Vermont Land Trust, every board issue on the board meeting agenda is framed in terms of policies. Similarly, every item on the Weaver Street Market board agenda is related to some aspect of one of the board's job products (linkage with ownership, written governing policies, and assurance of CEO performance), and every discussion is grounded in values and policies. Every board agenda is also part of a yearly plan the board wishes to follow. In the board meeting packet, every agenda item lists an objective and the way board members need to prepare for that item. The preparation references the relevant board policies for the item and any other applicable background material. An issue outside of the board's scheduled work can only be included on the agenda after it has been screened by the board president to make sure it is an appropriate board issue.

Champions. For most boards surveyed, the chair is the main champion of the board's self-discipline. This is not surprising, considering that under Policy Governance the job of the chair is to maintain the integrity of the board's process.

When the chair actually fulfills this role by actively advocating the board's self-discipline and by advocating Policy Governance principles, he or she causes the entire board to assume responsibility for its own process and to maintain consistency; every board member becomes a champion. The chair also plays an important role in guiding discussions—asking key questions, referring to policy, and creating an environment that encourages honesty, respect, and free expression.

Other boards have another board member, an outside consultant, the CEO, or a staff member as a champion. In all the organizations surveyed, the CEO was at least a participant in the initial inquiry and the gathering of data and training about Policy Governance. The CEO remains an advocate of the model in these organizations. Only in one case was CEO support inconsistent because of successive turnover in the position.

Board-CEO Relations. Having a CEO with a comprehensive knowledge of and commitment to Policy Governance significantly helps the board maintain discipline. In one case, "this has enabled the executive director to give feedback to the board as to where to proceed next or where it could turn for information." The most valuable contribution is when the CEO follows the role delineated by the model by only bringing the board appropriate information and by making requests at the appropriate policy level.

Boards that have maintained strong discipline have actively cultivated an effective relationship between the board and the CEO. The Southern Ontario Library Service provides an example of one such effective relationship. During the implementation of Policy Governance, the chair and the CEO assumed responsibility for distinguishing the new board and CEO roles and helping the board and staff to adjust. They were "scrupulous in respecting each other's spheres of authority" and thereby developed "openness and trust." The chair describes the relationship in this way:

> We would often have very open discussions about whose role it was to decide certain things (for example, inviting staff to board meetings, closing offices, terminating leases). When either of us thought we had an interest, we would try to bring it up and discuss our different perspectives. It was not just respecting each other's area but being open about different perspectives and the fact that sometimes it was unclear and needed to be hashed out together. We were not afraid to discuss it, because we were not afraid that we were trying to extend our areas of responsibility. That, to me, was so key.

Creating an effective relationship between the chair and CEO not only clarifies board and staff roles on every issue but also capitalizes on the organization's leadership capacity. The Southern Ontario Library Service chair invited the vice-chair, the staff Policy Governance consultant, and the CEO to advise and assist him in providing governance leadership. Freely requesting and receiving counsel is possible when roles and authority are understood and respected.

A trusting and cooperative relationship between the board and the general manager was also important for the Weaver Street Market board. Similar to the Southern Ontario Library Service's experience, Weaver Street Market's board president and general manager met regularly to sort through issues that would traditionally be on the board's agenda. Over time, distinguishing the roles of the board and the general manager became second nature. It is important to note that such clarification of roles comes *only* from careful study of the board's policies.

Coaching. Short of establishing an association to advise on Policy Governance, as one board wishes it had, boards may engage a coach to provide regular advice or support in helping the board stay on track. Whether they are board members, staff liaisons, or outside consultants, coaches are knowledgeable about Policy Governance and are in such a position that the board readily accepts their correction or counsel.

All of the boards surveyed have to some degree involved knowledgeable persons to provide information and support at the various stages of adopting and implementing Policy Governance. Many have gone further and also taken on a continuing coach. For example, Parkland Health District's board had assistance during implementation and now receives regular monthly feedback and suggestions from an external consultant to help it use the model even more effectively. Ongoing assistance has made it easier to understand how the principles of the model work in real life. Given "the tendency of human nature to revert to habit and already learned, comfortable ways of doing things," Parkland Health District believes that "most boards would do better with an outside, objective coach. . . . This should not become a dependency relationship but one in which, as the board gains experience, [it] gradually takes over the task of keeping itself on track." The Parkland Health District board likens its progress with coaching to taking "baby steps every month with a growth spurt resulting in a giant step every six months or so as . . . the import of a particular principle of the model really becomes second nature." In its Governance Process policy on Board Education, Parkland Health District even specifies that the board will use a coach (see Exhibit 8.8 later in this chapter).

The Southern Ontario Library Service board has found it helpful to use a consultant as a neutral guide. The consultant is a staff member, the manager of trustee training, but she is operating more as an external consultant throughout the process of developing policies and practicing Policy Governance, giving the board needed expertise at no additional expense.

At the San Francisco AIDS Foundation, the board liaison (a staff member) serves as a devil's advocate. He describes himself as "a sort of Carver purist" and comments, "If a discussion gets too *'meansy'* [focused on means], I just raise my hand and bring it to their attention. They trust me and have come to expect it from me." Similarly, the Early Childhood Community Development Centre believes that engaging a board consultant has been key in its ability to sustain Policy Governance and maintain enthusiasm.

Continued Training. Continuing to train board members significantly contributes to board discipline and helps the board stay on track. Reinforcement is a powerful way of keeping Policy Governance alive and in the forefront.

The Early Childhood Community Development Centre board really champions the model and stays "true to it by keeping informed through John Carver's newsletters, information from its board consultant, engaging in continued training, or hiring the board consultant to help when it hits a juncture in the road and is not sure how to proceed." Board training allows the board "to work from the same page," which commits members to the model and ultimately to the organization.

Most boards derive significant training simply from persevering with Policy Governance. With practice they understand and apply the principles and develop critical group process skills. The Vermont Land Trust board observes, "We are becoming more Carveresque as we learn more about and practice the model. It doesn't feel so scary and precipitous now that we have a couple of years under our belts."

Boards also supplement their specific Policy Governance training by developing other qualities and skills that enhance their work with the model. The past chair of the Southern Ontario Library Service board states, "We did a number of things to . . . make possible the sorts of challenging discussions the model allows or requires you to have. . . . The two-day workshop and the time we spent on Myers-Briggs were very important to developing the trust and safety to tackle the big issues."

The Vermont Land Trust's board refers to the need for training in conducting dialogues and managing meetings. The Colorado Association of School Boards suggests that boards receive training in discussion skills rather than simply being told to "do better." For the Parkland Health District board, continual work with the model naturally resulted in "team building" among board members: "A positive side effect of having to discuss and agree on a set of values proclaimed in policy is . . . developing a sense of unity as a group."

Sharing Learning. The City of Bryan has found that "learning by teaching" and sharing with other boards and members of the public enhance council members' discipline and enthusiasm. Individual council members make presentations to other communities, the Texas Municipal League, and to civic clubs and nonprofits. Explaining concepts and principles reinforces the board's own knowledge and proficiency in the model.

Using a range of media, the Bryan city council "goes to great lengths to involve the community" in a designated section on Ends development at each of its meetings (see Exhibit 5.3 for a full description). As a result, council members can communicate the council's vision better, and meetings are spent talking about and creating the future.

Taking Responsibility. Perhaps the most significant factor contributing to discipline is the extent to which a board takes responsibility for, and ownership of, Policy Governance. Taking responsibility means making the model's principles the foundation of all their work. "Commitment, understanding, and trust that the model does facilitate organizational strength" is a common theme expressed by the members of the Early Childhood Community Development Centre board. "With this commitment, board members desire to stay on track and check in with one another to ensure they are conducting business prudently."

In one case in which some board members still had some concerns about Policy Governance even after implementation, a relatively small group of board members worked to keep the whole board in line. Following a 50 percent turnover on the board, new members were oriented and trained to address any concerns thoroughly. Since then, more and more members have taken responsibility for keeping the board on track by saying things like, "This isn't what we are supposed to be doing" or "Is my understanding wrong, or are we out of our area?"

The most disciplined boards seem to be those that assume full responsibility for their jobs and do what it takes to fulfill that responsibility. As one organization notes, "Success takes 100 percent commitment of board members. It requires discipline and rigor." Discipline and rigor arise from commitment, which arises from discipline and rigor.

Building Enthusiasm. A consistent theme among the boards surveyed is that boards are "energized by the nature of the work." They are especially revitalized when connecting with owners and focusing on the future through their work on Ends. For the Bryan city council, linking with owners has energized the council, as well as the community. The council also feels encouraged as it listens to the struggles of other communities at gatherings of city councils and reaffirms that "Policy Governance is a better way."

Seeing results generates enthusiasm. For example, boards are excited by having more focused meetings, spending energy and time on important matters, and maintaining a consistent clarity of roles. On the Southern Ontario Library Service board, "Enthusiasm sustains itself. The benefits of the model in clarifying roles and shifting [the] focus to the future empower the organization, and this itself fuels the enthusiasm." Similarly, for Weaver Street Market, "The board was able to sustain its enthusiasm for Policy Governance by living the model, taking on the board's job products, scheduling and taking action on what it wanted to achieve, and abiding by Policy Governance principles. That's how it was sustained, but enthusiasm really arose from the . . . results. When something works, it's easy to be enthusiastic."

What Jeopardizes Boards' Discipline and Enthusiasm?

The boards that have contributed to this book have experienced a variety of threats to their ability to maintain Policy Governance. Because most of these threats have been covered in previous chapters (especially Chapter Three), they will not be covered extensively here.

Public Demands. Public boards need to work especially hard at staying focused. A political issue or precedent can easily take elected officials off track. Public sentiment for maintaining the status quo can also dampen commitment to Policy Governance. Educating their owners (the public) is an absolute priority for public boards.

Crises. A crisis such as a major funding cut, a strike, or a legal challenge can also cause a board to put Policy Governance discipline aside. Once Policy Governance is truly established, however, boards seem to recognize that holding onto Policy Governance principles and discipline is the very thing that will help them meet such challenges effectively.

Size of the Board. Large boards face particular discipline challenges. However, it is certainly not true that Policy Governance does not work for large boards. They just need to be all the more rigorous and imaginative about keeping discipline and enthusiasm alive.

Lack of Leadership. Boards that do not take responsibility for evaluating how well they are complying with their own policies will quickly fall off track. The lack of a chair committed to Policy Governance or the absence of some other champion causes boards to lose focus, momentum, and discipline.

Lack of Support. Trial and error can be excellent trainers, yet they can also create lingering frustrations that inhibit a board's motivation and thwart progress. A board that is not well versed in using Policy Governance and that encounters difficult issues and transitions may well blame Policy Governance and decide that the effort is not worthwhile. This is especially true if all board members do not take responsibility for making the model work. In addition, members who resist the board's overall direction can easily sap the board's energy and attention.

Going Overboard. Another threat to board discipline is when, as happened with one of the eleven organizations, a board misinterprets the model and goes overboard in some way. For example, the board can become so concerned about keeping the roles of managing and governing separate that board members feel they cannot speak with staff at all. This can create an unnatural strain that can jeopardize board-staff relations and undermine Policy Governance's intent of cooperative leadership.

The Loneliness of Pioneering. Fewer and fewer boards feel that they are the only ones implementing the model, as this book reflects. But when Policy Governance is not well known in a board's area or field of operation or when it is misunderstood or when it is known only as something that other boards have not implemented successfully, it is hard for a board not to feel alone and vulnerable. Public scrutiny early on can lead a board to sidetrack the best intentions.

Lengthy Processes. Lengthy processes also pose a threat to discipline, and there is no point in pretending that developing Ends or connecting with owners can be done overnight. During lengthy processes, boards need to invent new ways to keep initial enthusiasm alive. Sharing the task of getting background information for policy discussions can be a useful way of increasing board members' interest in their work. Breaking up the routine can also help maintain energy. For example, one board alternates its work on ownership and on Ends.

Lack of Immediate Results. Without the immediate results that they may have been used to, boards find that discipline can wane. This is especially true if board members harbor old expectations and yearnings to be involved in operations. Most boards find it helpful to alter members' expectations by frequently acknowledging that Policy Governance is a very different way of life. In any case, all this will change. As soon as a board begins experiencing the results of clearer board and staff roles, connecting with owners, and discussing the future, the members feel enthusiastic.

The biggest threat to discipline and enthusiasm is simply not keeping Policy Governance front and center, alive and well. As with any new way of life, the transition seems frustrating and difficult. Yet patience, training, discipline, consistency, and practice will overcome any barriers and produce the rewards that first drew a board to Policy Governance.

How Do Boards Recruit, Orient, and Train New Members?

Bringing new members into the board culture can be a critical turning point for good or for ill. For Policy Governance to be sustainable, new board members must be thoroughly oriented and trained as quickly as possible. A sign of the spread of Policy Governance is that boards now have the possibility of recruiting board members from other Policy Governance boards. But in most cases new board members (if they have prior board experience at all) come from the traditions of management rather than governance, of hands-on involvement rather than policy involvement, and sometimes of supporting a particular constituency rather than working for the ownership as a whole. Without a complete orientation and thorough training, such members can start off on very shaky footing. Where such education is provided, several of the organizations we have studied report that new board members with no prior board experience grasp Policy Governance more easily and enthusiastically than those accustomed to traditional governance practice.

The Colorado Association of School Boards holds a one-day intensive orientation for new board members and gives them a lot of reading material on the Policy Governance model. The reading material includes the principles of Policy Governance, back issues of the newsletter *Board Leadership,* a copy of the board's policy manual, and some of the materials written for the membership. Thus from their very first meeting the new members tend to be up to speed with the continuing board members. The CEO reports, "The new members appreciated the full-day training and have, essentially, hit the ground running on applying the model in the meetings."

Following a large board turnover, the Parkland Health District board developed a process to orient new board members and to help them gain a sense of owning the policies. After subsequent elections, the board prepared an orientation package for new members and arranged a one-day training session on Policy Governance. As with the Colorado Association of School Boards, the momentum of the board's work has been only minimally affected after elections.

At the San Francisco AIDS Foundation, new board member training is provided by the board's staff liaison, who is also the board's expert on Policy Governance. The training is done once a year, sometimes one-on-one and never with more than three new members. Reading materials include summary information about Policy Governance and the *CarverGuides* (details about the *CarverGuides* appear in Resource C).

The Southern Ontario Library Service's recruitment of new members includes preparing an information package prior to local elections. "The package notes that candidates must be willing to work under the Policy Governance model. It also requests that a minimum of one of three current board members be re-elected to provide for continuity. Once the new members are elected, they are invited to an orientation session." The orientation session includes an overview of Policy Governance principles (provided by the board's consultant) and background on how the Southern Ontario Library Service decided to implement the model and developed the policies (provided by board members). "New members are also invited to attend the last meeting of the outgoing board as observers. This gives them the opportunity to observe the actual process of a board meeting and the level and nature of discussion before they assume their new role."

What Roles Do the CEO and Staff Play in Keeping Boards on Track?

As discussed in the sections called "Champions" and "Board-CEO Relations," having a CEO who fully understands and practices Policy Governance principles plays a key role in keeping boards on track. In some instances, a CEO or other staff liaison is also the expert on Policy Governance who helps guide and support the board's process. But this cannot be allowed to detract from the board's sense of being responsible for itself.

By referencing applicable policies, CEOs can support the board's process when submitting monitoring reports and whenever they interact with the board. When submitting material for board discussions, other staff members can also help the board by stating the links between the material and the board's policies. The CEO and the staff also supply incidental information that allows the board to stay connected to the organization's activities. When the CEO of the Southern Ontario Library Service provides detailed monitoring reports, it enhances "the board's confidence in the model. The board feels informed but knows clearly what is in the CEO's bailiwick and what is open for board decision making." By clearly distinguishing which information is incidental, the CEO helps the board focus on its own job. See "Incidental Information" in Chapter Seven for more information on this CEO role.

Conversely, CEOs and staff members can easily sidetrack boards by presenting issues that the board should not handle, such as personnel and budget matters at levels below the board's relevant Executive Limitations policies.

☑ Key Learnings

This section summarizes the main lessons to be drawn from the eleven organizations' experiences in sustaining discipline and enthusiasm.

Discipline and Enthusiasm Are Critical

Without exception, boards say that implementing Policy Governance requires continual rigorous discipline. Without discipline and enthusiasm, boards cannot stay on track with Policy Governance or remain confident about their own abilities to use the model. Keeping Policy Governance in the forefront early on can set a valuable precedent for the long haul. Boards that initially work to make Policy Governance second nature have fewer difficulties later on with being disciplined and staying focused. Discipline and enthusiasm breed commitment, and vice versa.

Practice Pays

As a member of one organization says, "Perfect practice makes perfect, and that practice is called upon in times of stress to ensure optimum performance." Early in the process, boards are often anxious about whether or not they are "doing this right." They want to verify that every discussion is appropriate in terms of the board's newly defined job. After continual practice, they automatically know whether discussions are appropriate. At this point boards start to ask new and more searching questions, such as whether their tools for evaluating their total governance performance are as effective as they could be.

Boards that have come this far down the Policy Governance road seem confident enough to persevere despite not knowing how to do it all. To move themselves forward, they have generated their own processes and tools, including governance action plans, a neutral coach, chair monitoring reports, perpetual agendas, policy-linked agendas, refresher training events, skill-building sessions in meeting management, group dynamics exercises, and strategies to ensure that incoming board members understand and become advocates of the board's Policy Governance process.

Certain Things Help

Board discipline is enhanced by many factors, including the following:

- Self-evaluation and other means of self-monitoring
- Board and CEO discipline

- An active board chair
- Board member champions
- CEO and staff support
- Role clarity
- A coach
- A trustful and cooperative board-CEO relationship
- Board training and skill building
- Education of owners about Policy Governance
- Thorough orientation and training of new board members
- A board that fully embraces and owns Policy Governance

Stick to the Principles

It is quite clear from the experiences of the eleven boards that maintaining discipline derives from consistently adhering to Policy Governance principles. Indeed, not following the model reduces enthusiasm. Boards that see results from using the model recognize this.

The Road Is Not Always Smooth

People can get discouraged during long processes of developing Ends, linking with owners, or hammering out Executive Limitations. Sometimes boards are influenced by a skeptical member or stray into inappropriate discussions when the public seems to demand it. Boards are made up of human beings. Human beings err, but they also have the capacity to realign on a path toward fulfilling the board's role in the organization. The principles of Policy Governance provide that path.

Use It or Lose It

Principles, structures, tools, and mechanisms are only helpful and effective when people use them correctly. Owning Policy Governance—that is, trusting it and being fully committed to it—is the fundamental difference between success and struggle, enthusiasm and despair. Without ownership of both the principles and the process, boards find discipline difficult, enthusiasm diminished, and results scattered.

An analogy may best illustrate this point. A Policy Governance board that does not own Policy Governance is like a team that is playing soccer but that is not committed to following the rules of the game. The team intent is still to move the ball down the field into the opponent's goal. However, all the team members have not committed to the same strategy. Some are playing soccer correctly. Others keep turning it into an American football game; they insist on picking the ball up and moving into formation. Still others are not quite sure what they want to do. The team is more likely to score if everyone understands the rules, commits to playing by the same rules, handles the ball skillfully, and becomes a team player intent on the team's pursuit. As with any winning ball team, success comes with years of skill building and practice, practice, practice. What keeps the team going despite frustration, distractions, and slumps is the possibility of success.

○ Taking Action: Strategies for Where You Are Now

Once your board has fully implemented Policy Governance, it is still important to keep looking at how well you are staying on track. Understanding where your board is will help you know what to do from here. Unlike the previous "Taking Action" sections, this one contains a series of questions. The answers should identify any areas in which you need to improve.

Is Your Board on Track?

If your board is on track, it operates according to the principles of Policy Governance, and board members feel that they are adding value to the organization. Where is your board, given the following list of indicators that a board is on track?

- Board members are enthusiastic about their work.
- Board and organizational benchmarks are being met.
- Owners, customers, and staff members relate to the board at a policy rather than an operational level.
- Board agendas and discussions are solely at the policy level.
- During crises, the board relies on Policy Governance principles.
- The board can never justify failing to use the principles of Policy Governance.

Does Your Board "Own" Policy Governance?

Are your board members relating to Policy Governance as their way of governing? Are they proud of the work they have done to create policies that apply specifically to them?

Can Your Board Effectively Measure Whether It Is on Track?

Is your board monitoring its own work in compliance with its Governance Process policies? If so, does this happen at every meeting or at other regular intervals? Is the board satisfied with the way it monitors itself? Does the board catch itself when it strays? If so, does the board self-correct, or does it allow the issue to continue?

Is Your Board Excited About Its Work?

Is everyone contributing to discussions? Is attendance at meetings high? Are people bringing their concerns and ideas to the board table, or is all the action taking place somewhere else? Do members feel they are doing big things?

Is Board Turnover a Problem?

Does your board experience board turnover as a major hiccup in its progress, or do new members contribute from the moment they start work?

Is Your Board-CEO Relationship Working?

Are the board and the CEO operating in an atmosphere of trust and cooperation? Can the CEO be confident that the board will adhere to its policies? Does the board know that the CEO is adhering to its policies?

▶ Practical Tips and Tools

Here are some tips and tools for helping your board stay on track.

Go Back to the Principles and Policies

If you sense that your board is at all off track, invite members to revisit the Policy Governance principles, and comment on how well the board is complying with them. Maybe the board could assess itself on each principle, using the following scale: on track, getting there, off track. You can do a similar exercise with the board's Governance Process policies. If the board finds it is badly off track in several areas, this may indicate that it has not been self-monitoring frequently enough or that board members still have unresolved concerns. Unresolved concerns will persist until they are dealt with, and new ones can arise as board members join. You can use the worry list exercise in Chapter Two to help resolve board members' concerns. If training and orienting new board members is an issue, review this chapter to see how other boards bring new people up to speed.

Review Your Monitoring Process

If your board is having trouble monitoring its use of Policy Governance, a review of this chapter will show you how some other boards are tackling the issue. Examples of their methods include chair monitoring reports, board meeting monitoring reports, and regular reviews of Governance Process policies.

If your board does not catch itself when it strays, you are probably not asking the right questions. Make sure that your monitoring questions really use your Governance Process policies as the criteria.

If the board is taking no self-correcting action when monitoring reveals an issue, it could be that you are being too nice to yourselves and to each other! Try looking at what the inaction has cost in terms of effectiveness, board time, and results. Once everyone sees the cost, the motivation to get on track will almost certainly return.

Use Tools to Maintain Discipline, Enthusiasm, and Focus

Here are tools boards have used to keep themselves disciplined, enthusiastic, and on track:

• *Perpetual agenda.* This agenda can be used as a basic template for planning every meeting. It helps the board chair keep the discussions at a policy level. See Exhibit 8.1 for an example.

• *Agendas that encourage preparation.* Exhibit 8.2 shows an agenda that encourages board members to do work in advance of meetings. This ensures full and relevant policy discussions.

• *Annual calendar.* An annual calendar is another great tool for keeping a board on track and giving board members the overall picture of their work. See Exhibit 8.3 for an example.

• *Board Governing Style tracking form.* To create a policy tracking form, list each criterion from the board's Governing Style policy on the left side of a page. Allow space to the right of each criterion for examples of compliance or noncompliance. During the board meeting, an appointed monitor will record examples of how the board does or does not satisfy each criterion. At the end of the meeting, the monitor will report the results back to the board.

- *Board self-assessment.* The tool shown in Exhibit 8.4 can help the board evaluate itself and identify ways to improve its current performance. Before the meeting, circulate the questions. Depending on board size, split the board into groups of at least three people to discuss each question. Then bring the groups back together and share your findings. From this discussion, you should be able to say what needs to be done, prioritize those items, and schedule the actions into your board calendar. Exhibit 8.5 gives an example of the kinds of things your board might come up with after it has been through this process. At the end of the meeting, evaluate the tool itself and, if needed, adapt it to serve you better in your next self-assessment.

- *Board binders.* Exhibits 8.6 and 8.7 give examples of ways in which boards catalogue material to keep themselves organized and on track. The material in the Ends development binder (Exhibit 8.7) could be a section in the Board Notebook shown in Exhibit 8.6 or kept in a separate binder.

- *Board-staff exercise.* With this exercise, both the board and the staff can increase clarity and understanding of board and staff roles and board-staff relations under Policy Governance. At a retreat or a joint meeting, put the board in one group and the staff in another. Ask each group to respond to the following questions: What in the model works for you? What does not work for you? Then have both groups come back together and discuss the responses. Note how the different responses correspond to the groupings. Discuss any issues that arise from the different points of view (board and staff) and how they can be resolved in ways that are consistent with Policy Governance.

- *Displays.* Try printing definitions of Ends policies on the inside cover of the board package for every meeting, as well as on the sidebar of fax cover sheets sent to board members. You could also, for example, post Policy Governance principles on the boardroom walls.

- *Adaptation of other boards' useful ideas.* Other Policy Governance boards will already have tackled some of the issues your board is facing. Why not adapt some of their ideas? For example, see Exhibit 7.3, which gives a meeting monitoring form developed by the City of Bryan, Texas, and Exhibit 8.8, which gives Parkland Health District's policies on board education.

- *Separation of cause and effect.* Enthusiasm, sparked by the vision of a possibility, can be fleeting. It is human nature to doubt the wisdom of theory and process once the road gets bumpy. During rough moments, board members may blame any discontent on Policy Governance. The board can gain clarity about what it needs to do next by analyzing its problems. Have the board members consider these questions: Which problems have existed all along? Which would have arisen with or without Policy Governance? Which ones actually arise from the

EXHIBIT 8.2. AGENDA FOR PREPARATION.

Board of Directors Meeting
June 23, 1997
6:30–8:30 P.M.
Town Hall Room 100

Agenda

Time	Topic	Board Action	Leader
6:15–6:30	A. Gather and settle		
6:30–6:40	1. Preliminaries		
	Focus	Approve	John
	Agenda	Approve	John
	5/26/97 minutes	Approve	Ellen
6:40–7:50	2. Ends		Gary
	a. Policy development		
	Draft Ends policy	Edit for clarity	
	b. Process development		
	Communication with owners	Discuss	
7:50–8:00	3. Committee briefing		
	Draft plan for communication with owners	Assign and brief	Ellen
8:00–8:10	4. Next steps and board calendar	Discuss and agree	Ellen
8:10–8:15	5. Miscellaneous		
	Joint meeting with Commons Board	Schedule	Ellen

EXHIBIT 8.2. AGENDA FOR PREPARATION (*continued*).

Time	Topic	Board Action	Leader
8:15–8:30	6. Closings		
	Review decisions	Edit and agree	Anne
	Debrief and evaluate	Comment	John
	Adjourn meeting	Approve	Ellen
8:30	B. Leave		

Notes:

#2 Ends

Objectives: Continue discussion from last meeting. Discuss any preliminary input from non–board members, edit draft for clarity, and further discuss plans for getting feedback from owners.

Preparation:

- Review the Ends policy values discussion from the April meeting (Board Notebook, chap. 7, p. 71).
- Review the draft Ends policy (Policy Notebook, chap. 1, p. 9).
- Does the draft Ends policy express the board's stated values to the extent that the board can accept any reasonable interpretation?
- Review the board's policy on Communication with Owners (Policy Notebook, chap. 4, p. 6).
- Do the values expressed in the Communication with Owners policy sufficiently guide the board's dialogue with owners about Ends?

#3 Committee briefing

Objective: Create and brief a committee to draft a plan to have a dialogue with owners.

Preparation: Having reviewed the board's policy on Communication with Owners for the last item, think about any further parameters to guide the committee in drafting the plan for having a dialogue with owners, including the format of the report back to the board.

#4 Next steps and board calendar

Objective (carried over from the last meeting): Prioritize the board's activities for the rest of the year.

Preparation: Review 1997 board calendar information included in last month's board packet (Board Notebook, chap. 1, p. 9) and list your priorities for the remaining items for this year.

EXHIBIT 8.3. BOARD ANNUAL CALENDAR.

Date	Meeting Length	Category	Item	Action
January 27	3 hours	Policy	Executive Limitations (all)	Review
		Policy	Ends	Prepare for discussion
		Board	New members	Welcome
February 24	3 hours	Policy	Owners' input to Ends work	Determine
		Policy	Appointed board positions	Identify values, assign tasks
		Board	1997 annual calendar	Discuss and decide
		Board	Retreat location	Decide
		Board	Retreat process	Identify values, assign tasks
March 24	3 hours	Policy	Board-CEO Relations (all)	Review
		Policy	Ends	Discuss
		Policy	Appointed board positions	Discuss and decide
		Board	Retreat process	Decide
		Monitoring	Financial condition	Review
April 6 (Retreat)	4 hours	Policy	Ends	Discuss
		Board	Training conference	Discuss, decide, and schedule
May 26	2 hours	Policy	Ends	Discuss
June 23	2 hours	Policy	Ends	Review
		Policy	Communication with owners	Identify values, assign tasks
		Board	Annual calendar	Review and update
		Board	Joint meeting with Commons Board	Schedule
		Monitoring	Financial condition	Review
		Monitoring	Emergency management succession	Review
		Monitoring	Treatment of customers	Review

EXHIBIT 8.3. BOARD ANNUAL CALENDAR (*continued*).

Date	Meeting Length	Category	Item	Action
July 28	2 hours	Policy	Communication with owners	Discuss and decide
		Policy	CEO compensation package	Identify values, assign tasks
		Policy	Board member recruitment/election	Review
		Board	Owners' newsletter	Outline
		Monitoring	CPA's audit	Review and update
		Monitoring	Budgeting and financial planning	Review
August 25	2 hours	Policy	CEO compensation package	Discuss and decide
		Board	Focus groups with owners	Identify values, assign tasks
		Board	Meetings with other boards	Discuss
		Monitoring	General executive constraint	Identify values, assign tasks
		Monitoring	Treatment of staff	Review
		Monitoring	Asset protection	Review
September 22	2 hours	Monitoring	General executive constraint	Discuss and decide
		Board	Focus groups with owners	Discuss and decide
		Monitoring	Compensation and benefits	Review
		Monitoring	Communication and counsel	Review
		Monitoring	Financial condition	Review
October 27	2 hours	Board	Feedback from focus groups	Assess
		Policy	Ends	Review and revise
		Policy	New board member training	Review
November 17	2 hours	Policy	Board process (all)	Review
		Policy	Measures for monitoring	Identify values, assign tasks
December 15	2 hours	Policy	Measures for monitoring	Discuss and decide
		Board	Year-end evaluation	Discuss and decide
		Monitoring	Financial condition	Review

EXHIBIT 8.4. A BOARD'S SELF-ASSESSMENT.

The board's discussion should center on (1) its products, (2) the outcome of its work and its process, or (3) its conduct and behavior. The board should compare its actions with what it said it was going to do.

Linkage with the Owners

Think of the owners on whose behalf the board is acting.

- Has the board identified the owners?
- Who are the owners?
- Has the board stated how it will be a link or a bridge with the owners?
- What activities or methods have worked?
- Have the Ends of the organization been shaped by the owners?
- What would the owners say about the linkage?

Policy Development

Think of the policies the board has developed in the past year in the areas of Ends, Governance Process, Board-CEO Relationship, and Executive Limitations.

- Is the board content with what it has produced in these areas?
- Are there areas for improvement?
- How did the board approach policymaking?
- Were the right people involved in policymaking?
- Were the board's information needs met for policymaking?
- What would the board like to do differently?

Monitoring Performance

- Has the board set performance standards?
- Has the board established a monitoring system for determining performance?
- Does the monitoring system satisfy the board's need to be accountable?

Board Process

Think of a major issue before the board over the past year.

- What was the issue?
- How did the board determine if this was the board's issue (rather than the CEO's)?
- How did the board approach and discuss the issue?
- Did the board make a decision?
- If so, was it a policy decision?

EXHIBIT 8.4. A BOARD'S SELF-ASSESSMENT (*continued*).

Board Process (*continued*)

Refer to the board's written policies.

- What part of the policies related to the issue or to the board's behavior in dealing with this issue? Write down the policy or policies that seem to apply.
- In its activity at the meeting(s) and in the actions it took, did the board live up to its own standards as expressed in its policies?
- How did it show or not show this?

Next Steps

- Identify areas for improvement or further work.
- Validate the list of issues or tasks.
- Prioritize the tasks.
- Build a board agenda based on the work to be done.

Source: Queen's Regional Health Board, Prince Edward Island, Canada.

implementation of Policy Governance? Finally, how can Policy Governance help solve these problems?

- *Discussion of the future.* Try adopting the Vermont Land Trust's idea of rainbow sheets, wherein notepaper of different colors represents each possible Ends focus the board could take. Such a technique is certain to stimulate a lively discussion. Maintaining enthusiasm can be as simple as continuing to talk about what really matters to the board—the fulfillment of its vision. Keep Ends visible and alive everywhere: in the hallway, in newsletters, in presentations, in conversations with staff members, in communications with owners, and on your agenda.

EXHIBIT 8.5. SAMPLE SELF-ASSESSMENT REPORT.

On April 15, 1996, the board conducted a self-assessment that focused on the work of the board, specifically on board process and the outcome of the board's work. The findings of the board are summarized under four headings below. From the self-assessment, board members identified areas for improvement or further work. The board has yet to complete the next steps, which are to validate the list of issues or tasks, prioritize the tasks, and build a board agenda based on the work to be done.

Linkage with the Owners

Who the owners are: The board has identified the owners as the people of this province and the people of this district. The board recognizes itself as being open to the owners. The board believes that the owners see the board's job as complex but that the board is there for the good of the community. The owners see the board as trying to do a good job.

Successful methods of linking with the owners:

- Discovery meetings
- Meetings with other representatives of owners (for example, the city council and the Chamber of Commerce)
- Newsletter to the community
- Annual meeting with displays of services provided
- Community needs assessment project
- Community visioning process

Ideas for improvement:

- Increase follow-up with groups after meetings (for example, considering how well the board has responded to concerns).
- Hold open community meetings in other communities.
- Have individual board members link with local groups (for example, by attending meetings of service clubs).
- Continue the discovery meeting format with other groups (for example, school boards, the business community, families, students, and physicians).

Owners' role in shaping Ends: The Ends to this point have had much involvement from the owners, and the board wants to continue this. There is a need to engage the owners in helping make choices about "what good for which people" in the context of saying, "If we do this, we cannot do that."

EXHIBIT 8.5. SAMPLE SELF-ASSESSMENT REPORT (*continued*).

Policy Development

The board does not feel a strong ownership around the policies it is using. Board members do not feel fully familiar with all the policies, although they know they can turn to policies for guidance in times of uncertainty.

Some policies are incomplete. That is, there are blanks where the board plans to fill in specific dollar amounts. Also, the layout and numbering of the policies is too complicated for regular use. The board would like to test the workability of the policies by taking an issue or a scenario and working it through using the policies.

The board is continuing to develop Ends policies, including bringing more specificity to the Ends and prioritizing them. The board would like to understand how Ends will drive the organization and how the Ends will play out.

The information needs of the board in policy development were largely met.

Monitoring Performance

The board wants to set more specific performance standards in the policies it has developed.

The board will then need to hold itself accountable for ensuring that the policies are monitored. This means holding the CEO accountable for providing monitoring information.

Board Process

The board would like to take an issue and work it through to test the board process further.

The board sees a need to be more informed through more frequent and timely updates on relevant issues. Having a draft of the newsletter prior to publication would help board members respond to questions in the community. The board could develop standard responses to community members for situations in which board members are caught off guard and do not have all the information.

Other Outstanding Issues

The board needs to have a plan for orienting new members.

Source: Queen's Regional Health Board, Prince Edward Island, Canada.

EXHIBIT 8.6.
SAMPLE BINDER CONTENTS FOR BOARD ORGANIZATION.

All of the board's work is organized in two notebooks:

A. Policy Notebook

1. Articles of incorporation
2. Bylaws
3. Ends policies
4. Executive Limitations policies
5. Board-Staff Relations policies
6. Governance Process policies

(Because board minutes are part of the organization's legal documents, you may wish to include them in this Policy Notebook. That way, all documents pertaining to the board's legal obligations will be in one place.)

B. Board Notebook

1. *Organizational tools:* Board meeting dates, board directory, annual board agenda calendar and plan, committees, and membership
2. *Records of meetings:* Agenda cover letters, agendas, and meeting minutes
3. *Committee reports and minutes*
4. *Information on linkage with the owners:* Board strategy for linking with owners and any information, letters, reports, and so forth with regard to this topic
5. *CEO performance monitoring:* Monitoring reports as determined by Ends and Executive Limitations policies
6. *Board performance monitoring:* Board self-evaluation worksheets and, if used, chair monitoring reports
7. *Incidental information:* Any miscellaneous information provided to connect board members with the organization
8. *Resource material:* Training material or other resource material relevant to assisting the board with its job

---

EXHIBIT 8.7.
SAMPLE BINDER CONTENTS FOR INFORMING ENDS WORK.

---

1. *Ends development history:* Development stages of the board's Ends policies showing how they have changed over time
2. *The Policy Governance approach:* Articles that provide some insight into the Policy Governance approach (for example, a *Board Leadership* article on ownership issues)
3. *Environmental scanning information:* Information on what is happening in the organization's wider environment, such as demographics, other organizations' activities, and government plans
4. *Internal information:* Information and materials to provide background on the current business of the organization

EXHIBIT 8.8. SAMPLE BOARD EDUCATION POLICY.

Policy Name: Board Education   Date Approved: July 12, 1995
Policy Type: Governance Process   Review Date: Annually in March

The board recognizes that continual updating of skills and awareness of new issues are vital to a member's contribution to the board. Therefore, it is expected that

1. New board members shall receive a complete orientation to ensure familiarity with the health care system and issues, district structure and issues, and the process of governance. This orientation shall include but shall not be limited to the following:

   - An orientation to the district, the principles of governance, the board's policies, and major issues.
   - Attendance at a Policy Governance workshop.

2. Each board member shall complete a self-appraisal annually and identify specific areas in which he or she requires additional knowledge related to governance and health care system issues. Additional knowledge may be gleaned from attendance at appropriate seminars or conferences, selected reading, audio- or videotapes, or other programs of self-study.

3. Time shall be allotted at each regular monthly board meeting for board education purposes.

4. The board will subscribe to the governance coaching process for the June 1, 1997, to May 31, 1999, period and will review the coaching report at each regular board meeting.

Source: Parkland Health District.

CHAPTER NINE

BRINGING IT ALL TOGETHER

☐ The Challenge

In previous chapters we have looked at particular aspects of the Policy Governance model and the implementation process through the eyes of the organizations applying it. In this final chapter we draw all the learnings together to assess the total experience of Policy Governance implementation and the implications for the future development of the model. With these aims in mind, here are the particular questions we examine:

- Are boards successfully implementing Policy Governance?
- Which factors most strongly influence effective implementation?
- Can boards adapt the model successfully?
- What are the implications of experience for the future?

We conclude that Policy Governance is not being practiced perfectly anywhere. We also conclude that there is no board practicing any aspect of Policy Governance that is not making gains.

■ The Experience

Are Boards Successfully Implementing Policy Governance?

Before looking at the success of the boards we have studied, it is important to re-state that they were deliberately chosen to reflect different stages of progress. This is because, in our overall experience, the implementation of Policy Governance ranges from the immensely successful to the highly problematic. Our intention is to learn from experience, and that requires a willingness to deal with the real-ity of that experience. To examine how successful boards have or have not been with Policy Governance, we will consider two questions:

- Can boards put the structures and disciplines of Policy Governance in place?
- Is Policy Governance delivering on its promises, particularly its most funda-mental promise—organizations more powerfully fulfilling their missions?

Can Boards Put the Structures and Disciplines of Policy Governance in Place? Under Policy Governance the board's core tasks are to create policies, to ensure performance according to those policies, to evaluate itself, and to link with owners.

Creating Policies. The main structure of Policy Governance is the policy structure. Every organization we studied has created Executive Limitations. They have also agreed on policies in the Board-Staff Relationship and Governance Process cat-egories. This is encouraging and indicates that although many have called the process arduous, they have also found it feasible. Such progress is a tribute to these boards' desire for excellence, given that this work has had to take place along-side "normal business."

Ends policies are the most problematic to create. Eight boards have created fairly comprehensive Ends policies, but three have not. Not surprisingly, there seems to be a strong correlation between resolving the issue of ownership and suc-cessfully developing Ends. Of the three organizations that have reported major outstanding issues with ownership, none has developed a reasonably full set of Ends policies. In one case, the best Ends definition achieved to date is so vague as to allow for many different interpretations and for continued confusion among the owners, the customers, and the member bases. This organization's effort to de-velop Ends has been enriching and partly successful but considerably hampered by the amount of time it consumes. In another organization, the ownership issue produced an extremely heated debate and a major breakthrough. However, the subject is so sensitive that it is now being avoided. Work on Ends came to a halt before priorities could be clarified. In the last case, the ownership issue has not been tackled at all, and the Ends development process has bogged down.

It is undoubtedly positive that eight boards have developed a reasonably comprehensive set of Ends policies. Designing the process, finding the time to go through the process, and making the value choices involved are tall orders. Three organizations find the "at what cost" element of Ends particularly challenging. Every organization recognizes that, as John Carver suggests, work on Ends policies never ends. See Chapter Five for more on Ends development.

Monitoring Policies. Creating policies means having major pieces of the Policy Governance framework in place, but the power of that framework cannot be fully realized unless the board uses the policies and regularly monitors them.

- *Executive Limitations.* Eight of our eleven boards monitor these policies, but three have had mixed experiences. One is still formalizing its monitoring of Executive Limitations. Another consistently monitors only its financial policies. The third board is doing monitoring, but the chair questions whether members are really taking the time to read or understand the reports or compare them with policy.
- *Ends.* As with Executive Limitations, monitoring is essential for the full realization of the power of Ends. Two organizations have Ends monitoring fully in place, two have made significant progress, and four are just starting. In the other three cases, Ends development is not yet at a stage where monitoring can begin.
- *CEO evaluation.* Another crucial Policy Governance discipline is regular evaluation of the CEO's performance (in addition to the receipt of monitoring reports) against the board's Ends and Executive Limitations policies. Five organizations have at least an annual CEO evaluation process. In another four cases we have no information. The remaining two organizations indicate that a regular CEO evaluation process is under development.

See Chapter Seven for more on monitoring.

Evaluating Board Discipline. Seven of the eleven boards conduct self-evaluations in some form at every meeting, one board is actively struggling with the issue, two have nothing formal in place, and on one we have no information. Parkland Health District provides an example of an extremely thorough process. Weaver Street Market and the Colorado Association of School Boards have at least an annual assessment, as well as a self-evaluation process for each meeting. See Chapters Seven and Eight for more on board self-evaluation.

Linking with Owners. Seven of the eleven organizations report that they have processes in place for linking with their ownership. Among the seven boards there are many examples of impressive and extensive work in this area. One organization is actively developing plans to link with its owners. The remaining three organizations appear to have nothing under way yet. See Chapter Six for more on linking with owners.

Summary. The answer to the question "Can boards put the disciplines and structures of Policy Governance in place?" appears to be a pretty strong yes. Of the eleven boards studied, all have succeeded in creating Executive Limitations policies, which in most cases are being regularly monitored. Eight boards have reasonably comprehensive sets of Ends policies. In half of the cases these are being monitored regularly, and in the other half of the cases the boards intend to monitor the policies. At least five (and probably more) formally evaluate their CEOs at least annually. Seven boards conduct formal self-evaluation at every meeting to keep themselves on the Policy Governance track. Eight boards are creating formal linkages with their ownerships.

Significantly, there is a tendency for boards that are having difficulty in one area of Policy Governance implementation to have trouble in all areas. Conversely, boards that are succeeding in one area are likely to be succeeding in the other areas.

Even the boards that have fallen completely off the Policy Governance track still point to lasting benefits from their journey. One of the boards reports that although it has the structures in place, it is not operating them. That board has been unable to sustain the discipline required by the Policy Governance model. Yet the board has not given up on pursuing Policy Governance. Another board has had considerable problems with implementation, but its representative concludes, "Despite our own frustrations with the model (and it is less the fault of the model than of ourselves), I still see it as a viable way of managing governance. It can only benefit governance in the not-for-profit sector."

Is Policy Governance Delivering on Its Promises? To what extent are boards able to realize the promise of Policy Governance? Without major research, which we hope will one day be forthcoming, this question cannot be answered with statistics. Therefore, our response is inevitably subjective. Nevertheless, because it is probably the most important question asked in this book, we believe it is worth examining on the basis of the experiential evidence we have.

Initially, Policy Governance's appeal can be as simple as thinking, "There has to be something better than this." But as we have seen throughout this book, particularly in Chapters One and Two, the more possibilities a board sees in Policy Governance, the better the chance is that it will take hold. This positive rather than negative frame of reference is perhaps best expressed by the board of the

Southern Ontario Library Service. In a review of its pre–Policy Governance structure, it notes that "interest in Carver is not a criticism of the current structure." It
then describes the possibility that it sees the model as offering in terms of the organization's future and its links with the community.

The promises that attract a board to Policy Governance fall into four
categories:

- Clear distinction between board and CEO roles
- Efficient governance process
- Greater accountability to owners
- Fulfillment of the board's mission

Clear Roles. In almost every case, the promise of clearer roles and a better relationship with the CEO has clearly been realized. The Southern Ontario Library
Service reports that "board and staff roles are very clear, which removes many im-
pediments to decisive action." Before the introduction of Policy Governance,
the board of one organization had a difficult relationship with its CEO. Now a
representative of that board comments, "With discipline and constancy of purpose, the board was able to completely reverse any unfavorable perceptions about
the board, build unprecedented trust with the CEO, completely own its own work
and processes, and, through the development of policy and its own example, truly
provide powerful leadership to the organization."

It is not just board members but also CEOs who feel pleased about the clarity of roles. The same representative observes the CEO "knowing what information to provide to the board to what degree. Also, clearly knowing his role and
what criteria were set by the board, he experienced greater freedom and confidence in doing his job. Another gain was working as a partner with the board in
providing the organization with effective leadership." For the San Francisco AIDS
Foundation, Policy Governance has been "a gain for the CEO." It has brought
"clarity, documentation of what the board [members] said, how their words were
interpreted, not a lot of ambiguity. [Policy Governance] opens dialogue up. Both
staff and board acknowledge that it has given people a role to follow." Perhaps the
most telling quotation of all about the CEO's perspective comes from the CEO
of the Colorado Association of School Boards: "I think Carver underplays that
this is an equal partnership between board and staff. Carver makes it sound more
hierarchical than it really is. This is a marriage."

One of the biggest surprises for the authors of this book has certainly been
that boards report few disagreements with CEOs about the "reasonable interpretation" of their policies. Of the eleven boards, only two have had issues, which
have been resolved without a problem.

In fact, the promise of clearer roles is often delivered at a level that goes well beyond the board and the CEO. For the City of Bryan, Texas, "This is a model that captures the best of everyone's abilities and translates them into actions that work. Owners participate, board members govern, and staffs implement." The Law Society of Upper Canada believes that its most significant gain has been identifying the public as its moral owners and realizing that it is not a professional association. "While painful to discuss, this has been the result of the model's ability to clarify roles."

Efficient Governance Process. A more mixed but still positive picture emerges when it comes to the promise of improving governance processes. There is no doubt that boards wish for a more effective process and that the group discipline required by Policy Governance represents a major challenge to many boards.

• *Better discussions.* Since introducing Policy Governance, the Law Society of Upper Canada reports that "council agendas have improved" and that the focus has moved "away from committee reports." The Southern Ontario Library Service reports, "For the first time, the board was having freewheeling discussions with opposing ideas and thoughtful responses." That board has seen its discussions improve in another way: "The model also facilitates the participation of people of diverse cultures and styles. Whereas the traditional model of governance relies on strict parliamentary style, Policy Governance encourages open discussion and more consensual decision making." The Colorado Association of School Boards cites "more focused board meetings" as one of its biggest gains from Policy Governance. The Vermont Land Trust notes that conversations are of a "much higher quality, more exciting. For years, the questions about the budget never got more knowledgeable. Now there is a context for them. . . . This goes to the heart of fiduciary duty."

• *Improved budget processes.* The Early Childhood Community Development Centre makes a similar point about the board's budget process: "It was a challenge creating a budget that responded to the board's words. However, [it was] not impossible. In fact, in the end it proved more informative about what the board really cares about." The YMCA-YWCA of London reports that the "budget process is definitely less complex, less detailed, and less time-consuming."

• *Reduction in board work.* Another possibility organizations see in Policy Governance is that they will be able to manage more with less. For the City of Bryan, "Without a framework such as Policy Governance, there is just too much to keep everyone's arms around." Parkland Health District agrees that "the model allows board members to cope with the blizzard of information that threatens to bury many boards. They know exactly the reason for each piece of information they receive; it is . . . there to help them make a decision, to monitor, or [it is] nice to know. The latter category they can choose to ignore if they wish." The Vermont Land Trust's board adopted Policy Governance after a doubling in the number of projects that it had obliged itself to approve directly. With Policy Governance in place, the board can confidently delegate this work to the staff.

• *Reduction in number of committees.* Most of the organizations we studied have reduced the number of board committees and have prevented any remaining committees from usurping the board's role.

• *Improved crisis management.* Some organizations see Policy Governance as helping them to stave off or manage crises. Indeed, the Southern Ontario Library Service has survived a 37 percent budget cut and reports, "The model has proven effective in difficult times." The Vermont Land Trust has successfully used Policy Governance to manage a crisis provoked by a donation of several million dollars. Two of the eleven organizations did not share this success; they were overtaken by crises shortly after deciding to introduce Policy Governance. In both these cases, the organizations were in the very early stages of implementing the model, so it would be a mistake to say that Policy Governance failed them.

• *Gains in discipline and unity.* Before introducing Policy Governance Weaver Street Market and the Early Childhood Community Development Centre saw the possibility of gains in board discipline and unity; they and the majority of organizations we have studied have since realized that promise. Parkland Health District comments that the "positive side effect of having to discuss and agree on a set of values proclaimed in policy is team building among board members."

Greater Accountability. Boards also see Policy Governance as enabling them to be accountable in a more meaningful way. The CEO of the Colorado Association of School Boards clearly addresses the difference that Policy Governance makes for CEOs: "It isn't possible any longer for me to fail to deal with things the board has said are important—and I know what the board has said. Strategic plans and goals didn't hold me accountable like the policies do. This adds a dimension of accountability that wasn't there before, and I like it." In terms of his accountability to the council, the Bryan city manager says, "The most exciting thing about Policy Governance is that for the first time [the] staff is truly responsible for implementing council policy." He adds that this is also the most challenging thing about the model! The CEO of the Early Childhood Community Development Centre reports, "From the executive director's perspective, the development of the monthly monitoring reports on scheduled policies has reinforced the power of Policy Governance in assuring accountability for the organization."

It is not only the CEO who becomes more accountable under Policy Governance; it is also the board as it engages in linking with owners. The City of Bryan observes that the "Citizens of Bryan could be engaged in . . . thinking about the future of the community in concert with the council. In the final analysis, it was this promise of reconnecting with the citizens and the council that proved to be the most alluring."

The clearest evidence that Policy Governance really can increase accountability lies earlier in this chapter, where we have reviewed the extent to which boards are both monitoring their policies and linking with their owners.

Fulfillment of Mission. Every board hopes that by adopting Policy Governance it will be moving closer to achieving its mission. What evidence is there that Policy Governance will enable it to do so? Following are reports from some of the organizations we studied that indicate their progress.

For the Southern Ontario Library Service, Policy Governance has provided an enhanced ability to pursue and defend its mission. As a result of its Ends process, it reports that it "is well prepared to deal with upcoming issues. For example, our principal funder embarked on a study of the outcomes that each of the several related organizations ought to be achieving. The board's work on Ends provided an excellent foundation that enabled us to be proactive in providing input." The board cites its clarity of purpose as enabling more vigorous pursuit of joint initiatives and quicker responses to new opportunities and threats. The chair gives an example: "The future of free access to library service in Ontario was under threat. We had a new chair and a new CEO. . . . And [in] implementing and working with the Carver model, we dealt with all these issues and had considerable success. I think there is a relationship between these two [events]. We felt like we were doing important things. We were!"

For Weaver Street Market, Policy Governance has enabled the board not only to clarify its goals but also to spend more time focusing on their accomplishment. Still in the early stages of Ends development, the board's chair reports, "Even if the Ends statements are not completely refined, they paint a possible future that necessarily provides some direction. Such knowledge gives the board a clearer view on everything that it currently deals with. It is truly freeing to move beyond the details of what is happening inside the organization to see that the organization can indeed define, strive for, and achieve something bigger in the world."

The City of Bryan reports significant progress in establishing a shared vision with its owners, and it is producing results. "The council is able to articulate [its] vision for the community more clearly than ever before. This future focus has spilled over into the community. Residents are feeling better about Bryan than ever before. [The] staff is coming to see that the model provides the framework for the kind of successful community that each of them has devoted their career to help create." Similarly, the San Francisco AIDS Foundation board members decided to implement Policy Governance "understanding that their basic role was to provide a vision. This model has allowed the board to establish a shared vision.

[It] has made it very easy to grasp some of the issues. Staff [members] have embraced and implemented it."

Parkland Health District has also had success. "The biggest gain experienced by the board [members] from their use of Policy Governance is the clarity of direction that it provides. They have gradually moved their focus from a preoccupation with means, and in particular finances, to much more concern about the results from the district's efforts on health for the ownership."

The Early Childhood Community Development Centre wanted a model that would make "the organization accountable to the constituency it served and allow for the board to attend to its most critical need—that is, creating a clear vision and direction for the organization." A board member describes the impact of adopting Policy Governance in this way: "We want the Early Childhood [Community] Development Centre to be the best place it can be. To indulge in operations narrows the board's focus and doesn't allow the organization to move forward. To be on the leading edge in terms of what services the organization offers can only be achieved through the board's focusing on the Ends of the organization. From the board perspective, the greatest gain has been the freedom to focus on the vision and look forward to the future instead of approving the past."

According to the Vermont Land Trust, the Ends discussion has produced several significant shifts in organizational focus, and "It is very interesting to go back and look at our Strategic Plan [from] the early 1990s. It is all about programs. Now the conversation is about outcomes."

Summary. It is clear that Policy Governance is very much a work in progress for all the boards we have studied. Given this and the fact that Policy Governance is a relatively new approach, it will likely be several more years before one can see (and therefore measure) tangible results in terms of fulfilled missions; however, it also seems that the majority of those we have studied feel that Policy Governance is delivering much of the promise that they saw when they decided to implement it. It is possible that boards bring extra vigor to aspects of the model that most appeal to them and that they get commensurate results.

Organizations that have realized only a few of the promises of Policy Governance seem to have no quarrel with the model itself, only with the ease of its implementation. In the next section we will briefly examine the factors that most strongly influence boards' ability to implement Policy Governance.

Which Factors Most Strongly Influence Effective Implementation?

Throughout this book you have read about many factors that influence the successful implementation of Policy Governance. We propose that these factors fall into three groups:

- Seeing a possibility
- Being committed
- Having a structure

Seeing a Possibility. If board members do not hear something about Policy Governance that they feel could make a powerful difference for their organization, they will not even start to look at it. It doesn't seem to matter where they hear it or from whom; it only matters that they become interested and begin learning about the model. All the boards we studied saw Policy Governance as offering a possibility. For all of them that possibility still exists.

One contributor expresses the possibility this way: "Policy Governance provides a framework for understanding and expressing the organization's unique role in the community and its relationship with stakeholders. It facilitates big-picture thinking. . . . A board must believe that this, and not day-to-day administration, is its real reason for existing."

Being Committed. Unfortunately, seeing the possibility is not enough. The board, and we mean the whole board, must be committed to the model.

Voting to adopt Policy Governance indicates commitment but is not conclusive evidence. The board must want to learn about the principles of the model, to understand it thoroughly. Board members should be willing to speak up, ask questions, read, discuss the ideas, and talk to others about it. They also need the ability, desire, and time to think about it.

Oddly, Policy Governance is very simple but can take a while to grasp. We know many intelligent people who have understood the model right away and many other equally intelligent people for whom the light did not go on until much later. The language or the jargon of the model (particularly the negative framing of Executive Limitations) is sometimes identified as a potential barrier, but it does not seem to be a very serious one, as only two of our eleven organizations have made any reference to it.

It is clear that commitment needs an agent. Ideally (but not necessarily) this agent is the chair. It is also clear that the CEO must support the model. Every organization we have studied has had that support. Although one started with a less-than-happy relationship with its CEO, there was an obvious atmosphere of trust in almost all cases.

This matter of trust could influence boards' ability to commit to Policy Governance. Many of the initial concerns that the model provokes are about power and control. We feel that Policy Governance gives boards far more real power and control than traditional governance practice and that the issue of trust should therefore be irrelevant. However, we recognize that a board may need a level of trust to get to the point of believing us!

Having a Structure. The third vital component of successful implementation is undoubtedly structure. Excitement about the possibility will carry you so far, and commitment will take you even further, but without structure it all starts to fall apart. If boards do not actually live their policies, use them fully at each meeting, and implement them in relation to every issue they face, old familiar ways creep back, and before you know it the policies are not worth the paper they were written on. From the staff's point of view, if board members have forgotten one policy, they have forgotten them all. For the model to work, boards must keep saying what they mean and meaning what they say. An agenda format requiring that every agenda item be linked to a policy is one of the tools that boards have found most effective in helping to make Policy Governance real. From the experiences of the organizations in this book, it is apparent that living the policies is the most important structure and discipline of all. If that is in place, then all the other disciplines—such as monitoring and evaluation—naturally follow.

Can Boards Adapt the Model Successfully?

We often hear people speaking of "model consistency," normally when they are telling someone that they are doing something wrong. This can be damaging, for boards need to and can adapt Policy Governance in ways that pose no threat to the potential benefits and that may increase their ownership of the model.

There is a tendency (and we are sure John Carver will agree) to treat some of Carver's advice as if it were written in stone. Contrary to Carver's recommendations, you can have a large board, you can have committees, the CEO can be on the board, and it can all work out beautifully. Carver's advice, and it's good advice, is simply that these things could endanger your ability to practice Policy Governance. What matters is strict adherence not to this advice but to the *principles* of Policy Governance (see "The Principles of Policy Governance Explained" for a full description). It is important to distinguish between the essential components of the model and best practice (that is, the practice most likely to achieve the desired result—good governance). As you get the hang of using the model, you will be able to recognize the dangers and avoid them.

For example, Weaver Street Market's CEO is a member of the board but "clearly exhibits complete discipline in handling both roles." Many organizations in our sample have subgroups of the board. Although these subgroups mostly prepare material for meetings of the whole board and pose no threat, other groups really do jeopardize the board's ability to speak with one voice.

What Are the Implications of Experience for the Future?

When we started thinking about this book, we proposed that practice tests theories. We also hypothesized that testing the model through examining practice could teach us things that would influence the theory. We think we have tested the model. The experiences of the eleven organizations gave us extensive and valuable information. They have told us what it's really like to work with Policy Governance. So what have we learned about the theory and the practice of Policy Governance?

Theory. We learned that the theory is fine. Policy Governance can and does work for most organizations. Its promises are being fulfilled. As the organizations themselves recognize, the breakdowns along the way are not reflections on the model. The model requires a degree of group discipline that most boards find extremely challenging. None of the organizations would claim to be total Policy Governance masters. But in the vast majority of cases, their experience belies the accusation that boards cannot rise to that challenge. The only question is, do they really want to?

Practice. We asked the organizations what implications they saw from their experience for the future development of Policy Governance across the whole field of governance.

We Want More. Four boards want more guidance in dealing with the "big policy issues" involved in Ends development and monitoring, particularly the question "At what cost?" One CEO says, "I know Ends work is not as generic as Executive Limitations, but I think boards could use help with process templates. It would be a big contribution to the field and to the success of the model."

Tailor It. One board suggests that there be policy templates for organizations in similar circumstances, such as school boards. In a similar vein, the Bryan city manager remarks, "Having to have been the pioneer on so much of the municipal component of the model has been time-consuming. It will be nice when the model proliferates to the point that we have a large group of colleagues to share successes with."

Show and Tell. One organization thinks it would be helpful to see how other organizations' policies have evolved over time, to see "examples of before and after, what led to the changes, and how those changes impacted the organization."

Discussion Skills. Several boards want to see more training resources for boards on discussion skills and group dynamics.

Ways to Keep the Sense of Connection. When boards are completing their initial policies and have not yet moved on to Ends work, they often feel or fear a sense of loss and disconnection with the organization. Boards and staffs need ideas about keeping the sense of connection without jeopardizing their hard-won clarity of roles.

Staff Can Do It Too. More than half of the contributing organizations mention the possibility (and in some cases the actuality) of extending Policy Governance principles throughout the organization. CEOs are developing Ends and Executive Limitations for their staffs. They want guidance in this endeavor.

More Emphasis on Partnership. One organization suggested that the presentation of the model (rather than its content), underplays the "equal partnership between board and staff. Carver makes it sound more hierarchical than it really is. This is a marriage."

OK, Coach. Several boards mention the need for support in the form of coaching. They want ongoing advice and feedback from someone who is really familiar with the model. Finding the right person is not always an easy task.

The interesting thing about all of these points is that they are about continuing to develop the model in practice and not, as they could have been, about rewriting the theory. These are ideas about moving on from here and taking more and more people along. John Carver has written the introduction, but maybe, in a sense, the story has only just begun.

TOOL FINDER FOR
BOARD DEVELOPMENT

When you want to . . .	Try this . . .	Agenda guides Exh. 3.4, 8.1, 8.2, pp. 54, 165, 180	Annual calendar Exh. 8.3, p. 182	Board binders Exh. 8.6, p. 188	Board orientation and education Ch. 8, p. 172	Board presentations Ch. 6, p. 131	Board self-evaluation Ch. 7, 8, pp. 145, 162	Board-staff exercise Ch. 8, p. 179	Board-to-board meetings Ch. 6, p. 131	CEO newsletter Ch. 4, p. 78	Color-coded board material Ch. 3, p. 40
Avoid traps							●				
Bring discipline to the board		●		●	●		●				●
Build ownership of Policy Governance					●	●		●	●		
Check for understanding of policies					●			●			
Collect data											
Conduct board self-assessment							●				
Decide whether to adopt Policy Governance					●				●		
Determine ownership values						●			●		
Develop group process							●				
Disseminate information						●			●		
Ease the implementation of Policy Governance		●	●	●	●		●				
Educate the ownership						●			●		
Ensure that Policy Governance fits board values											
Explore issues for Ends development						●			●		
Feel connected with the organization						●		●		●	
Find causes of board discontent							●	●			
Fulfill accountability to ownership						●			●		
Get input on Ends policies						●			●		
Hear customer needs and concerns						●			●		
Imagine the future						●			●		
Improve board performance		●	●		●		●				
Keep board work focused		●	●	●			●				
Make the transition to Policy Governance		●	●								
Organize board work		●	●	●							●
Plan board work		●	●								
Quickly develop policies											
Set priorities											
Stay the course		●	●		●		●				

When you want to . . .	Consultant or coach Ch. 8, p. 167	Demographic data Ch. 6, p. 128	Discussion of principles Ch. 2, p. 33	Displays Ch. 8, p. 179	Educating owners Ch. 6, p. 127	Ends development techniques Exh. 5.11, p. 112	Fishbowl (roundtable) Ch. 6, p. 128	Focus groups Ch. 6, p. 132	Framework for ethical decision making Exh. 6.1, p. 124	Governance action plan Ch. 3, p. 38
Avoid traps	•									
Bring discipline to the board	•		•							•
Build ownership of Policy Governance			•	•	•	•	•			•
Check for understanding of policies			•							
Collect data		•								
Conduct board self-assessment	•									
Decide whether to adopt Policy Governance	•		•							
Determine ownership values					•		•	•	•	
Develop group process	•									
Disseminate information					•	•				
Ease the implementation of Policy Governance	•									•
Educate the ownership				•	•					
Ensure that Policy Governance fits board values			•							
Explore issues for Ends development		•			•	•	•	•		
Feel connected with the organization										
Find causes of board discontent										
Fulfill accountability to ownership										
Get input on Ends policies		•			•	•	•	•		
Hear customer needs and concerns		•			•	•	•	•		
Imagine the future						•				
Improve board performance	•		•							•
Keep board work focused									•	•
Make the transition to Policy Governance	•		•							•
Organize board work										•
Plan board work										•
Quickly develop policies	•									
Set priorities		•							•	
Stay the course			•							•

When you want to . . .	Ground rules Ch. 3, p. 52	Group Process Tool Finder Resource B, p. 211	Identification of governance issues Ch. 1, p. 17	Identification of governance possibilities Ch. 2, p. 31	Impact study Ch. 6, p. 128	Meeting liturgy Ch. 3, p. 52	Meeting management Ch. 3, p. 52	Mock conversations Ch. 2, pp. 22, 33	Myers-Briggs Type Indicator Ch. 3, p. 41	Needs assessment Ch. 6, p. 128
Avoid traps										
Bring discipline to the board	•	•				•	•			
Build ownership of Policy Governance				•						
Check for understanding of policies								•		
Collect data					•					•
Conduct board self-assessment										
Decide whether to adopt Policy Governance			•	•				•		
Determine ownership values										•
Develop group process	•	•				•	•		•	
Disseminate information										
Ease the implementation of Policy Governance			•	•				•		
Educate the ownership										
Ensure that Policy Governance fits board values			•	•				•		
Explore issues for Ends development					•					•
Feel connected with the organization										
Find causes of board discontent			•							
Fulfill accountability to ownership										
Get input on Ends policies										
Hear customer needs and concerns					•					•
Imagine the future										
Improve board performance	•	•					•			
Keep board work focused		•					•			
Make the transition to Policy Governance			•	•				•		
Organize board work						•				
Plan board work						•				
Quickly develop policies										
Set priorities		•								
Stay the course										

When you want to . . .	Try this . . . Ownership Linkage Tool Finder Exh. 6.2, p. 126	Owners' exercise Ch. 6, p. 137	Owners' newsletter Ch. 6, p. 132	Parking lot Ch. 4, p. 63	Policy blitz Ch. 4, p. 63	Policy-consistent staff reports Ch. 8, p. 173	Policy review Ch. 7, p. 149	Retreat Ch. 3, p. 40	Search conference (discovery) Ch. 6, p. 133	Self-monitoring Ch. 7, 8, pp. 145, 162
Avoid traps						•				•
Bring discipline to the board						•	•	•		•
Build ownership of Policy Governance										
Check for understanding of policies							•			
Collect data										
Conduct board self-assessment										•
Decide whether to adopt Policy Governance										
Determine ownership values	•	•							•	
Develop group process								•		•
Disseminate information	•		•							
Ease the implementation of Policy Governance					•	•		•		•
Educate the ownership	•	•	•						•	
Ensure that Policy Governance fits board values							•	•		•
Explore issues for Ends development	•		•						•	
Feel connected with the organization						•				
Find causes of board discontent										•
Fulfill accountability to ownership	•		•							
Get input on Ends policies	•		•						•	
Hear customer needs and concerns										
Imagine the future								•	•	
Improve board performance										•
Keep board work focused						•	•			•
Make the transition to Policy Governance								•		
Organize board work								•		
Plan board work										
Quickly develop policies				•	•			•		
Set priorities										
Stay the course						•	•			•

When you want to . . .	Self-test on policies Ch. 4, p. 75	Survey Ch. 6, p. 128	Telephone polling Ch. 6, p. 133	Template of policies Ch. 4, p. 62	Traps exercise Ch. 3, p. 53	Undiscussables Ch. 4, p. 76	Worry list Ch. 2, p. 31
Avoid traps	•				•		
Bring discipline to the board							
Build ownership of Policy Governance	•				•		•
Check for understanding of policies	•						
Collect data		•	•				
Conduct board self-assessment							
Decide whether to adopt Policy Governance							•
Determine ownership values		•	•				
Develop group process							
Disseminate information							
Ease the implementation of Policy Governance				•	•		•
Educate the ownership							
Ensure that Policy Governance fits board values							•
Explore issues for Ends development		•	•				
Feel connected with the organization							
Find causes of board discontent						•	•
Fulfill accountability to ownership							
Get input on Ends policies		•	•				
Hear customer needs and concerns		•	•				
Imagine the future							
Improve board performance	•						
Keep board work focused	•				•		
Make the transition to Policy Governance				•			
Organize board work							
Plan board work							
Quickly develop policies				•			
Set priorities							
Stay the course	•				•		•

TOOL FINDER FOR GROUP PROCESS

When you want to . . .	Try this . . .	Affinity diagram Exh. 5.13, p. 115	Balancing advocacy with inquiry Exh. 2.2, p. 32	Brainstorming Exh. 3.6, p. 56	Different point of view Exh. 2.3, p. 33	Fishbowl (roundtable) Ch. 6, p. 128	Focused group discussion Ch. 3, p. 52	Focus groups Ch. 6, p. 132	Force field analysis Exh. 5.14, p. 117	Listen to dissenting voices Exh. 2.1, p. 32	Mind mapping Exh. 5.12, p. 114
Consider many possibilities			•	•	•					•	•
Determine strengths and opportunities			•						•		
Determine the best solution											
Expand people's thinking			•	•	•	•			•	•	•	•
Find common threads		•					•				
Find out what others think			•	•	•	•				•	•	
Focus the discussion on a topic							•	•			
Generate lots of ideas in a short time		•		•							•
Get everyone involved				•							•
Hear different points of view			•	•	•				•		•	
Identify priorities											
Imagine the future											•
Listen for possibilities			•	•		•	•	•			•	•
Organize large amounts of information		•									
Prioritize possible directions											

When you want to . . .	Try this	Multiple voting Exh. 6.3, p. 138	Nominal group process Exh. 3.2, p. 51	Round robin Exh. 3.1, p. 51	Search conference (discovery) Ch. 6, p. 133	Undiscussables Ch. 4, p. 76	Weighted voting Exh. 6.4, p. 139
Consider many possibilities			•	•			
Determine strengths and opportunities			•				
Determine the best solution		•	•				•
Expand people's thinking			•	•	•	•	
Find common threads			•		•		
Find out what others think		•	•	•	•	•	•
Focus the discussion on a topic							
Generate lots of ideas in a short time			•	•			
Get everyone involved			•	•	•		
Hear different points of view			•	•		•	
Identify priorities		•	•				•
Imagine the future					•		
Listen for possibilities			•	•	•		
Organize large amounts of information							
Prioritize possible directions		•					•

FURTHER READING AND RESOURCES

In this section we present information about all the books, articles, and other resources that we have mentioned in this book, together with information about other resources that could help you in working with Policy Governance.

Policy Governance Source Materials

Books

Carver, J. *Boards That Make a Difference: A New Design for Leadership in Nonprofit and Public Organizations.* (2nd ed.) San Francisco: Jossey-Bass, 1997.

Carver, J., and Carver, M. M. *A New Vision of Board Leadership: Governing the Community College.* Washington, D.C.: Association of Community College Trustees, 1994.

Carver, J., and Carver, M. M. *Reinventing Your Board: A Step-by-Step Guide to Implementing Policy Governance.* San Francisco: Jossey-Bass, 1997.

CarverGuides

Carver, J., and Carver, M. M. *CarverGuide No. 1: Basic Principles of Policy Governance.* San Francisco: Jossey-Bass, 1996.

Carver, J., and Carver, M. M. *CarverGuide No. 2: Your Roles and Responsibilities as a Board Member.* San Francisco: Jossey-Bass, 1996.

Carver, J. *CarverGuide No. 3: Three Steps to Fiduciary Responsibility.* San Francisco: Jossey-Bass, 1996.

Carver, J. *CarverGuide No. 4: The Chairperson's Role as Servant-Leader to the Board.* San Francisco: Jossey-Bass, 1997.

Carver, J., *CarverGuide No. 5: Planning Better Board Meetings.* San Francisco: Jossey-Bass, 1997.

Carver, J. *CarverGuide No. 6: Creating a Mission That Makes a Difference.* San Francisco: Jossey-Bass, 1997.

Carver, J. *CarverGuide No. 7: Board Assessment of the CEO.* San Francisco: Jossey-Bass, 1997.

Carver, J. *CarverGuide No. 8: Board Self-Assessment.* San Francisco: Jossey-Bass, 1997.

Carver, J., and Carver, M. M. *CarverGuide No. 9: Making Diversity Meaningful in the Boardroom.* San Francisco: Jossey-Bass, 1997.

Carver, J. *CarverGuide No. 10: Strategies for Board Leadership.* San Francisco: Jossey-Bass, 1997.

Carver, J. *CarverGuide No. 11: Board Members as Fundraisers, Advisers, and Lobbyists.* San Francisco: Jossey-Bass, 1997.

Carver, J., and Carver, M. M. *CarverGuide No. 12: The CEO Role Under Policy Governance.* San Francisco: Jossey-Bass, 1997.

Board Leadership Newsletter

Jossey-Bass publishes *Board Leadership: A Bimonthly Workshop with John Carver,* a newsletter that contains many useful articles. It costs $105 for a personal subscription and $135 for a board subscription. Here are the *Board Leadership* articles that have been mentioned in this book:

"The Board of a Trade Association Establishes Its Ends Policies." *Board Leadership* no. 31, May–June 1997, pp. 4–6.

Carver, J. "Free Your Board and Staff Through Executive Limitations." *Board Leadership* no. 4, Nov.–Dec. 1992, pp. 4–5.

Carver, J. "What Do You Want from Your CEO? How to Express Board Concerns in *Unmistakable* Language." *Board Leadership* no. 16, Nov.–Dec. 1994, pp. 4–5.

Carver, J. "Board Approvals and Monitoring Are Very Different Actions." *Board Leadership* no. 24, Mar.–Apr. 1996, pp. 3–4.

"A City Council Creates Ends Policies." *Board Leadership* no. 33, Sept.–Oct. 1997, pp. 4–5, 8.

Conduff, M. "Guest Presentation." *Board Leadership* no. 24, Mar.–Apr. 1996, pp. 7–8.

Gabanna, C., Paszkiewicz, D., and Raso, C. "Guest Presentation." *Board Leadership* no. 34, Nov.–Dec. 1997, pp. 7–8.

"A Hospital Board Creates Ends Policies." *Board Leadership* no. 34, Nov.–Dec. 1997, pp. 4–5.

"Nine Steps to Implementing Policy Governance." *Board Leadership* no. 13, May–June 1994, pp. 4–6.

"A Public School Board Establishes Ends Policies." *Board Leadership* no. 32, July–Aug. 1997, pp. 4–6.

Internet Resource

Carver, J. "Policy Governance in a Nutshell." [http://www.policygovernance.com/model.htm].

Audiovisual Resources

Carver, J. *Empowering Boards for Leadership: Redefining Excellence in Governance.* San Francisco: Jossey-Bass, 1992. (Two-hour audiocassette.)

Carver, J. *John Carver on Board Governance.* San Francisco: Jossey-Bass, 1993. (Two-hour VHS videocassette.)

Other Useful Resources

Baldwin, C. *Calling the Circle: The First and Future Culture.* Newberg, Oreg.: Swan-Raven, 1994.

Borden, V., and Banta, T. (eds.). *Using Performance Indicators to Guide Strategic Decision Making.* New Directions for Institutional Research, no. 82. San Francisco: Jossey-Bass, 1994.

Brassard, M. *The Memory Jogger Plus: Seven Management and Planning Tools.* Methuen, Mass.: GOAL/QPC, 1989.

Bryson, J., and Crosby, B. *Leadership for the Common Good.* San Francisco: Jossey-Bass, 1992.

Buzan, T., and Buzan, B. *The Mind Map Book: How to Use Radiant Thinking to Maximize Your Brain's Untapped Potential.* New York: NAL/Dutton, 1994.

Chrislip, D., and Larson, C. *Collaborative Leadership: How Citizens and Civic Leaders Can Make a Difference.* San Francisco: Jossey-Bass, 1994.

Covey, S. *Seven Habits of Highly Effective People.* New York: Simon & Schuster, 1989.

Covey, S. *Principle-Centered Leadership.* New York: Simon & Schuster, 1990.

Doyle, M., and Straus, D. *How to Make Meetings Work.* New York: Jove, 1976.

Drucker, P. *Leader of the Future.* San Francisco: Jossey-Bass, 1996.

Flower, J. "Future Search: Power Tool for Building Healthier Communities." *Healthcare Forum Journal,* 1995, *38*(3), 34–56.

Gozdz, K. (ed.). *Community Building: Renewing Spirit and Learning in Business.* San Francisco: New Leaders Press, 1996.

Goodspeed, S. *Community Stewardship: Applying the Five Principles of Contemporary Governance.* Chicago: American Hospital Publishing, 1998.

Greenleaf, R., Fraker, A., and Spears, L. *Seeker and Servant: Reflections on Religious Leadership.* San Francisco: Jossey-Bass, 1996.

Greenleaf, R., Frick, D., and Spears, L. *On Becoming a Servant Leader.* San Francisco: Jossey-Bass, 1996.

The Memory Jogger™ II. Methuen, Mass.: GOAL/QPC, 1995. Order from GOAL/QPC, 13 Branch Street, Methuen, MA 01844–1953; phone (978) 685–3900, fax (978) 685–6151.

RE-THINK Group. *Benefits Indicators: Measuring Progress Towards Effective Delivery of the Benefits of Parks and Recreation.* Calgary, Alberta, Canada: RE-THINK Group, 1997.

Schwarz, R. *The Skilled Facilitator.* San Francisco: Jossey-Bass, 1994.

Schwarz, R. "Groundrules for Effective Groups." Chapel Hill, N.C.: Institute of Government, University of North Carolina at Chapel Hill, 1995. To obtain a copy, write to Publications Sales Office, Institute of Government, CB#3330 University of North Carolina at Chapel Hill, Chapel Hill, NC 27599–3330; phone (919) 966–4119.

Senge, P. *The Fifth Discipline.* New York: Doubleday, 1994.

Senge, P., and others. *The Fifth Discipline Fieldbook.* New York: Doubleday, 1994.

The Team Memory Jogger™. Methuen, Mass.: GOAL/QPC-Joiner, 1995.

Weisbord, M. "Future Searches." In K. Gozdz (ed.), *Community Building: Renewing Spirit and Learning in Business.* San Francisco: New Leaders Press, 1996.

A Note About Using the Internet for Research

The primary Internet resource about Policy Governance is *www.policygovernance.com,* John Carver's Policy Governance web site. It offers information about publications; training opportunities; general introductory material on Policy Governance;

and a forum for debate, questions, and sharing in which John and Miriam Carver occasionally participate.

When it comes to venturing further on the Internet, Raymond Lemieux of Raymond Lemieux Gouvernance offers the following advice: "If you have never searched for Policy Governance on the Net, you are missing an important source of information. But here, quantity beats quality. Be prepared to find the useful and the useless on the Internet. Unless you are selective in your search you can easily spend hours and days getting nowhere fast."

Although the Internet does have many references to the young and limited literature about Policy Governance, you will be amazed to find hundreds of thousands of references that have little to do with what you are seeking. Use multiple keywords to restrict your search or you will get everything. Unfortunately, the only way to be sure that the information fulfills your needs is to read it, and there is no guarantee that it is good information. If you have no time limit and great patience, it is worth the experience. Otherwise, you are better off reading the main books on Policy Governance, which give a true sense of the wholeness of the concept and which benefit from the well-structured presentation that the Internet currently does not offer.

THE HISTORY OF POLICY GOVERNANCE IN PRACTICE

In the Foreword to this book John Carver outlines how he developed the theory of Policy Governance. Here we trace the history of the translation of that theory into practice and examine the extent to which it influences boards today. We also look at the model within the wider context of other thinking on governance and examine the criticisms that have been directed at Policy Governance.

How Policy Governance Began

At one level, the history of the practice of ideas is simple. A person has an idea. That person speaks about the idea to others, who start to apply the idea. They in their turn tell other people about the idea, and eventually the practice becomes widespread.

The story of the practice of Policy Governance begins in 1976 when John Carver became CEO of a mental health center now called Quinco Behavioral Health Center in Columbus, Indiana. In an unusual arrangement, the board of this organization contracted with its new CEO to use his fledgling model, thus becoming the very first practitioner of Policy Governance.

In 1979, Carver was asked to make a keynote speech to mental health board members at the National Council of Community Health Centers' annual meeting in Washington, D.C. Carver, a founder and past chair of the organization, decided that this would be his "coming out"—the moment when he would publicly present his radical ideas about the basis for mental health boards. According to Carver, "I recall saying to myself, this is 'no guts, no glory time.' . . . One of the difficulties of the early days was dealing with the presumptuousness of what I had come to believe. Trying not to belittle people while launching an outright attack on the accepted process was not easy. It isn't always easy now."

His presentation went well, and word spread via networks, conventions, and one or two published items. As a result, the model was adopted by other agencies, including the El Paso Mental Health and Mental Retardation Center in Texas, the Ohio Society of Architects, and the Ross County Community Action Commission in Chillicothe, Ohio.

"Columbus, Indiana, was home for almost eight years," he says. "Eight years in which the model was used, demonstrated, and honed. What had begun as an intellectual inquiry had now become a crusade! [After] a few consultancies early in my Indiana time, [I] grew into becoming known across the U.S. and some parts of Canada as a writer and consultant for boards. Pretty soon, I had branched out far beyond mental health boards."

Word Spreads

In 1983 Carver left his job as CEO to devote himself entirely to writing and consulting. He began the manuscript for *Boards That Make a Difference*. As Carver reports, "The intellectual inquiry had become a mission, and that had now become a business." Take-up was slow, but recognition and interest increased each year. The organizations that took on Policy Governance were "the bold ones, the ones willing to try whatever made sense to them, rather than just do what everyone else was already doing."

Carver traveled extensively and especially tried to appear at events that were attended by the broadest range of people. The Indianapolis Chamber of Commerce, the National Association of Community Leadership Organizations, and the Management Services Division of the Wilder Foundation are early examples of organizations that gave Carver a platform. He notes, "The word-of-mouth factor is far more powerful than I can conceive. . . . Once rolling, it has the momentum of a massive object."

Boards That Make a Difference (see Resource C for details) was published in 1990. The idea for the book had been turned down by several publishing companies before it reached Lynn Luckow, now chief executive officer of Jossey-Bass. Luckow and later editor Alan Shrader saw the potential. Their judgment has been vindicated; *Boards That Make a Difference,* now in its second edition, has been a bestseller in Jossey-Bass's Nonprofit and Public Management Series. Carver reports, "Publishing has worked miracles. I run into people all over North America and even all over the world who are familiar with Policy Governance through publishing."

As his work has become more established, Carver has trained others to teach Policy Governance. He has often done this by allowing someone to be exposed repeatedly to his presentations and consultations until the model has become second nature. Since 1995, he has run weeklong Policy Governance Academies specifically to train those acting as internal and external consultants to boards. So far almost one hundred people have undertaken this latter form of training. "I hope other consultants find it easier to convince, to teach, [and] then to coach boards, because some of the resistance has been broken down. So many people . . . need to know an idea is popular. Well, now it is more popular, though a long way still from becoming the norm."

Policy Governance Today

The question of exactly how popular Policy Governance has become is not currently answerable. To date no one has taken an overall survey. That would be a massive task, not least because the spread of Policy Governance is patchy, both geographically and sectorally. The nonprofit sector provided the first examples of adoption and is probably still the main venue in which Policy Governance is used. Development among governmental organizations came a bit later, but there are now a vast number of examples. Development among business organizations is slow and, as far as Carver knows, there are probably only a handful of corporations in the world that have seriously adopted Policy Governance at any level— something he intends to change.

Difficulties in Evaluating Progress. In attempting to evaluate the progress of Policy Governance we inevitably need to address the question of what it means to adopt Policy Governance. Certainly, it does not mean using one or two tips or some new words. Ultimately it is a whole way of being. Fashion designers can tell how many of their jackets have been sold. What they cannot tell is how many of the people who bought the jackets have truly adopted their total "look." They have no idea how many people have bought good or bad copies of the jacket from other sources. They cannot even tell if someone who bought the jacket a month ago is still wearing it today!

John Carver and his co-consultant and wife, Miriam Carver, are well aware of how difficult it is to track the model's use: "If our experience is any guide, we know that boards are far more likely to use part of the model than all of it. That tendency testifies to the eclecticism and independence of judgment of boards, but unfortunately it also means that most boards that profess to follow the Policy Governance model are not getting anywhere near its full power to transform board leadership."

Here is one reasonable working definition: "A Policy Governance board is any board that has a policy manual containing policies in the four Policy Governance categories and that governs entirely by those policies." Many boards who consider themselves to have adopted Policy Governance, including several that have provided source material for this book, are excluded from such a definition. Even though the others do meet the definition, can we really be confident that they have adopted Policy Governance unless we know more about the content of the policies themselves and the way the board and CEO operate from them?

According to Jeffrey Brudney, professor of political science and director of the Doctor of Public Administration Program at the University of Georgia,

> As governments and the citizenry have come to rely more heavily on nonprofit organizations for the delivery of important social and human services, the need for effective governance and management of these institutions has grown apace. John Carver has offered a provocative model that spells out a new role for boards of directors of nonprofit organizations to provide effective governance. The difficulties in studying the implementation and efficacy of Carver's model are considerable; they include issues related to sampling, selection of nonprofit organizations for study and the choice of respondents within them, possible impact of application of the model on the board versus on the nonprofit organization itself, and change over time. Careful inquiry can potentially resolve these issues, and it is a good thing, for research on Carver's Policy Governance model is much needed. The results should prove beneficial not only to researchers but also to practitioners in the nonprofit community.

Evidence of Progress. With all the aforementioned issues in mind, we can still look for evidence of the extent to which Policy Governance has been adopted. John and Miriam Carver estimate that they have personally helped more than one thousand boards at some stage of the Policy Governance development process (but they note that they do not know how most of them are faring now). In addition, many boards have taken on Policy Governance under their own steam using the now-extensive range of the Carvers' publications or the help of consultants. Taking this into account, the Carvers say, "The . . . boards whose leadership has been substantially influenced by the Policy Governance model clearly number in the tens of thousands, and perhaps far beyond that."

For further evidence of the influence of Policy Governance, we turn to some sources. Most are Canadian, although similar evidence could undoubtedly be found in the United States.

• From the end of 1994 to early 1995, Jeffrey Brudney and Vic Murray (a professor in the School of Public Administration at the University of Victoria, British Columbia) conducted a survey on board change. It was published in *Nonprofit World,* the journal of the Society for Nonprofit Organizations, in an article titled "Improving Nonprofit Boards: What Works and What Doesn't?" (Vol. 15, No. 3, May–June 1997, pp. 11–17). Out of the 851 leaders (mainly CEOs) of Canadian nonprofit organizations who responded, 25 percent had chosen Policy Governance and another 12 percent had partially adopted the model.

• Gerry Cragg, director of association services for YMCA Canada, estimates that 75 percent of YMCAs in Canada have been influenced by John Carver's work without necessarily having adopted the Policy Governance model.

• Policy Governance is given prominence in the United Way of Canada's "Board Basics Kit," produced for its Leadership Development Program. This training manual identifies Policy Governance as one of four possible board models. The other models cited are the policy board (which is characterized as the "traditional" board), the working board (in which members act as hands-on operators, as well as governors), and the collective board (in which staff and board substantially or totally overlap).

• A report called "The Road Ahead II," published by the government of Ontario's Education Improvement Commission in December 1997, identifies Policy Governance as having been developed by John Carver, paraphrases its principles, and proposes that all Ontario school boards adopt a model reflecting those principles.

• Raymond Lemieux of Raymond Lemieux Gouvernance reports that at the time of this writing, the AltaVista search engine offers 791,852 web pages for policy governance, and the Excite search engine registers 1,227,855 hits (queries) for the same subject. This welter of information includes theoretical concepts, forums, policy samples for nongovernmental organizations or universities, references, success stories, consulting programs and fees, and information on such specialist organizations as institutes and centers on governance in Canada and the United States. Most references do not relate to the distinct model of Policy Governance examined in this book, but a growing number of them do. Carver's own web site (http://www.policygovernance.com) is also increasingly used by practitioners looking to share and discuss Policy Governance issues.

Although this evidence is circumscribed by many reservations, it is clear that at least since the 1990 publication of *Boards That Make a Difference,* Policy Governance has been vigorously taken up across North America. It is also worth noting that Carver has spoken or consulted in Australia, Ethiopia, Turkey, Bulgaria, Austria, Switzerland, Germany, the Netherlands, England, Argentina, and Mexico, bringing Policy Governance to an international audience.

General Views on Governance and Leadership

In assessing the progress of Policy Governance, it is interesting to review what well-respected people are saying about governance in general. We will again refer to some Canadian examples.

In a 1994 video script called "In Search of Effective Governance" from the Canadian Comprehensive Auditing Foundation (55 Murray Street, Suite 210, Ottawa, Ontario, Canada K1N 5M3; phone 613–241–6713), several corporate and public sector leaders give their views. Here's a typical quote from a corporate president and CEO: "I would see the directors attempting to look forward to the future and engaging themselves very much in the strategic direction of corporations, finding ways they can enhance that future, develop the future with the management, and find ways of assuring that managers are acting in consistency with that strategic direction." The chair of another corporation says, "I seek an independent board that basically works in a collegial manner, but a management that realizes that managements come and go, but boards last forever in the institutional and legal sense." The presentation suggests six principles of good governance that board members should embrace:

1. Knowledge, ability, and commitment
2. An understanding of the board's purpose and of whom the board is representing
3. An understanding of the objectives and strategies of the organization
4. An understanding of and reasonable information about good governance
5. Preparedness to ensure that objectives are met and that performance is satisfactory
6. Accountability to those they represent

Many of these principles accord with Policy Governance, but Policy Governance goes further. That is, it places a responsibility on the board for creating the vision in communication with the organization's owners, rather than merely understanding what management is doing.

Similarly, in its December 1994 report, the Toronto Stock Exchange Committee on Corporate Governance recommends that the board of directors of every corporation explicitly assume responsibility for the stewardship of the corporation and for the following matters:

- Adopting a strategic planning process
- Identifying the principal risks and ensuring the implementation of appropriate systems to manage these risks
- Planning for succession, including appointing, training, and monitoring senior management
- Creating a communications policy for the corporation
- Ensuring the integrity of the corporation's internal control and management information systems

Again, much of the thinking here matches the concepts of Policy Governance, but Policy Governance proposes that the board take direct responsibility for creating the vision, rather than simply "adopting a strategic planning process." Carver's model also goes further toward defining explicit and distinct roles for the board and the management in the other matters.

In terms of more general thinking on leadership, it is also notable that there is considerable synergy between the principles of Policy Governance and those espoused by writers such as Stephen Covey on principle-centered leadership and Robert Greenleaf on servant leadership.

Criticism of Policy Governance

Policy Governance has had some mixed reviews.

Criticism One: The Policy Governance Model Is Not for Everyone. When Vic Murray was director of the Voluntary Sector Management Program at York University, he wrote an article titled "Is Carver's Model Really the One Best Way?" which the Canadian Centre for Philanthropy published in September 1994 *(Front & Centre,* Vol. 1, No. 5, p. 11). Murray criticizes the Policy Governance model on the grounds that many of its assumptions are unrealistic and unduly limiting. Specifically he asserts, "The history, culture, personalities and environmental conditions of many nonprofits make it impossible for a Carver-type model to be sustained over time." He concludes, "When it comes to board governance patterns, hardy hybrids of many models can flourish. There really is no one best way." From "Improving Nonprofit Boards: What Works and What Doesn't?," his aforementioned survey conducted with Jeffrey Brudney, he comes to a similar conclusion: "Carver-users were no more satisfied than users of any other model or combination of models."

Before looking at this criticism in detail, we need to consider the notion that boards can choose from many models. Yes, boards practice governance in all sorts of ways, but can they really be said to be operating a model? Policy Governance is a model in the sense that it provides a theoretical foundation for governance and puts forward a set of principles and practices that flow from the theory and that are integrated with each other (see the Foreword of this book for more discussion on this topic). Using this definition, Policy Governance is the only real model of governance to have been clearly distinguished and widely published thus far. As more people apply their minds to this critical area of organizational and democratic life, we hope that there will be more models, but they don't exist now.

Leaving aside the question of alternatives, we must turn to the important criticism that the traditions, personalities, and circumstances of many nonprofits make it impossible for Policy Governance to be sustained over time. Interestingly enough, this is not actually a criticism of Policy Governance as a theoretical foundation for governance but rather a commentary on boards' ability to apply it. Fundamental criticisms of the model would be objections to its precepts, such as that board leadership is group leadership or that the board's raison d'être is to hold the organization in trust for a wider group or that the board's primary function is to define and ensure fulfillment of the wider group's vision.

It is possible to say that Policy Governance represents an ideal—one that is tough to put into practice. Certainly, the study of eleven organizations undertaken in this book provides plenty of evidence of the challenges involved. Boards do struggle with the discipline of speaking with one voice, of identifying and linking with their ownership, and of defining vision in terms of specific outcomes for specific people at a specific cost. However, the book also shows that it is possible to do all these things and to sustain the discipline over time. There are generally accepted principles of well-being, including eating balanced meals and getting plenty of rest and exercise. The vast majority of us do not question these principles, even though applying them consistently can be a struggle because of habit, personality, or circumstance.

Criticism Two: Policy Governance Is Too Rigid. Some people say that the Policy Governance model is too rigid. This criticism is strongly related to the first. Because the precepts, principles, and practice of Policy Governance form a coherent whole, John Carver's assertion is that you cannot adopt bits of it and still say you are practicing Policy Governance. There is a very natural tendency for people to object to such an all-or-nothing recommendation.

Fundamentally, we subscribe to the need to treat the model holistically in order to secure its full promise. We also believe that boards need to and can "adapt" Policy Governance in ways that are consistent with its principles, pose no threat to the potential benefits, and may indeed increase boards' sense of owning the model. The important thing is to distinguish between the essential components of the model and simply "best practice." Changes to the essential components of the model, such as the board speaking with one voice, would definitely preclude delivery of the model's promise. Changes to best practice, such as having a large board, would put the model's promise at risk but would not necessarily prevent its realization.

Criticism Three: Policy Governance Separates Boards from the "Real World." Tom Plunkett reviewed the first edition of *Boards That Make a Difference* in the Fall 1995 issue (Vol. 3, No. 2) of *Board Talk*, a publication of the Centre for Quality Governance. In this review, Plunkett, professor emeritus of public administration at Queen's University and chair of the board of directors of Kingston General Hospital, Ontario, suggests, "The model fails to recognize that the means selected to achieve a particular policy objective may be, in some circumstances, no less important than the policy itself" (p. 7). He also says, "For a Board to develop effective policy it must utilize information from both external and internal sources" (p. 8). For both reasons, Plunkett is concerned that separating policy from its implementation "would force a Board to operate in a virtual vacuum."

The first part of this criticism fundamentally challenges an important precept of Policy Governance—that the board's role in means selection is to define and monitor the Ends and to define what would *not* be acceptable (in relation to ethics, law, and prudence). In the abstract, this sounds like it gives the CEO carte blanche in selecting means. However, the Policy Governance concept of Ends is far more rigorous and specific than the kinds of goals most organizations produce; Policy Governance boards also have a duty to specify and prioritize Ends to the extent where they feel they can responsibly accept any "reasonable interpretation" by the CEO on how those Ends should be achieved. For example, the City of Bryan, Texas (one of the organizations described in our book) takes its definition of Ends through four levels of specificity until at the most specific level it has statements such as, "There is a lack of visible junked vehicles." If a board believes that it cannot trust the CEO and the staff to make more detailed decisions within its policies, perhaps it is not a board that should undertake Policy Governance.

Plunkett also speaks to the board's need for information from both internal and external sources and implies that by operating with less information, the board that adopts Policy Governance will be less informed in its policymaking. Certainly, the Policy Governance board may well end up with a smaller *quantity* of information, but it will also have a far higher *quality* of information. The Policy Governance board requires information that proves that all of its policies are being fulfilled. It also requires information that supports Ends policy development (such as impact studies, owners' views, customer's views, staff reports, and environmental scanning information). In addition, the board is free to ask for any incidental information it would like to see. The information *is* from both internal and external sources, but the most important thing is that the board has defined in advance what information it wants and why. It is not wading through vast piles of documents simply for the sake of it.

There is some validity to Plunkett's statement that separating policy from implementation would force a board to operate in a vacuum. At some point in the Policy Governance implementation process, many of the boards we studied did experience a sense of separation from the ongoing activities of the organization. The constant and abundant flow of information from the CEO dwindled to a limited number of reports addressing compliance with specific board policies. Board members no longer had a mandate to get involved in everything and anything at whim. Many board members wondered, "Now what?" The good news is that as soon as board members began developing Ends policy and linking with their owners, this uneasiness was replaced by a sense that they were, at last, doing work that really mattered.

General Assessment of the Criticism. Assessing the validity of the criticism of the Policy Governance model basically centers on two questions:

1. Is the criticism based on a thorough understanding of the model?
2. Does the criticism arise from flaws in the principles and design of the model, or from flaws in the way it is generally being practiced?

John Carver believes that the most meaningful criticism that can exist of the model is "that it cannot work with real people acting the way real people act, no matter how flawlessly designed." However, he asserts, "Any newly drawn ideal is not practical in the 'real world' into which it is thrust. It serves to create a new world and can do that despite its never being perfectly delivered in reality."

The ultimate question is, does Policy Governance make a difference for organizations? Because the model is an ideal—and a very recent one in the history of governance—this is a question not likely to be answered definitively in the near future; however, this book provides promising evidence that Policy Governance can produce positive results for people and organizations.

The Future of Policy Governance

Policy Governance seems to be alive and well; it has undoubtedly already influenced a significant proportion of boards in North America. As more boards reach maturity in operating with Policy Governance, there is every reason to assume that a new world of governing is truly on its way.

ABOUT THE SOURCE ORGANIZATIONS

What follows are brief descriptions of the organizations on whose experience this book is largely based.

City of Bryan, Texas

The City of Bryan is a Texas municipality located in east central Texas. The original home of Texas A&M University, Bryan is the county seat of Brazos County and had a population of sixty-five thousand in 1997. Bryan is a full-service municipality and owns and operates the area's electrical utility. The 1998 budget was $140 million. Bryan has approximately eight hundred regular full-time employees. The city council sets policy, which is implemented by the city manager. A mayor and one council member are elected at large, and five council members are elected from single-member districts. The City of Bryan has actively worked with Policy Governance since early 1995.

Colorado Association of School Boards

The Colorado Association of School Boards (CASB), founded in 1940, represents and serves Colorado's 176 local school boards by offering a large menu of contract services, one of which is Policy Governance. CASB itself uses Policy

Governance, having been formally introduced to the model in 1996. CASB has facilitated numerous Policy Governance projects for its members.

Early Childhood Community Development Centre

The Early Childhood Community Development Centre of Saint Catharines, Ontario, Canada, is a nonprofit charitable resource and development organization governed by a volunteer board of representatives from both the private and the public sectors. The organization was created in March 1993 by a task group of agencies, practitioners, and educators. With twelve full-time staff members and a varying number of part-time staff and volunteers, it provides a broad range of services that holistically support the delivery of quality care and education to children and families. The board's move to Policy Governance began with an exploration of governance options in late 1995.

The Law Society of Upper Canada

The Law Society of Upper Canada is the governing body of Ontario's legal profession. Founded in 1797 and incorporated in 1822, it is one of the oldest professional organizations in Canada. The Law Society is responsible for educating, licensing, supervising, and disciplining the province's lawyers to ensure that the public can obtain competent and professional legal services. The Law Society's affairs are governed by forty-four governors known as *benchers*. Forty of them are elected by members of the profession every four years. The other four are non-lawyers (lay benchers); they are chosen from the general public and appointed by the lieutenant governor-in-council. There are also several nonvoting ex officio benchers. The Law Society's council began working with Policy Governance in June 1996.

Parkland Health District

Parkland Health District was created in 1994 after the Saskatchewan, Canada, government decided to create thirty health districts in the province. The health district is responsible for ensuring that the health needs of all the residents of the area are met. Saskatchewan is an area of 17,000 square kilometers with a population of 20,500. The district employs about 650 staff members (320 full-time equivalents). When it was first formed, the board replaced nineteen individual boards—four hospital boards, eight nursing home boards, three ambulance boards, and portions of home care and public health that had previously been in the jurisdiction of four additional boards. The twelve-member Parkland Health District board has been working with Policy Governance since May 1995.

San Francisco AIDS Foundation

The San Francisco AIDS Foundation was one of the first AIDS service organizations in the United States. Founded in 1982, it is San Francisco's response to HIV and AIDS. Now the San Francisco AIDS Foundation is firmly established as a global leader in the fight against AIDS. With an annual budget of $18 million, more than a hundred employees, and 350 volunteers, it served 150,000 individuals in 1997. The San Francisco AIDS Foundation continues to face challenges with compassion, dignity, and a sense of purpose. The board decided to implement Policy Governance in 1993.

Southern Ontario Library Service

The Southern Ontario Library Service (SOLS) is an arm's-length agency of the Ontario government mandated to increase cooperation and coordination among public library boards and other information providers. In Ontario, 400 public libraries, governed by independent boards and funded mainly by local municipalities, serve a population of 10.75 million people. SOLS serves 255 of these libraries. Its sister organization, OLS-North, serves the other 145. The City of Toronto operates as a separate library system. SOLS's client libraries operate in English or French or both, and they include seventeen First Nation libraries. SOLS currently employs fifty staff members. The twenty-member board (fifteen elected from client libraries and five ministerially appointed) was introduced to Policy Governance in June 1993.

United Way of Burlington, Hamilton-Wentworth

The United Way of Burlington, Hamilton-Wentworth, is an umbrella fundraising organization. Since 1927, it has raised more than $90 million (in Canadian dollars) for almost a hundred agencies. Through customer-oriented fundraising and a fund distribution system, the United Way ensures that when people make a donation, their charitable gift represents an investment in the community with a high return. Other innovative programs include Loaned Representative, Leadership Development Services, Labor Community Service, and Gifts-in-Kind. The twenty-two member board began the transition to Policy Governance in February 1993.

Vermont Land Trust

The Vermont Land Trust (VLT), one of the most successful land trusts in the United States, protects the productive, recreational, and scenic lands that give Vermont and its communities their rural character. Since 1977, VLT has worked with landowners, as well as with state, government, and other conservation organizations, to protect more than 165,000 acres permanently. Nearly 3 percent of Vermont's privately owned farm and forest land is now under VLT's steward-ship. VLT conserves productive agricultural land, protects forestland for a healthy wood products industry, sustains critical wildlife habitats, and helps communities protect land for recreation and scenic enjoyment. VLT is a private, nonprofit, member-supported organization with seven local offices and an eighteen-member board that adopted Policy Governance in February 1996.

Weaver Street Market, Inc.

Weaver Street Market, Inc., is a community-owned natural foods store in Carrboro, North Carolina. Incorporated under state statutes as a cooperative corporation and financed by an innovative mix of community investment, it is unique in being owned by both workers and consumers. Opened in 1988, it is the largest and most successful natural foods cooperative in the Southeast. The founding intention was to integrate the best of what is possible in cooperatives with the best of what is possible in privately owned stores. The result is a community-owned enterprise with an entrepreneurial spirit. The seven-member board of Weaver Street Market (the two owner groups elect four of the seven members—two members each) was first introduced to Policy Governance in June 1994.

YMCA-YWCA of London

The YMCA-YWCA of London has operated as a joint association in Canada since 1951. It has three health, fitness, and recreation branches; a child-care ser-vices branch operating twelve centers across the city and in neighboring coun-ties; a camping services branch that operates day and resident camps; an employment training program for new Canadians; and a unit providing associ-ationwide marketing, accounting, and other finance services. The London Y is a $10 million operation with an asset base of $8 million (both figures in Canadian dollars). The Y has 150 full-time staff members, as well as some 300 active volunteers and a part-time payroll of up to 400 other staff members, depending on the season. The eighteen-member board was introduced to Policy Governance in the winter of 1994.

INDEX